LOVE THY LEGUMES
Sonali Suratkar, MHS

COPYRIGHT

Copyright © 2016 Sonali Suratkar

All Rights Reserved. No part of this publication may be reproduced, stored in a retrieval system, or transmitted, in any form or in any means – by electronic, mechanical, photocopying, recording or otherwise – without prior written permission.

Concept, Design, Layout, and Photography by Sonali Suratkar.
Recipes developed, standardized, and/or authored by Sonali Suratkar.
Cover co-designed with Neeraj Sonalkar.

Print ISBN # 978-0-692-78840-0

Published by Sonali Suratkar. Printed in the United States of America in 2016.

DISCLAIMER

The taste of the recipes can differ from region to region as the quality of the produce and ingredients can be variable. As such, adjust the recipes per your palate preferences.

This publication contains ideas and opinions of its author and is designed to provide useful information in regard to the subject matter covered. Any diet-related suggestions made in this book are only guidelines. Work with your physician and/or dietitian if you are on medications, and let them know your intention to incorporate more legumes in your diet, as legumes have the potential to affect your dose of medication required by influencing your blood parameters, especially for diabetes, hypertension, polycystic ovary syndrome (PCOS), and hyperlipidemia.

The author expressly disclaims any responsibility for any liability, injury, loss, risk, or health-related issues, personal or otherwise, which is incurred as a consequence, directly or indirectly, of the use and application of any of the contents of this book. Diet is not the only factor that affects one's health and overall well-being. Various aspects of diet, level of physical activity, mental stress, sleep, genetics, medication, and environmental factors play an important role in one's well-being. Decisions should be made in the light of these other factors, and in some cases, under the guidance of one's physician.

All nutrient values are approximate and have been calculated in most cases using available online resources and textbook references.

TABLE OF CONTENTS

Acknowledgments viii
Reviews ix
Introduction x

HUMBLE LEGUMES - A TREASURE TROVE

Introduction To Legumes 2
Carbs, Fiber 3
Fat 5
Protein 5
Minerals 7
Vitamins 7
Anti-Nutrient Substances 7
Phytochemicals 8
Soybeans 8

COOKING LEGUMES THE QUICK & EASY WAY

Healthy Cooking Practices & Some Food Pairing Ideas 12
Dals (Split Legumes) 14
Whole Legumes 16
Flours 18
Dried Legume Cakes (Vadis) 19
Germination 19
Fermentation 20
Pressure Cooking 22
Steaming 27
Using an Aebleskiver Pan (Appe Pan) 27

MENU PLANNING

Tips for Balancing Meals 30

LET'S GET STARTED

Spices, Herbs & Aromatics 40
Tempering 44
How to Customize these Recipes 45
Highlights of the Recipes 47
Stay Connected 48

BUBBLING CURRIES & STEWS

Restaurant-Style Dal Makhani / Black Gram Curry 50
Zhatpat Masur / No-Fuss Lentils Curry 52
Kala Chana Curry / Black Chickpeas Curry 53
Adrakwali Mung Dal / Ginger-Infused Mung Dal 55

Dal Haryali / Dal with Spinach 56
Rojana Masur Dal / Everyday Pink Lentils Soup 58
Simply Chole / Chickpeas Curry 60
Sambar / South Indian Vegetable Stew 61
Rajma Masala / Kidney Beans in A Silky Curry 63
Ragda Patties / Potato Patties with Dried Peas Curry 64
Hara Vatana Shorba / Dried Green Peas Soup 66
Lasooni Palak Chana / Spinach & Chickpeas Stew 67
Matki Chi Amti / Simple Moth Beans Curry 69
Dhaba Dal / Roadside Eatery Dal 71
Bengali Ghugni / Bengali White Peas Soup 73
Lasooni Mung Dal / Garlicky Mung Dal Soup 74
Dhanshak Dal / Mixed Dal & Vegetable Stew 74
Palak Chole / Chickpeas in Spinach Sauce 74
Chawli Chi Amti / Black-Eyed Peas Curry 76
Jain Lauki Chana Dal / Simple Split Peas & Calabash Soup 77
Dal Methi / Fenugreek & Pigeon Peas Soup 78
Zhatpat Misal Pav / Quick Mixed Beans Spicy Curry 79
Paneer Dal Fry / Dal with Indian Cottage Cheese 81
Black Beans Curry 82
Mexican Beans Soup 83
Turkish Carrot & Pink Lentils Soup 85
Italian Hearty Beans Soup 87
French Fusion Lentils Soup 88

SIZZLING STIR-FRIES & KEBABS FOR SALADS, WRAPS & SANDWICHES

Chole Chaat / Curried Chickpeas Salad 90
Sprouts Chaat Salad 92
5-Minute Dressings & Chutneys 93
Kachori-Inspired Mung Chaat Salad 94
Punjabi Chana Masala Salad 96
Mediterranean Beans & Pasta Salad 97
Peruvian Sprouts Ceviche 98
Swadishta Matki Usal / Delicious Moth Beans Stir-Fry 100
Pan-Fried Pakoras Wrap with Kadhi 102
Kadhi / Soulful Yogurt Soup 104
Kadhi Pakodi / Yogurt Soup with Fritters 104
Pan-Fried / Baked Samosa with Spiced Carrot Lentils 106
Chatpata Chana Salad / Black Chickpeas Salad 108
Black Beans Kebabs / Burger Patties 109

NON-VEGETARIAN & SORT OF NON-VEGETARIAN

Chicken Dhanshak / Chicken Curry with Vegetables	112
Dhanshak Salad / Cabbage with Caramelized Onion	114
Turkey Chili With Soy Granules	115
Fennel-Infused Chicken Mung Beans Stew	117
Soy Kheema / Vegetarian Minced Meat	118
Mediterranean Chicken Hummus Wrap	119
Spanish Chickpeas Bravas	121
Turkey / Chicken Kebabs	122

FOR THE LOVE OF RICE

Brown Rice & Lentils Pulao	124
Nutrient-Dense Khichadi / Nutrient-Dense Porridge	126
Protein-Packed Khichadi / Protein-Packed Porridge	127
Bisibele Bath / South Indian Rice Stew	128
Veggies & Lentils Pulao	129
Black Chickpeas Fried Rice	131
Mexican Rice & Beans Bowl	132

ANYTIME MEALS FROM IDLIS & APPE TO CREPES & PANCAKES

Mung Dal Appe & Dosas / Mung Dal Puffs & Crepes	134
Chana Dal Appe / Light Falafel	136
Whole Mung Dosas & Koftas	137
Cheese & Whole Mung Kebabs or Dosas	138
Dahi Vada / Black Gram Puffs in Yogurt	141
Dahi Tadka / Tempered Yogurt	142
Instant Toasty Idlis / Instant Steamed Cakes	143
Protein-Packed Idlis & High Fiber Idlis	145
Idli Variations / Steamed Cake Variations	146
Protein-Packed Dosas, Uttapam / Protein-Packed Crepes	149
Dosa Variations / Crepe Variations	151
Uttapam / Indian Pizza	151
Masala Dosa Filling	153
Flavored Dosa & Paneer Uttapam	154
Tomato Omelet	155
Nutrient-Dense Thalipeeth / Multigrain Pancakes	157
Oats Dosa / Oats Crepe	158
Instant Methi Chilla / Fenugreek Crepe	159
Instant Ragi Dosa / Instant Finger Millet Crepe	160
Squash & Oats Crepes / Pancakes	161

TOTALLY TOFU

Tofu in Thai Green Curry	164
Tofu in Thai Yellow Curry	165
Palak Tofu / Tofu Pakoras in Silky Spinach Gravy	166
Tofu Bruschetta	168
Tofu Bhurjee / Tofu Scramble	169
Korean-Style Hot Tofu Soup	171
Quinoa Tofu Pulao	172

FOR THE SWEET MOMENTS

Puran Peda / A Sweet Treat	174
Puran Poli / Sweetened Flatbread	175
Strawberry / Blueberry / Spinach Smoothie	177
Kesariya Mung Dal Kheer / Saffron-Infused Mung Porridge	178
Mocha Tofu Soufflé	179
Chocolate Crepes	180
Vanilla Pancakes with Mango	182
Badam Mung Dal Kulfi / Almond Mung Dal Ice Cream	184

HOT OFF THE PAN

Low-Glycemic, Nutrient-Dense Rotis or Tortillas	186
Missi Roti / Protein-Packed Rotis or Tortillas	187
Dal Pudina Thepla / Minty Dal Flatbread	188

CALL THEM CHUTNEYS OR DIPS

Curry Leaves & Chana Dal Chutney	190
Chana Dal & Peanut Chutney	190
Instant Chutney Podi / Instant Dry Chutney	191
Hummus	192
Hummus Variations	192

References	194
Glossary	195
Index	200

Note: Recipes contain variations and ideas for pairing.

ACKNOWLEDGMENTS

The reason I was drawn to cooking and learning more about food is my Aai. To me, she is the world's best cook! I love everything she cooks, not because she is my mother, but because it tastes so good that you can't help but ask for the recipe to make the dish again and again. She is always very eager to learn new recipes and techniques, and she generously passes on her knowledge and skills to others. My cooking is strongly influenced by her style and techniques; she is my teacher and inspiration for all my endeavors.

I started putting together my recipes because of my husband Neeraj. His constant encouragement and appreciation of my experiments in the kitchen has provided much needed strength and support. He is my favorite critic and undoubtedly a very objective one, having become the guinea pig for experiments gone awry. In spite of his busy schedule and travels, he doesn't forget to appreciate my photography while also sharing tips for improvement.

My dad has supported me in all of the unconventional decisions I have made in my life. He is always there to cheer me on with his motivational words and thoughts to keep me going in spite of all difficulties. His actions always remind me to give generously.

I dedicate this book to my parents and my husband. My parents, for being the greatest teachers I could have hoped for and my amazing husband, for making this journey of publishing a book a reality.

I am indebted to my family and friends for their support and encouragement throughout the process of testing recipes, giving feedback, sharing my recipes, etc. I am grateful to my mother-in-law, Radhika, Yogita, Amit, Jyoti, Shweta, Ketaki, Mayank, Snehal, Saurabh, David and Sanjeev for their input, encouragement, and help sharing my work.

Last but not least, I would like to extend my sincere appreciation to my reviewers – Amber, Heather, Purvi, Becky, Lara and my father-in-law, for the long hours they spent thoroughly reviewing the content and giving me detailed feedback.

REVIEWS

Sonali Suratkar's debut book "Love Thy Legumes" is a great addition to anyone's healthy-eating toolbox. Having practical and appealing recipe ideas on hand is of high priority for being consistent with goals to reach or maintain optimal health, and this educational cookbook delivers. Not only does this book provide recipes, but also the myriad nutritional benefits from legumes and other healthy foods that pair well with them. As a legume-lover myself, I found the book full of ways to use one of my household staples in new and exciting dishes while keeping my plate healthy and balanced. I look forward to sharing this resource with my vegetarian and non-vegetarian nutrition clients, friends, and family, and I recommend that others do the same.

-Amber C. Summers, PhD, RDN, CHES

Whether you are a vegetarian or not you'll learn to "Love thy legumes" after reading this book. Filled with delicious healthy recipes and useful tips on incorporating legumes into your diet, this cookbook includes a wide variety of ways to prepare legumes. While there is an Indian influence to many of the recipes, there is also something for every taste.

-Lara Ho, RN, PhD

In her debut cookbook, nutritionist and legume enthusiast Sonali Suratkar celebrates the often overlooked, but high-nutrient legume. Teeming with dozens of varied recipes and complimented with beautiful photos, "Love they Legumes" will inspire readers reach for this high-protein, high-fiber food group. Whether as the centerpiece of your meal, or paired with other dishes, Suratkar invites readers to appreciate the deliciousness of legumes. Readers will learn about the nutritional content and health benefits of legumes as well as practical advice to incorporate legumes into their diets.

-Heather Lukolyo, MD, MHS

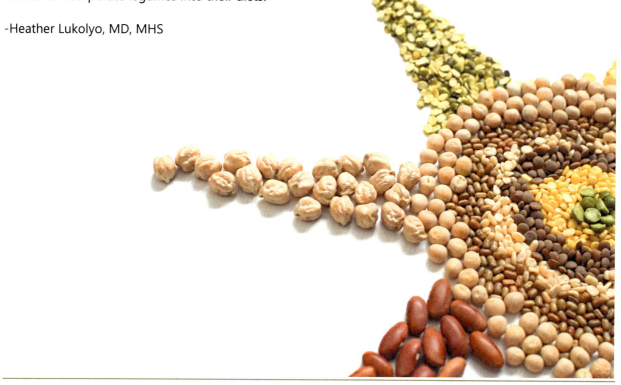

INTRODUCTION

In a world of foodies and budding amateur chefs, I am just another foodie with a passion for cooking, but the geeky nutritionist in me springs up whenever I cook, talk, or write about food. My love for cooking and interest in food began at home, in my mom's kitchen in Mumbai, India. Her cooking inspired me to cook great dishes, just like she does. My husband, Neeraj, especially supports and encourages me to pursue my interests.

Intrigued by the healing power of food, I obtained a Dietetics Degree and then pursued my Master of Health Science Degree from the Johns Hopkins Bloomberg School of Public Health. There, I had the golden opportunity to be involved in nutrition programs that aimed to help ethnic minority groups shop, eat and cook healthy food, while working on ways to improve their access to healthy foods in a food desert.

"Healthy eating" is a colloquial term, but what does it really encompass?

I realized that everyone, in general, needs to have a better understanding about "healthy eating." We are all prone to chronic diseases such as diabetes, hypertension, heart disease, etc., either by genetic factors, environmental factors, or both. Healthy eating is an important component of a healthy lifestyle, which is generally recommended as the first step towards prevention of modern day lifestyle-related diseases.

Today, there is a compulsive desire to dissect the exact nutritive value of the food we consume. Although it is a step forward in our societal evolution about how we look at food, the fact is that healthy eating is much more than a simplistic understanding of nutritive details.

Eating healthy requires going beyond a food's nutritive value and learning to understand:

RIGHT PERSPECTIVE: Understanding the nutritive value of the meal as a whole, rather than considering individual foods by themselves. **"Whoa, ½ cup of cooked whole beans is 100 calories!!"** Yes, but that ½ cup of beans can provide important nutrients that you would not find in a typical 100 calorie dessert, grain or protein food. Whole legumes can add good amounts of bulk or fiber in a meal to help you feel full sooner and curb over-eating. **One teaspoon of sugar** added to any bean stew or curry that yields 6 servings, is a very small amount. However, 1 to 2 teaspoons of sugar per cup of tea or coffee can be significant if you drink several cups a day.

QUICK FIXES AND COOKING PRACTICES: Turning nutritious foods into delicious dishes can be simple and easy. **"Raw broccoli and kale do not taste good!"** Why not sauté them in olive oil and garlic to make them delicious?! Similarly, Brussels sprouts need not be baked in the oven for a long time; they taste better when lightly roasted in a pan in butter or oil (check out the recipe on my website http://quicklydelicious.com).

Short cooking time also retains the anti-cancer phytochemicals of these foods. Light cooking also reduces the anti-nutrients (goitrogens) in these foods, which can affect your thyroid functioning. Explore some more healthy cooking practices in this book.

FOOD PAIRINGS: Knowing how to balance a meal with food pairings can guide you to improve the overall nutritive value of your meal. For example, pairing nutrient-dense foods with foods that are relatively less nutrient-dense, or eating smaller portions of less healthy foods with larger portions of the healthier foods, etc. **"I love white rice and may not be able to switch to brown rice!"** Pair your low-fiber white rice with equal amounts or more of high fiber whole beans and vegetables! Skip the high calorie dessert after an indulgent restaurant meal and grab an apple (or a pear) instead to add some fiber.

HOW MUCH, HOW OFTEN, HOW MANY: Knowing how much to eat, how often to eat and how many types of foods to eat is central to our understanding about what is a healthy diet. **"I eat vegetables and legumes daily!"** That is fantastic, however, eating less than one cup of cooked legumes or two cups of vegetables daily may not provide the nutrients required to maintain good health. While eating out less frequently will most likely give a big boost to your health, you need to choose healthy options at home as well! Choosing to eat only a few types of vegetables may significantly limit your nutrient intake.

PLANNING AHEAD: Planning balanced meals for the family not only ensures that we have accounted for our nutrient requirements, but it takes away some of the stress of cooking or fixing a meal. Doing some preparation over the weekend is an efficient way to ensure you are eating healthy food for the rest of the week. For example, **cooking 2-3 types of beans** over the weekend can ensure you have some protein ready for any weekday. Preparing ginger paste or other marinades, and storing them in the refrigerator can save some prep time.

Now that you briefly understand healthy eating from my perspective, let me give you an overview of this book. Given the rising rates of obesity, diabetes, hypertension, polycystic ovarian syndrome (PCOS), etc., I felt that a general shift towards eating more legumes and cooking them the right way could be an important step towards alleviating or preventing these health issues. **Love Thy Legumes** emphasizes the **importance of eating legumes in different ways on a regular basis, whether you follow a vegetarian diet or not.** This book is the first of a series of educational media that I am working on, to **empower you to plan and cook delicious, nutrient-packed meals** even on a tight schedule.

Although nutrient-dense legumes are a staple in many ethnic diets, they have been replaced by the more alluring fast-food, processed snacks, and sweets that are easily accessible and harmful to our health. Fast-food options are just around the corner, a phone call away, or delivered in a click. A diet that can afford protection from several diseases has been transformed into a diet of low fiber carbohydrates, high fat foods and few vegetables and fruits. Low levels of physical activity and a diet low in legumes, fruits and vegetables have contributed to a steady increase in people developing diabetes, hypertension, gallstones, polycystic ovarian syndrome (PCOS), heart disease, and other chronic diseases. Even children and young adults are no longer spared from these disorders.

Today we need to be more proactive and aware than ever before if we wish to ensure a healthy and bright future for ourselves and our children.

Vegetarians especially need to ensure that they consume enough protein and fiber in every meal so that they don't overload on carbohydrates or fat in any particular meal. **"Legumes," especially whole legumes, play a very important role in the health of vegetarians and vegans. Including whole legumes regularly is a great way to help meet daily protein, fiber, and other important nutrient requirements.**

The educational component of the book will walk you through the benefits of eating legumes while describing efficient ways of cooking legumes so that you do not lose some of the important nutrients in the usual cooking practices. The Menu Planning section will guide you to plan meals that are nutritionally balanced, and the easy-to-follow recipes will get you excited to eat legumes more often!

Involving family in the process of planning, grocery shopping, cooking and setting the table can be a fun activity and a great opportunity to teach children about healthy eating. This will lay a strong foundation for your children's long-term health. Be sure to get your family members involved.

I am glad that my book is published in 2016, the year declared by the United Nations as the International Year of Pulses. Join me in my journey that extends the celebration of these humble foods beyond this year!

I hope you enjoy this journey exploring new strategies for eating healthy on a regular basis.

HUMBLE LEGUMES -
a treasure trove

INTRODUCTION TO LEGUMES

Every year a new hype about a food creates a rippling trend as being a "superfood," whether it is blueberries, chia seeds, flaxseeds, kale, coconut, oats, or any other food. But the humble legumes have been around for a long time and have never received celebrity status. The beauty of consuming legumes is that they include such a wide range of split and whole beans, peas, and lentils that you can consume them on a daily basis without getting bored. They can also unleash many health benefits that go beyond what other so-called superfoods offer. This book is my tribute to the humble legumes!

Let us begin by briefly understanding some terms. Pulses are commonly defined as the dried seeds of leguminous plants that are harvested exclusively for the consumption of the dried seed. The legume species, on the other hand, extends beyond pulses and includes leguminous plants that are harvested as vegetables (green peas, green beans), for oil extraction (soybeans, peanuts), or sowing. The focus of this book is on the dried seeds of the legume family (leguminosae), rather than pulses, in order to include dried green peas and soybeans, which have a unique nutrient profile and may not be classified as pulses.

For the scope of this book, I will be referring to the dried seeds as legumes. These include:

- ☼ **Whole beans** – kidney beans (rajma), black beans, mung beans (mung, green gram), black-eyed peas (chawli), chickpeas (kabuli chana, Bengal gram), soybeans, etc.

- ☼ **Dried peas (sukha vatana)** – dried white peas (whole) or dried green peas (whole)

- ☼ **Whole lentils (sabut masur)** – red, brown, green, black, etc.

- ☼ **Split variety (dals, dhals)** – split mung beans (mung dal), split pigeon peas (split red gram, toor dal), pink lentils (split red lentils, masur dal), split green peas (sukha vatana ki dal), etc.

Since **peanuts** are nutritionally more similar to nuts, they are not covered in detail in this book. **Beans, dried peas and lentils** (except pink lentils, which is a split variety) are the whole, intact, dried seeds. Dals are the split versions of the whole legume and are available as dals with the skin or seed coat (chilka) or without the skin (dehusked).

The term "**lentils**" technically refers to masur (lens culinaris), or the lens shaped lentils that are available as whole red/brown, black, or green lentils or the split red (pink lentils). However, in some countries, most of the split beans (dals) are also generically referred to as lentils, which can be confusing while one is shopping. For example, yellow lentils could mean split mung beans (mung dal), split pigeon peas (toor dal) or split yellow peas (chana dal) because they are all yellow in color. Similarly, black lentils could refer to the black colored beluga lentils or the black gram (urad). It may not matter what terminology you use, so long as you make them part of your weekly menu and include a variety. If you do this, then you are on the right track.

Considered a poor man's meat, legumes are in fact more valuable than meat in terms of their **overall nutritive value, lower cost, long shelf-life, and ease of availability and cooking.** They are also **good for the environment,** as they require less water, improve soil quality and have a low carbon footprint. Legumes are nutrient-dense – they provide a lot of the nutrients (macro and micro nutrients) required for optimal health. They also contain non-nutritional components that can provide health benefits.

Let us explore the nutrients in legumes that can help those with **excess weight, diabetes, pre-diabetes, high blood pressure, polycystic ovary syndrome (PCOS), high cholesterol or triglycerides, constipation, and other chronic diseases.**

CARBS, FIBER

The high content of **fiber and slowly digestible carbohydrates (carbs)** in whole legumes and dals with skin make them **low glycemic index foods** (foods that do not cause a sudden rise in blood glucose after consumption). Therefore they can help prevent or delay the development of **diabetes** or help diabetics to control their blood sugar. Their high fiber content also provides satiety (feeling of fullness) to help you cut back on calories per meal and boost your efforts to **lose weight**. The fiber also relieves **constipation** when the intake of whole legume is complemented with plenty of fluids. Of all the energy-providing food groups, whole legumes have the highest fiber content per 100 calories. Most whole legumes also contain **soluble fiber** that can help lower **blood cholesterol**.

Oligosaccharides, a type of carbohydrate present in legumes, are not digested in our body. They pass into the large intestine and ferment, causing gas or flatulence. These oligosaccharides function as **prebiotics**, which help to maintain health-promoting and immunity-boosting bacteria in our intestines, and may protect against **colon cancer**.

Don't let the discomfort deprive you of the myriad benefits.

Gas or flatulence can be alleviated by:

- ☼ cooking legumes thoroughly
- ☼ adding ginger to the dish
- ☼ discarding soaking or cooking liquid*
- ☼ incorporating whole legumes in your diet in a gradual manner
- ☼ pairing high fiber whole legumes with lower fiber grains and vegetables (details in menu planning section, page 30-38) to prevent fiber overload in a meal
- ☼ consuming mint (pudina), fennel (saunf) or carom seeds (ajwain) after the meal
- ☼ doing simple yoga asanas (for example, pavan muktasana, bringing one or both legs close to the chest while lying on the back)
- ☼ maintaining an active lifestyle – taking a walk, marching on the spot, etc.

*Some may prefer to discard the water used for soaking or cooking (soaking or cooking liquid) in order to reduce flatulence or gas formation, but that also translates to a loss of water soluble vitamins and minerals (B-complex vitamins, potassium, etc.), which are **important for cardiovascular health**. In that case, be sure to include other foods that are high in these nutrients to compensate for the loss.

How much fiber do I need? **Adults need 25-35 grams of fiber a day.** Just ½ cup of cooked **whole** beans, dried peas or lentils can provide you an average of 7 grams of fiber, which is more fiber than is contained in 1 apple (5 grams), 1 cup of cooked rolled oats (4 grams), 1 slice of whole grain bread or roti (3 grams), 1 large carrot (2 grams), ½ cup of cooked brown rice (1.8 grams), or 1 cup of tightly packed spinach (1 gram). One cup of cooked whole legumes a day can easily help you reach 50% of your fiber requirement.

½ CUP COOKED CHICKPEAS HAS MORE FIBER (SOLUBLE & INSOLUBLE) THAN 1 CUP COOKED ROLLED OATS OR ½ CUP OF COOKED BROWN RICE

FAT

Most legumes are **low in fat** (around 2.5%), except for soybeans (8%) and peanuts (47%). Legumes, therefore, make for a great food choice while giving you the freedom to increase your usage of healthy cooking oils. Soybeans contain essential **omega-3 fatty acids,** while peanuts contain a high proportion of monounsaturated fatty acids. Mungo beans (black gram, urad), kidney beans (rajma), black-eyed peas (chawli), and black chickpeas (kala chana) contain small amounts of omega-3 fatty acids. These fatty acids are important because they can help lower inflammation and LDL cholesterol levels.

PROTEIN

Legumes are an **important source of protein**, especially for vegetarians and vegans, and are a good alternative or complementary protein for non-vegetarians (those who consume poultry, seafood, meats, etc.). Just ½ cup of cooked **whole** beans, dried peas, or lentils can provide an average of 7 grams of protein, which is more protein than is contained in 1 slice of whole grain bread or 1 whole wheat roti (4 grams), 1 egg (6 grams), ¾ cup milk (6 grams), or ~⅛ cup or ½ oz. of almonds (3 grams). (Chart on page 6)

How much protein do I need? An adult needs about 1 gram per kilogram of body weight for optimal growth and health, and more during pregnancy, lactation, high physical activity, recuperation, etc.

For example, a woman weighing 50 kg (110 lbs) would need 50 grams of protein on a daily basis. However, certain medical conditions may dictate lower amounts of protein. This does not mean that you should start counting your protein intake to every gram, but the general guidelines in the Menu Planning section (page 30 - 38) and in the recipes will help you build your meal appropriately to get enough protein. Including whole legumes in your meals can help you increase your protein intake.

Combining legumes and grains or cereals, as is traditionally done in many cultures, can provide all essential amino acids required for growth and good health. Some tasty ways to combine these include:

- ☼ Mexican: rice and beans or tortilla and beans

- ☼ Indian: rice and dal, khichadi, puran poli, Pongal, rajma chaval

- ☼ Mediterranean: pita bread and hummus , lentils and rice

- ☼ English: baked beans on toast

Similarly, pairing legumes with dairy, poultry, or meat can also provide all of the essential amino acids.

When your diet is imbalanced in terms of macronutrients (contains more servings of carbohydrate and/or fat, and fewer servings of protein than required by the body) it can gradually lead to **weight gain, muscle weakness, gallstones, and decreased strength and stamina**.

MINERALS

All legumes are an important source of minerals such as **potassium** and **magnesium,** which can help **lower your blood pressure.** In order to retain these nutrients and get maximum benefits, one way is to cook them at home and not discard any soaking or cooking liquid. People with high blood pressure can especially benefit from the regular consumption of whole legumes, more so if they cook their legumes rather than using canned legumes. [Note: high intake of potassium and other minerals may be of concern for those with kidney (renal) or other conditions]. Most legumes contain **iron** and **zinc**, however, some are particularly good sources. These minerals are important as they help build **immunity** to diseases and maintain **blood hemoglobin levels**, along with many other functions.

Cooking practices and food pairings can improve the availability and absorption of these minerals. These are covered in detail in the Cooking Legumes section (pages 12-28).

LEGUMES WITH IRON

Soybeans
Moth beans (matki)
Lentils (masur)
Mung beans (mung)
Kidney beans (rajma)
Mungo beans (black gram, urad)
Roasted Bengal gram (roasted chana)
Pigeon peas (toor)

LEGUMES WITH ZINC

Soybeans
Lentils (masur)
Kidney beans (rajma)
Dried peas (sukha vatana)
Pigeon peas (toor)
Mung beans (mung)

VITAMINS

Legumes contain B-complex vitamins such as folate, thiamin, niacin, etc. Fermentation can further increase the content of these vitamins and produce vitamin B-12 and vitamin C, otherwise not present in legumes. **Folate and B-12** are required for maintaining healthy **blood hemoglobin** levels and reducing blood homocysteine levels, which in turn can **reduce cardiovascular risk**. Vitamin C, an antioxidant, helps repair damaged tissues, reduces acidity, and is required for cholesterol metabolism, among other functions. Since most of these vitamins are heat-sensitive, they can be easily lost during cooking. The Cooking section shares tips on reducing these losses and ways to increase their content. To ensure you get these nutrients, **include yogurt, nuts, seeds and fresh fruits in your diet as snacks, in your breakfast, or in a main meal**.

ANTI-NUTRIENT SUBSTANCES

Legumes contain certain anti-nutrient substances (phytates, trypsin inhibitors, goitrogens, etc.) that can inhibit the digestion and absorption of nutrients such as proteins, iron, zinc, etc.; however, most of these anti-nutrient substances are broken down during cooking. **Make sure you cook your legumes thoroughly.**

In the case of flours, it is better to roast the beans before grinding them into flour in order to reduce the effect of anti-nutrient substances. Ready-made bean flours may be a better option if you are unable to roast and grind them at home. Some flours, such as soybean flour, have high fat content and may need to be refrigerated, otherwise the fat could go rancid, making the flour unsafe for consumption.

PHYTOCHEMICALS

Phytochemicals are plant chemicals that afford special health benefits. Flaxseeds, sesame seeds, legumes, and especially soy, contain important phytochemicals such as lignans and isoflavones (phytoestrogens), which have the potential to **improve colon, cardiovascular and bone health, hormonal imbalances seen in PCOS, or relieve some menopausal symptoms.** Soybeans and other soy products are commonly used in Asian cuisines. These include tofu, tempeh, soy milk, miso paste, soy sauce, etc. and contain varying degrees of isoflavones that can affect estrogenic activity in our body depending on the type and amount consumed. These are better choices than soy protein isolates or soy supplements. Consumption of soy nuggets (soy chunks) and soy granules, also known as textured vegetable protein, can also help increase your protein and phytochemical intake in a meal.

SOYBEANS

Soybeans (also known as soya beans) are slightly different from most legumes. They contain higher amounts of protein, fat, fiber, B-complex vitamins, iron, calcium, magnesium and phytochemicals, as mentioned earlier. Their protein quality is similar to that of meats and eggs, and are considered a **very good source of protein for vegetarians.** The impact of soy consumption on health is an active area of research.

Raw soybeans, or soybean flour made without roasting the soybeans, can contain high amounts of phytates (an anti-nutrient) which can inhibit absorption of some nutrients. However, thoroughly cooked soybeans and most commercially available products, including soybean flour, have reduced phytate content. The immature green soybeans are known as edamame. Soybeans are processed by various techniques to produce several fermented products such as tempeh, soy sauce, miso paste, and natto, and non-fermented products such as tofu, soy milk, and soy nuggets and granules (also known as textured vegetable protein or meat alternatives).

Soybeans are naturally rich in iron, calcium and magnesium. Coagulants used for making tofu can increase the calcium or magnesium content, multiplying the benefits for those with high blood pressure. Soybeans also contain small amounts of omega-3 fatty acids and are low in saturated fats.

The phytochemical content of soy products varies with the type, depending on how each of these is processed. Soybeans and soy products may offer protection against heart disease, some cancers, osteoporosis and can help alleviate some symptoms of menopause and PCOS. These effects may be afforded by the phytochemicals, fiber, protein or other nutrients present in them. About **1 to 2 servings** once or twice a week may work well for adults, leaving room for you to enjoy other legumes. Work with your dietitian, who can help you tailor your soy intake for any of your health concerns such as PCOS, thyroid disorders, menopause, etc.

Although whole soybeans and products made using whole soybeans have high fiber content, most other soy products may have lower fiber content. This is because processing the beans may require removal of the seed coat, or may cause breakdown of carbohydrates and proteins. A positive side-effect of the lower fiber content, however, is that the final product is easier to digest. Such products are favored because they do not cause flatulence. Consider pairing tofu, which is low in fiber, with high fiber vegetables and/or brown rice to ensure the meal is balanced and filling.

Here are some soy products that I have personally tried:

Tofu, also known as bean curd, is made by curdling soy milk, similar to the way paneer (Indian cottage cheese) is made. It makes for a great substitute for paneer, which is high in saturated fat. **Tofu contains protein, iron, calcium, magnesium, and B-complex vitamins, and phytochemicals that are not present in paneer.** It has been consumed by Asian cultures for a long time and is now gaining popularity in other cultures.

Soybean flour (soy flour), when added to other flours to make breads and flatbreads (tortillas, rotis, etc.), can increase the protein, fiber, vitamin, and mineral content of the bread and lower its glycemic index. So, feel free to substitute part of your whole grain flour with soybean flour and enjoy a more nutritious bread, roti, or tortilla. Commercially prepared soybean flour may be better than homemade flour if it is made without roasting the bean, because it is generally treated to reduce the phytate content. If you want to make your own soybean flour or add soybeans to your whole wheat grains, just remember to roast them before grinding. Full-fat flour is better than the non-fat version as it contains essential fatty acids (omega-6 and omega-3). **Store soybean flour in the refrigerator to prevent the fat from going rancid**.

Soy sauce can add a wonderful aroma and flavor to your dish. If you are concerned about the sodium content of soy sauce, use it sparingly, rather than opting for the low sodium sauce and using a generous amount of it. You do not have to worry about the sodium content of soy sauce if you use a small amount (1 teaspoon per serving) with tofu and whole beans, and generous servings of vegetables, as the potassium and magnesium in these can help reduce the impact of sodium in the meal. Please refer to the tofu recipes to understand these pairing ideas (pages 163-172).

Soy milk is the boiled extract obtained after soaked soybeans are puréed. It is a good source of protein and can be used as a substitute for cow's milk. It contains about 2% fat and its caloric value is similar to whole milk (cow's). Choose soy milk that lists whole soybeans in the ingredients.

Soybean meal (textured vegetable protein), also known as textured soy protein, includes **soybean nuggets (soy chunks), soy granules, soy flakes, soy strips, etc.** that are produced from the residue that remains after the soybean oil is extracted from the beans. These soy products contain high amounts of many nutrients such as protein, iron, potassium, magnesium, B-complex vitamins, etc. and do not contain any fat. They also contain some phytochemicals present in other soy products.

Choose to consume a **VARIETY** of whole & split legumes **REGULARLY**

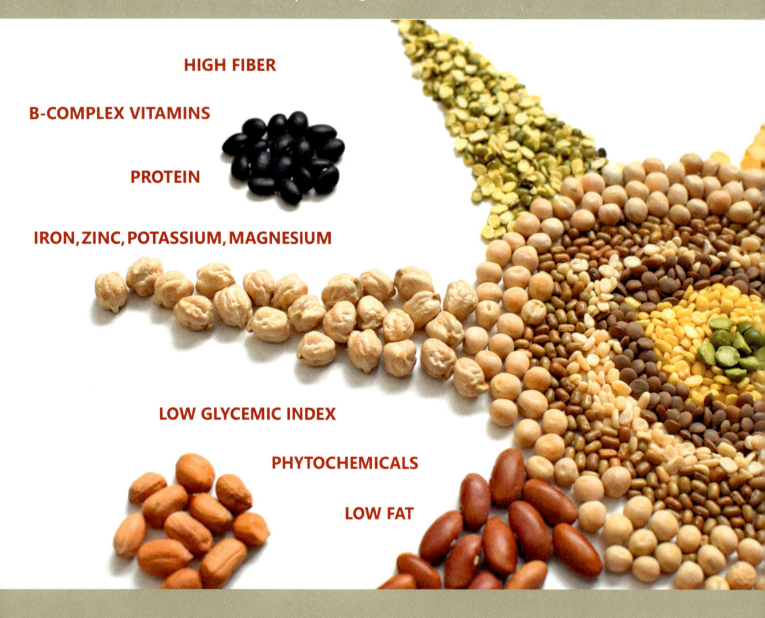

HIGH FIBER

B-COMPLEX VITAMINS

PROTEIN

IRON, ZINC, POTASSIUM, MAGNESIUM

LOW GLYCEMIC INDEX

PHYTOCHEMICALS

LOW FAT

COOKING LEGUMES -
the quick & easy way

Legumes are generally considered foods that take a long time to cook, and you may hesitate to include them in your weekly menu. As such, **canned beans** can be a very convenient alternative to cooking legumes. However, they may contain **preservatives, salt and/or sugar. Draining and rinsing the canned beans leads to loss of water soluble nutrients** that get leached into the liquid. They can also occupy **a lot of space in your pantry** if you decide to include more legumes in your diet. Depending on how often you use them and how many family members you prepare for, you may need to stock several cans. You can keep a few cans handy for the days when you need to cook something more quickly and skip dining out, but for regular consumption it is best to learn to cook legumes at home.

With some planning and efficient use of a pressure cooker, you will be able to incorporate legumes in your diet on a regular basis and without much hassle. It is **less expensive to buy and cook dried beans** than to buy canned beans. Once you get accustomed to eating home-cooked legumes, you will realize that you can make much larger quantities for a given price, while reducing your dependence on commercially processed foods. You will taste the **full flavor of the beans**, and enjoy the freedom to adjust the salt per your health requirements or taste preferences. You do not have to eat bland food if you follow healthful cooking practices at home and include a range of whole and split legumes (pages 12-38).

Legumes are available in different forms and can be treated differently. Here are some guidelines to help you cook legumes regularly. If you prefer a different cooking method, that is fine too, so long as you follow healthy cooking practices and food pairings to get maximum health benefits.

HEALTHY COOKING PRACTICES & SOME FOOD PAIRING IDEAS

Whether you are cooking dals, whole beans, legume flours or other legume-based products, here are a few healthy cooking practices and food pairing ideas to boost your nutrient intake from these nutrient-rich foods.

WAYS TO REDUCE LOSS OF B-COMPLEX VITAMINS AND MINERALS:

- ☼ Instead of discarding the water used for soaking or cooking, **re-use the soaking or cooking liquid** as a stock for your soups, curries, or dals, or use it to make rice, doughs, or batters. This can prevent loss of important water soluble nutrients, valued for lowering blood pressure and cardiovascular risk. Discarding the soaking or cooking liquid also leads to loss of flavor. If you are concerned about flatulence or gas, then please refer to the tips discussed on page 4.

- ☼ **Avoid using large amounts of water** for soaking or cooking unless you intend to utilize all of it, else it can lead to significant loss of nutrients.

- **Cut back on the use of** sodium bicarbonate (soda bicarb) in the form of **fruit salt baking soda, or baking powder.** It also increases the sodium content of the dish.

- **Keep cooking time short** as much as possible.

- **Add salt at the end of cooking**, rather than at the beginning, to prevent the legumes from becoming tough in texture and help to keep the cooking time short.

- **Add acidic foods at the end of cooking** if you are boiling legumes on the stove. This can prevent the dals from becoming tough; however, this is not a concern if you are pressure cooking.

- **Do not bake** cooked beans for a long time.

WAYS TO INCREASE VITAMIN CONTENT AND MINERAL ABSORPTION:

- **Cooking the legumes thoroughly** can make most minerals more available while reducing the effect of anti-nutrient substances that could otherwise interfere with the absorption of some minerals.

- **Avoid tea or coffee with a meal or immediately after a meal**, as tannins present in tea and coffee can inhibit the absorption of iron, zinc and other minerals.

- **Germination and fermentation** can increase the content of these vitamins and also break down some of the proteins to make them easier to digest. Anti-nutrient substances that inhibit the absorption of some nutrients are also reduced.

- **Combining legumes with animal proteins** (dairy, poultry, meat) can improve the quality of protein in the meal and/or iron absorption.

- **Including soybeans** or its products such as tofu in the diet can increase your protein, vitamin, and mineral intake.

- **Complementing iron rich legumes with vitamin C rich foods** can enhance iron absorption from plant-based foods, especially for vegetarians. Vitamin C can overcome the inhibitory effects of phytates (anti-nutrient substances) in legumes that may be present. Simple ways to pair legumes with vegetables is to prepare a fresh salad or a quick stir-fry with vitamin C rich vegetables or eat a fruit that is rich in vitamin C at the end of the meal. Kindly refer to details shared in the Menu Planning section.

DALS (SPLIT LEGUMES)

Split pulses, split legumes, dhals, or "dals" are available with or without the skin (seed coat) and are the easiest to cook. **Plain dals without skin (dehusked) have less fiber compared to the whole legumes or dals with skin.** As such, dals tend to cause less flatulence as compared to whole legumes, and are therefore preferred over whole legumes. However, they also have lower content of minerals and vitamins, which are lost during processing. **In Indian cuisine, the term "dal" is also used to refer to the dish that is prepared using split legumes or whole beans.**

If you are not accustomed to cooking legumes or find yourself frequently checking on the doneness of legumes, measuring the dals and the amount of water to use for cooking can be a great way to start. **Using excess water and then discarding it, or cooking for an unnecessarily long period of time, reduces the vitamin and/or mineral content of foods.** Measuring the legumes also trains you to prepare food for the desired number of servings, ensuring you and your family get enough protein and fiber.

Here are some practices that can guide you to cook dals efficiently while retaining most nutrients.

Adding water two times the measure of dal should be sufficient, whether it is for pressure cooking or for soaking and grinding to make a batter. For example, 1 cup of dal can be pressure cooked with 2 cups of water without the need for soaking. More water (>3 times the measure of dal) is required if you boil it on the stove. Measuring the water, rather than eyeballing the water level, usually yields consistent results and prevents uneven cooking.

Soaking is not required for most dals (except chana dal) if they are boiled on the stove or cooked in a pressure cooker, making them easy to include in your diet. *Al dente* or less tender dals may cause flatulence; so cook the dals thoroughly. Soaking reduces the cooking time and makes the proteins and carbohydrates easier to digest; so soak the dals if you are not pressure cooking. There are recipes that call for soaking of dals, especially if you need to grind, ferment and/or steam the batter or pan-fry it. For example, idlis (lens shaped steamed cakes), dosas (crepes), dhoklas (steamed cakes), appe (puffs), etc. are made using soaked dals. I find an overnight soak (8-10 hours) most convenient and works well for most recipes. However, for fermented batters (idli, appe, dosa, etc.) you can soak for as little as 4 hours before grinding and fermenting. Likewise, non-fermented batters used for pakoras (fritters) and some types of dosa, appe, etc. only require 2 hours of soaking.

Stove top boiling may take 20-30 minutes depending on the type and size of the dal and tenderness desired. Older or aged varieties take longer to cook; soaking such varieties can shorten the cooking time.

Pressure cooking the dals up to the first whistle (or after the pressure regulator starts to rock steadily in case of a whistle-free pressure cooker), is usually sufficient to cook them thoroughly, even without a soak. However, split dried green peas (sukha hara vatana ki dal) may take around 10 minutes of pressure cooking after the first whistle. Similarly, chana dal (split chickpeas, yellow split peas) is more resilient and requires 1 hour of soaking and 5 minutes of pressure cooking after the first whistle. The final outcome is a dal with a soft and smooth consistency. Some people may opt for pressure cooking by counting the number of whistles, however the results may vary with the type of dal, whether or not it is aged, the amount of water used in the pressure cooker, and/or whether the dal was soaked, etc. For detailed instructions on pressure cooking, please refer to the Pressure Cooking section (pages 22-25). By using stackable containers, you can pressure cook 2-3 types of dals simultaneously and store them in the refrigerator for up to 7 days.

USES:

- Split legumes can be used to make a variety of dishes – plain dals, spiced dals, soups with herbs, and stews with vegetables, poultry or meat.

- Soaked dals can be ground into batter and used to make appe (puffed spheres or pancake puffs) or dhoklas (steamed savory cakes), or fried to make pakoras (fritters).

- Leftover dals can be transformed into parathas (flavored flatbreads), muthias (fried spiced snacks), dhoklas (steamed savory cakes), or dosas (crepes).

- Soaked dals can be ground and fermented to make South Indian dosas (gluten-free crepes), idlis (mini steamed cakes), etc.

- Roasted dals and pan-fried dals are also used as snacks either by themselves or added to rice flakes or puffed rice. For example, chivada is an Indian snack mix of rice flakes or puffed rice and roasted chana dal.

- Some dals are also used for tempering, for example, urad dal and chana dal.

- Sweets can also be made using dals. For example, in Maharashtra, cooked chana dal is sweetened with sugar or jaggery and used as a stuffing for flatbreads, called puran polis. In the south of India, sweet pongal is a non-dairy porridge made with sweetened dal and rice and is served during the harvest festival.

- Deep fried dals are used in snacks such as Indian farsaan, or as salad toppings, for example, in Burmese tea leaf salad.

- Roasted dals are also ground to make flavorful moist chutneys or even dry chutney powders such as chutney podis in South Indian cuisine.

WHOLE LEGUMES

Consuming whole legumes a few times a week can be an important dietary change that you can make if you want to gain better control over your **blood glucose, blood pressure, and blood lipids, or to alleviate constipation and PCOS.** Whole legumes can also aid in **weight loss** by increasing your intake of fiber (to provide the much needed fullness to reduce overall caloric intake) and protein (to help repair or retain muscle mass). **Cooking whole legumes need not involve hours of cooking.** By using pressure cookers to cook whole legumes, you can eat these healthy foods on a regular basis, without any hassle.

Try some of the **healthful cooking practices** covered on pages 12 and 13 to ensure you get maximum health benefits.

Here are a few tips to cook whole legumes efficiently while retaining most nutrients:

Soaking is optional for small beans and black-eyed peas, as you can pressure cook them even without soaking. If you wish to boil them on the stove, soaking is very important to reduce the cooking time.

Soaking is a must for large beans whether you pressure cook them or cook on the stove. You need to soak them 8-10 hours before cooking – overnight if you cook in the morning, or during the day if you cook in the evening. Alternatively, you can soak 2-3 types of beans over the weekend and pressure cook them simulaneously using stackable containers. You can refrigerate the cooked beans for a week or freeze for a longer time. Cooked beans retain their flavor better than cooked vegetables that are refrigerated or frozen. They also make for convenient yet healthy weeknight dinners or weekday lunch boxes.

Adding water two times the measure of beans should be sufficient, whether it is for soaking or for pressure cooking to make curries or stews. If you prefer intact beans for stir-fries or salads, use an equal amount of water as the beans. More water (>3 times the measure of beans) is required if you are boiling on the stove. Measuring the water, rather than eyeballing the water level, usually yields consistent results and prevents uneven cooking. For example, 1 cup of beans can be soaked in 2 cups of water and pressure cooked using the soaking liquid.

Total cooking time varies with the size of the legume, cooking method and whether or not they were soaked. Please refer to the guidelines summarized on page 27. The cooking time may need to be adjusted if you use aged varieties.

Soaked black-eyed peas (chawli) and small beans such as mung beans (mung), moth beans (moth or matki), and lentils (masur) can be cooked on the stove within 20-30 minutes. However, without soaking, you can still cook them in the pressure cooker for 5 minutes on low heat after the first whistle or after the pressure regulator starts to rock in case of a whistle-free pressure cooker. Older or aged varieties may take longer.

Soaked large beans such as chickpeas (kabuli chana), kidney beans (rajma) and dried peas, however, should generally be pressure cooked, as stove top boiling takes much longer (>1 hour). Pressure cooking only takes 10 minutes at the most after the first whistle or after the pressure regulator starts to rock steadily, in the case of whistle-free pressure cookers.

USES: Whole beans can be:

- used to make curries, stews, soups
- boiled or sautéed in spices, and used as a salad or pizza topping
- mashed and made into patties
- ground into a paste to make hummus
- mashed and used in cakes or brownies
- sprouted and used for salad toppings or curries
- soaked and ground to make dosas (crepes), appe (puffed spheres or pancake puffs) or dhoklas (steamed savory cakes), or fried to make pakoras (fritters)

A FEW GUIDELINES FOR COOKING SPLIT AND WHOLE LEGUMES*:

Legume Type	Boiling on Stove Method	Pressure Cooking Method
Dals Dals with skin	20-30 mins, without soaking 10-15 mins, if soaked	1 whistle or when pressure regulator starts to rock
Small beans Lentils Black-eyed peas	>30 mins without soaking or 20-30 mins if soaked	5 mins on low heat after 1st whistle or after pressure regulator starts to rock (without soaking)
Large beans Dried peas	>1 hour, 8-10 hour soak needed	10 mins on low heat after 1st whistle or after pressure regulator starts to rock, 8-10 hour soak needed

* Duration of boiling and pressure cooking is a rough estimate and can vary with the type of legumes and whether or not they are older varieties. See exceptions on page 15.

FLOURS

Gram flour (besan) is the most commonly used legume flour and is made from roasted chickpeas. However, other bean flours such as kala chana besan (black chickpea flour), black gram flour (urad flour), mung bean flour (mung flour) and soybean flour are becoming popular as well. Flours inherit the nutrition profile of the whole legume, however, some fiber, vitamins, and minerals are lost when the husk is removed and the bean is processed.

THE ADVANTAGE OF LEGUME FLOURS is that they can be used to increase our plant-based protein intake, and by healthy pairings we can compensate for the lower fiber and other nutrient content. They can be used to substitute all-purpose flour, or low fiber grain products like couscous, rice flakes (pohe), semolina (sooji), and vermicelli (sevayan) to make more nutritious instant recipes. They can also be added to flatbread doughs to increase the protein content while lowering the glycemic load.

Note that it is better to consume whole legumes more often than dals, and dals more often than flours, on account of the nutrient content and health benefits associated with whole legumes.

USES: Flours can be used to make delicious:

- ☼ homemade instant batter for vegetarian omelets, pancakes, instant crepes (dosas) or pancake puffs (appe) that do not require fermenting

- ☼ dough for different types of flatbreads (rotis, tortillas), especially to increase protein and potassium content

- ☼ filling for stuffed flatbreads (parathas)

- ☼ batter for fritters (pakoras) or for coating

- ☼ steamed cakes (muthias, dhoklas)

DRIED LEGUME CAKES (VADIS)

Just like textured vegetable protein (soy granules and soy chunks), dried mung dal cakes (mung dal vadis), dried urad dal cakes (black gram dal vadis), Punjabi vadis, etc. are also available in the market (Indian stores). They can be boiled for a few minutes and drained to use in curries, stir-fries, salads, or pulaos. They are pre-cooked dals or whole beans, sometimes mixed with spices and then dried. They may not share the nutrient profile of whole legumes, but can be conveniently used to add some extra protein to your meal. Read the ingredient list to make sure they do not contain all-purpose flour.

GERMINATION

Sprouted beans such as mung sprouts, chickpea sprouts, lentil sprouts, moth bean sprouts, etc. are available in supermarkets, however, they can be germinated at home as well.

The process of germination involves the following steps:

- ☼ **Soak** the beans for 8-10 hours.

- ☼ **Drain but do not discard** the water (reuse it as a stock in soups and stews, or for cooking rice and vegetables).

- ☼ **Wrap** the beans in a cheese cloth or muslin cloth for 12-36 hours (or more) depending on the length of the sprouts desired. Place the wrapped beans in a colander, cover them with a lid or plate and if needed, place the colander over a smaller size bowl to ensure some aeration. Shuffle the sprouts every 12 hours. To facilitate the sprouting process, the wrapped beans should be kept in a cool, dry, and dark place.

ADVANTAGES OF GERMINATION

Germination makes the proteins and carbohydrates in the beans easier to digest. The vitamin and mineral content is increased, especially that of B-complex vitamins and vitamins C and E. Discomfort or flatulence is also lessened with germination.

Sprouts can be used raw, steamed, or lightly sautéed. They can be served as a side salad, a topping for a main course salad or a filling for a sandwich or wrap. They can also be toasted to serve as a snack, added to yogurt to make a raita (yogurt dip), or mixed with chutneys to include in Indian chaats (street-side savory snacks), etc.

FERMENTATION

Fermented foods such as Greek yogurt, sauerkraut, kimchi, etc. are gaining popularity in the US and are finding a regular spot on the shelves in the supermarket. However, fermented foods have been an integral part of many cuisines. Here are a few examples:

Indian: chaas/ chaach (buttermilk), lassi (a yogurt-based sweet or salted thick beverage), raita (a yogurt-based side flavored with chunks of fruit or vegetables, herbs and ground spices), yogurt mint chutney, shrikhand (Indian dessert made with strained yogurt, with or without fruits and nuts), fermented legume batters, etc.

Mediterranean: Greek yogurt (plain or flavored with honey, nuts and fruits), tzatziki (Greek dip made with strained yogurt, cucumber, and herbs), etc.

European: sauerkraut (cabbage fermented with or without other vegetables)

Korean: kimchi (seasoned and fermented cabbage)

Japanese: miso (fermented soybean paste), tempeh, natto, etc.

American: sourdough bread

ADVANTAGES OF FERMENTATION

Fermented foods are valued because fermentation can:

- improve gastro-intestinal health **by increasing health-promoting bacteria (probiotics),** and thereby reduce the risk of colon cancer

- boost **immunity** or resistance to infections

- make proteins and carbohydrates **easier to digest**

- make minerals more available and **easy to absorb**

- increase B-complex and vitamin C levels, **especially vitamin B-12**, making fermented foods an important source of B-12 for vegetarians and vegans. However, if these foods are heated, the content of these vitamins is reduced.

The process of fermentation involves the following steps:

☼ Soak beans or dals for 4-10 hours (depending on the recipe, type of legume, etc.).

☼ Grind them into a fine or coarse batter.

☼ Ferment the batter overnight (8-16 hours) at 25-30° C (75-85° F), for example, in a warm place (inside an oven) in the cold months.

☼ Alternatively, to expedite the process of fermentation, home-ground bean flours can be used instead of dals or whole beans, and fermented for 8-10 hours with yogurt to introduce health-promoting bacteria.

Complementing legumes with yogurt adds good quality protein, calcium, vitamin A, vitamin D (if fortified), B-complex vitamins, and probiotics to your meal, thereby considerably improving the nutritive value of the meal. It can also make legumes more appealing and easier to digest. Much of the lactose is broken down in the process of fermentation, making it a low lactose food. You can strain the yogurt to further reduce the lactose content. Fat from the yogurt can also give you a feeling of fullness that will last for a while. Yogurt also provides vitamin A, an antioxidant, and important B-complex vitamins, especially B-12, which is needed for lowering blood homocysteine levels, a risk factor for cardiovascular diseases. Many vegans and vegetarians who do not consume yogurt, are likely to consume lower than required amounts of vitamin B-12; they should consider including other fermented foods in their diet.

WAYS TO INCORPORATE FERMENTED FOODS:

If fermented foods are not currently part of your diet, here are a few ways you can add these to your meal.

Fermented vegetables: Add a side of fermented vegetables, such as sauerkraut or kimchi, to your meals.

Miso, tempeh: Have some miso soup or soy sauce, while being mindful of the salt content. Try pairing these foods with a generous serving of tofu, whole beans, and colorful vegetables. Include some tempeh instead of tofu in your meal.

Fermented batters: Ferment legume batters to make idlis (lens shaped steamed cakes), dosas (crepes), uttapams (thick crepes with toppings), appe (pancake puffs), etc. (details in the respective recipes).

Yogurt: There are several ways to enjoy yogurt (dairy or non-dairy). Here are some ideas to get you started:

- ☼ Make a chutney with yogurt (tamarind yogurt chutney, mint yogurt chutney, yogurt-based red garlic chutney, etc.) and use as a salad dressing.

- ☼ When craving sweet things, try a mixture of yogurt, nuts, and chopped fruits.

- ☼ Serve ½ cup yogurt on a daily basis, either in homemade Indian buttermilk (½ cup water + ½ cup yogurt blended together with cumin powder or mint leaves) or in a lightly salted lassi (½ cup yogurt + ¼ cup water, rock salt, and black pepper), or just serve as a side with an optional ½ tsp honey.

- ☼ Make a yogurt dip (raita or tzatziki) by adding chopped vegetables or fruits to yogurt and seasoning with ground cumin and dried or fresh herbs.

PRESSURE COOKING

Pressure cookers use high pressure, which increases the temperature above the boiling point of water and thereby cooks tough foods in a shorter amount of time. The water in the pressure cooker reaches around 121°C (250°F), which is lower than the usual baking temperature of 180°C (350°F). **Pressure cooking can be a better method of cooking than baking,** as baking exposes food to a higher temperature and for a longer duration, which can deplete the nutritive value of the dish. Besides, baking also requires the use of leavening agents such as baking powder or baking soda (that further reduces B-complex vitamins) and/or a higher proportion of fat or sugar (increasing the caloric value). **Pressure cooking is ideal for dry and tough foods** such as legumes, cereal grains (rice, cracked wheat, etc.), and root and tuber vegetables (carrot, potato, yams, etc.). **Tender vegetables or leafy greens should not be pressure cooked** as they can be cooked faster without pressure, and the high heat can reduce their nutrient content.

ADVANTAGES OF USING A STOVE TOP PRESSURE COOKER:

Reduced cooking time: By pressure cooking for 5-10 minutes, more nutrients can be retained than in slow, longer-duration cooking methods.

Efficient: Large cookers can cook multiple items simultaneously (rice, beans, potatoes and other starchy vegetables, meat, chicken, etc.) by using stackable containers (as shown here).

Large Quantity: They are great for cooking large batches of food for a family or party.

Multi-purpose use: Pressure cookers can be used for steaming by removing the whistle or pressure regulator, with no need for separate steaming equipment. (Picture of steamer basket on page 22)

Cleaning: A stove top pressure cooker is easy to clean and maintain.

Durability: They are very durable and usually last for several years.

Replacements: Small parts such as safety valves, gaskets, etc. are readily available.

Reasonably priced: Stainless steel cookers are easily available for any budget. Please visit the **SHOP section** of the website (quicklydelicious.com) for reviews and recommendations on pressure cookers.

TYPES

Stove top pressure cookers are designed either **with whistles or pressure regulators** which indicate that the optimum pressure has been reached. **Try pressure cookers with pressure regulators if you do not like the loud whistle of traditional pressure cookers.** That is how I switched over from the traditional Indian pressure cooker to the one I currently have. Check out the SHOP section of the website for details. Electric pressure cookers, on the other hand, are standalone appliances with many control features.

pressure cooker with whistle

MATERIAL AND SIZE

Stove top pressure cookers are available in aluminum, stainless steel, and anodized aluminum or as standalone electric appliances with non-stick pots. Stainless steel cookers are the most durable and easy to maintain, while aluminum ones are less expensive. Anodized pressure cookers and non-stick pots used inside an electric pressure cooker have limited usage because of the special coating. I have not used any electric cookers for the purpose of cooking beans, so all of my tips relate to the use of stove top pressure cookers.

pressure cooker with pressure regulator

Pressure cookers come in a wide variety of sizes, ranging from ½ liter (½ quart) to more than 20 liters (20 quarts). You may want to buy one small cooker and one large cooker for different purposes. The small size cookers or pressure pans can cook one food item at a time – these are good for beginners or when you want to make a one-pot dish or cook in smaller quantities. However, if you want to be more efficient you can purchase the larger size cooker to cook one dish in a large quantity or get stackable containers to cook multiple items (rice, beans, chicken, meat, starchy vegetables, etc.) simultaneously.

Choose a size based on the number of items you want to cook at a time (2, 3 or more) or the quantity of food you typically prepare. Steamer baskets are usually purchased separately. A variety of steamer baskets and idli stands are available in the market. However, you can steam food in your stackable steel containers as well.

STEPS FOR USING A PRESSURE COOKER

Place the stand or cooking rack inside, at the bottom of the pressure cooker, and **fill it with water** until the stand or rack is just submerged.

Wash your measured legumes in a steel container **and add double the amount of water** or the amount mentioned in the recipe. Stack containers of any other foods, such as rice or root vegetables, that need to be cooked along with the beans. If you want to cook only beans, then you can cook them directly in the small cooker without using any container.

Place the containers on the stand and close the lid per the instructions in the manual. **Make sure the whistle or the pressure regulator is well placed** on the lid and the lid is sealed per the instructions of your model.

Turn up the heat to high and wait until it **whistles or until the pressure regulator begins to rock steadily.** It takes around 5 minutes on electric stoves, but can be faster on gas stoves.

Turn the heat down to low after the first whistle or after the pressure regulator starts to rock steadily, and let the beans or dals cook for **5-10 minutes** or as instructed in the recipe. You can set a timer on your cooking range or cell phone. This method yields more consistent results than counting the number of whistles in case of a traditional pressure cooker. If you miss the count you may overcook or undercook the dish. However, if you are more experienced and prefer to keep track of the count, then that is fine too.

Turn off the heat and wait until the pressure is released. This usually takes about 5 minutes. The safety valve in your cooker is typically raised during pressure cooking, and will return to its normal position when the pressure is released.

Your legumes, starchy vegetables, or rice are **ready.** Total cooking time is about 20-25 minutes. Add the legumes to the sauce, curry, sautéed vegetables or tempering that you have prepared while the legumes were cooking in the pressure cooker. Alternatively, you can store the legumes in the refrigerator for up to one week for later use.

For the **one-pot cooking method**, you can prepare your sauce, curry or tempering directly in the cooker, add the rinsed legumes, and then pressure cook them. The final dish will taste slightly different, but it is good to try some variations. You can include combinations of rice, legumes, and starchy vegetables.

STEAMING

Fermented or unfermented legume batters, or yogurt-based batters can be steamed in a steamer, or in a pressure cooker after removing the pressure regulator or whistle from the lid. When using a pressure cooker, place the stand at the bottom of the cooker and add enough water to submerge the stand. Then place the lid on the pressure cooker and turn the heat to high. Make sure the whistle or pressure regulator is removed. Once you see the steam emerging vigorously and steadily through the vent, turn off the heat and wait until the lid is easy to slide and it is safe to open the lid. Be careful to keep a safe distance from the cooker and open the lid in a way that the steam is directed away from you. Then quickly transfer the container with the legume batter to the cooker using tongs. Put the lid back on, turn the heat to medium and let the batter cook for 12-15 minutes. For making idlis, use the greased idli stand. Once the required steaming time is up, turn off the heat and wait until the lid is easy to slide and it is safe for you to open the lid. Check with a knife or toothpick to see if the batter is cooked – the knife or toothpick should come out clean. If not, then steam for a few more minutes. For pictures, please refer to page 148.

USING AN AEBLESKIVER PAN (APPE PAN)

An Aebleskiver pan (appe pan, paniyaram pan), used to make appe, paniyaram, or pancake puffs, offers a quick and easy way to steam batters – it cooks with the steam generated from the moisture in the batter itself. They are available as cast iron or non-stick pans, with 6 large or 12 small wells as shown in the picture on page 26. The pan is heated on medium to high heat after greasing the wells with a brush or by pouring a few drops of oil or ghee (clarified unsalted butter) into the wells. Once the pan is hot enough, but not smoking, pour 1-2 teaspoons of batter (depending on the size of the well) in each well, and cover it with a lid. Steam the puffs for about 2 minutes on medium heat or until the puffs are easy to flip. Flip them over with a fork, knife tip or the pointed wooden spatula that some manufacturers may provide with the pan., Cook the other side until done. You may pour a few drops of oil or ghee before flipping so that the puffs are not too dry. Serve when both sides are done! This method has become very popular for making quick and delicious breakfast dishes, and provides an interesting way to incorporate more legumes in your diet.

Summary

- **Cook a variety of legumes a few times a week**
- **Eat more whole legumes than dals or legumes flours**
- **Always soak large beans**
- **Utilize the soaking and cooking liquid**
- **Pressure cook to save time and retain nutrients**
- **Cook thoroughly**
- **Germinate/ Sprout/ Ferment whenever possible**
- **Avoid fruit salt, baking soda or baking powder as much as possible**
- **Add salt and acidic foods at the end of cooking**
- **Pair legumes with vitamin C rich foods**
- **Avoid tea and coffee with legumes**

MENU
planning

TIPS FOR BALANCING MEALS

Whether you have a great selection of recipes from your repertoire or you want to add some from this book, **balancing meals** is important to ensure that you and your family's health requirements are met. Many commercially available foods and meals, or even recipes available online may be labeled as "healthy," based on the presence of one or two popular "healthy" ingredients; however, this does not necessarily make them healthful or well-balanced. The amount of that healthy ingredient used, how often you eat that food, and how well it is complemented by other components of the meal or other foods during the day – all these factors contribute to making it really beneficial for you. And of course, if your diet is part of a healthy lifestyle, then it will have the most positive impact.

Throughout this book I have shared tips on how to increase the nutrient content of a meal, or minimize the loss of nutrients from foods. Most of the recipes come with '**pairing ideas**' that you can use in your unique way as well, by combining them with recipes that you already cook. These simple practices can help you develop your own healthy diet.

It is easy to meet one's protein and B-complex vitamin requirements on a non-vegetarian diet that includes meat, poultry (egg, chicken, turkey, etc.), dairy, and seafood. However, it is also easy to exceed one's caloric intake and not meet one's fiber requirements. On the other hand, a vegetarian diet that predominantly features grains (cereals such as wheat, rice, etc. and millets such as sorghum, finger millet, etc.) or dairy (milk, yogurt, paneer, cheese, etc.) and lower amounts of legumes, fruits and vegetables, can also exceed one's caloric requirement, without meeting protein and/or fiber requirements. Over a period of time, the excess calories, if not burned by physical activity, can lead to weight gain and other health problems associated with excess weight.

If you are on a vegetarian diet and still find yourself **gaining weight**, or have developed **diabetes, PCOS, high blood lipid levels, or high blood pressure,** then evaluate your food choices to see if your diet is characterized by sweet foods (other than naturally sweet fruits and dry fruits), fried foods, and lower or infrequent consumption of whole legumes, fruits and vegetables. Are you also getting enough physical activity per day? Reflect on other lifestyle factors as well. No matter what diet you follow, including more whole legumes can help improve your health. Consider some of the following tips to help gain better control over your blood pressure, glucose or lipids, treat constipation and even lose weight.

The first step is to include more whole legumes in your diet.

- ☼ Prefer **whole beans or dals with skin** over dals without skin or flours.

- ☼ If you currently consume whole legumes 1-2 times a week, then consider 3-4 times a week.

- ☼ If you consume only 2-3 types of whole and split legumes a week, then try other kinds and enjoy the greater variety. Include some large and some small beans. See the Legume Calendar (page 38) for some ideas.

- ☼ Replace some of your dal recipes with whole beans, lentils or dals with skin. Small beans can be easily pressure cooked without soaking, so add them to your khichadis or tadka dals.

The next step is to understand the amount of legumes to consume on a daily basis, especially for vegetarians.

- ☼ The recipes in this book are constructed in a way to help you include enough protein and fiber per serving and to help you feel full.

- ☼ For practical purposes, one can note that **1 cup of dry large beans or ¾ cup of dry small beans or dals** yields about 6 servings. Serving size will vary with recipes depenging on the amount of water and vegetables that are added to the dish. Similarly, 1 cup flour is about 4 servings.

- ☼ You are **not limited to consume just a single** serving in one meal. Depending on your age, physical activity and other biological needs, you can consume more or fewer servings.

- ☼ For smaller quantities, remember that **⅓ cup of dry large beans** will yield about 2 servings. When cooked they grow about 2.5-3 times in size and you will get 1 cup of cooked beans.

Amplify your efforts by replacing some of your grains (wheat, rice, etc.) with more legumes and vegetables.

- ☼ Prioritize finishing legumes and vegetables on your plate before consuming your second roti, slice of bread, or additional ½ cup of cooked rice.

- ☼ Get a second serving of legumes and vegetables instead of grains.

- ☼ Skip the grains (wheat, rice, sorghum, maize, etc.) in one meal a day for a few times a week. Have a salad or chaat with whole beans, or a soup with mixed beans and vegetables for either lunch or dinner, a few days a week. You can also make legume puffs (appe) for breakfast, or legume crepes for lunch or dinner and serve them with a vegetable stir-fry. Learn to enjoy your legume dishes by themselves – make them so delicious that you do not feel the need to have them with roti or rice.

- ☼ If you eat 2 rotis with ½ cup cooked legumes and ½ cup cooked vegetables in a meal, then consider 1 roti with 1 cup cooked vegetable and 1 cup cooked legumes. Adjust your roti, rice, bread or tortilla servings to make room for more legumes and vegetables. Don't feel full yet? Then have some fruits, yogurt or Indian buttermilk. Contrary to popular belief in India, fruits do not ferment or cause discomfort in the stomach when consumed with other fruits. In my next book I will get into the details of this topic and other myths.

- ☼ Serve pan-fried legume kebabs or patties along with a vegetable soup to make the meal more interesting. Or try vegetable patties with a beans soup. Make legume-based crepes or dosas to pair with your vegetable stir-fry or curry. I bet you will not miss the grains.

- ☼ If you are unable to include more legumes in your lunch or dinner, don't fret. You can replace the grain in your breakfast by making legume-based appe (puffs), dosas (crepes), idli (steamed buns) or dhoklas (steamed cakes) for breakfast, or have some roasted chana chaat as a snack, or hummus and vegetables.

Pair your legumes with a generous helping of fresh, raw salads or subzi (vegetable stir-fries) in each meal.

- ☼ Include vitamin C rich vegetables such as colorful bell peppers, kale, cabbage, cauliflower, broccoli, Brussels sprouts, radish, bok choy, tomato, etc. as a salad or quick stir-fry to improve iron absorption. Avoid overcooking or cooking these vegetables for a long time as it reduces the vitamin C content and other health benefits.

- ☼ Alternatively, enjoy some vitamin C rich fruits such as oranges, strawberries, guava, papaya, etc. at the end of the meal. Vitamin C can also help relieve acidity or heartburn.

- ☼ Eating more legumes does not mean eating fewer vegetables. The goal is to replace some grains with more legumes and vegetables; so do not skimp on your vegetable side.

Follow healthy cooking practices and methods as often as possible.

- ☼ Cooking methods that will preserve or improve nutrient content of legumes have been discussed in detail in the educational portion of the book (pages 12-22). Implementing these practices will give a boost to your nutrient intake.

- ☼ Pressure cook, boil on the stove, steam, pan-fry or use an appe pan to create healthy dishes for your family, instead of baking for a long time or deep-frying. Ferment and germinate whenever possible.

Complement legumes with yogurt (dairy or non-dairy) to ensure some vitamin B-12 and probiotics in your diet.

- ☼ Be sure to include fermented foods, especially if you follow a vegan diet. Please refer to the Fermentation section (pages 20-22) for details on fermented foods and their benefits. Discuss with your dietitian or physician if you need to supplement your diet.

Pair the lower fiber foods with high fiber foods for a good balance of fiber in a meal.

- ☼ Pairing whole beans with lower fiber grains or millets can prevent fiber overload in a meal, if you tend to develop flatulence. For example, whole beans such as chickpeas (chana), kidney beans (rajma), mung beans (mung), or dried green peas (sukha vatana) can be paired with rice, sorghum (jowar), maize or pearl millet (bajra) rotis, etc. However, when you do so, it's best to have a generous helping of the beans and lesser amounts of the grain.

- ☼ Complement your lower fiber wheat products such as semolina, vermicelli, pasta, couscous, etc. with whole beans as well.

- ☼ In khichadis, use equal proportion of legumes and grains and consider whole beans such as whole mung, or mung dal with skin, whole lentils (sabut masur) or black-eyed peas (chawli) to make your khichadis. You may recall that small beans, lentils, and black-eyed peas can be pressure cooked even without soaking. Substitute rice with whole grain barley, dalia, or rolled oats if you are using dals.

- ☼ Instead of making idlis or dosas with 3 or 4 parts rice and 1 part urad dal, use 2 parts rice and 1 part urad dal and serve with chana dal chutney or sambar to include more protein and/or fiber. Try the high fiber idli recipe (page 145) that uses dal with skin, which packs in more fiber and protein than brown rice.

- ☼ Similarly, pairing whole beans with lower fiber vegetables (page 35) can reduce fiber overload in a meal, and thereby reduce discomfort.

☼ On the other hand, pairing dals and legume flours, which are lower in fiber, with high fiber whole grains (whole grain rotis, bread, brown rice, etc.), vegetables or fruits can increase the fiber content of the meal. For example, a tomato omelet made with besan (gram flour) can be served with an apple. There is a misconception that all millet flours have a lower glycemic index than whole grain flours. Most millet flours such as sorghum flour (jowar) and pearl millet flour (bajra) have lower fiber and protein content compared to whole grain wheat flour, but are more nutrient-dense than rice. So, pairing millet flours with whole beans can help you enjoy a variety of grains and their health benefits.

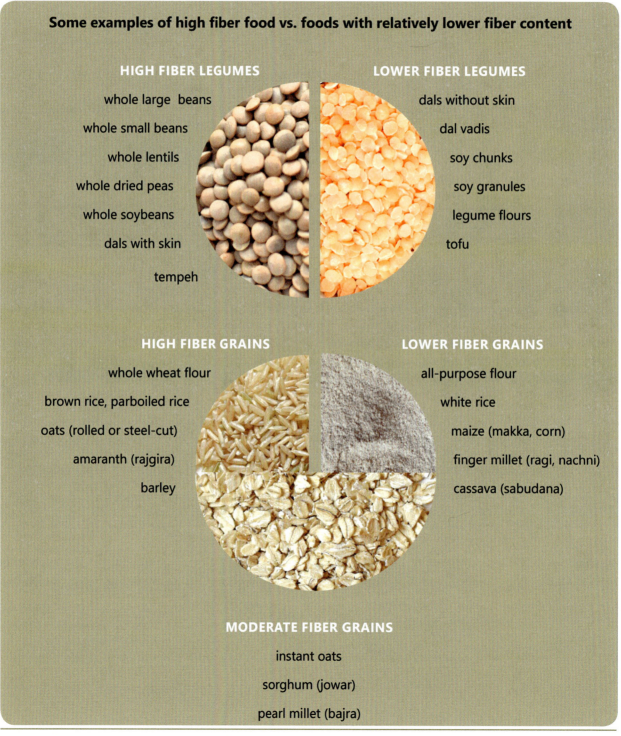

Some examples of high fiber food vs. foods with relatively lower fiber content

HIGH FIBER LEGUMES
- whole large beans
- whole small beans
- whole lentils
- whole dried peas
- whole soybeans
- dals with skin
- tempeh

LOWER FIBER LEGUMES
- dals without skin
- dal vadis
- soy chunks
- soy granules
- legume flours
- tofu

HIGH FIBER GRAINS
- whole wheat flour
- brown rice, parboiled rice
- oats (rolled or steel-cut)
- amaranth (rajgira)
- barley

LOWER FIBER GRAINS
- all-purpose flour
- white rice
- maize (makka, corn)
- finger millet (ragi, nachni)
- cassava (sabudana)

MODERATE FIBER GRAINS
- instant oats
- sorghum (jowar)
- pearl millet (bajra)

HIGH FIBER VEGETABLES

Avocado, Okra, Eggplant, Drumstick vegetable (moringa oleifera pods), Carrots

Green beans, Green peas, Edamame

Bitter gourd, Ridge gourd with seeds (turiya)

Cabbage, Cauliflower, Kale, Broccoli

LOWER FIBER VEGETABLES

Onion, Tomato, Cucumber, Lettuce

Spinach, Mustard greens, Colocassia greens, Bok Choi

Mushroom, Zucchini

Potato, Sweet potato, Bell peppers, Calabash (doodhi), Ridge gourd without seeds (turiya)

Pairing soluble fiber rich whole legumes may counteract the adverse impact of coconut or sugar on blood cholesterol or glucose respectively, depending on the amount of sugar or coconut used. Adding a small amount of sugar or coconut to some recipes to increase palatability of the dish does not make the dish unhealthy. Coconut is now valued for its medium chain fatty acids and potential to increase HDL cholesterol. It can be part of a healthy, active lifestyle. Discuss with your dietitian how much coconut will work for you. It is an important source of saturated fatty acids, especially for vegans.

Be aware of the salt and sugar content of processed foods, ready-to-eat, or instant foods such as canned foods, sauces (pasta, soy, etc.), flavored instant oats, dips, snacks, Indian condiments (papads, pickles, etc.), sweetened beverages, bakery foods, frozen treats, etc. that may easily bump up your salt and sugar intake. Be mindful of the sugar that you add to your beverages and homemade desserts or sweets. Each teaspoon of sugar contains about 4-5 grams, which amounts to 16-20 calories per teaspoon. If you consume 4 or more teaspoons a day then you are consuming 80-100 empty calories, that do not provide any other nutrient.

Include 1-2 servings of soybeans in your diet either as whole beans or soybean products – tofu, soybean flour, soy milk, soy chunks, soy milk, soy yogurt, etc., especially if you have PCOS or menstrual problems. Using tofu or soy chunks in place of paneer or cheese can increase the health benefits. Choose from a variety of recipes to include soy in some form or another.

Cook a few types of whole beans in advance, so you will have them on hand during the week, to simplify preparing dinners or packed lunches. Most of the 30 minute recipes in this book can be ready in 15 minutes if the legumes are cooked in advance. Soak 2-3 types of whole large legumes on the weekend, pressure cook them in stackable containers, and allow them to cool down to room temperature before refrigerating (up to one week). Then use them over the next 5 weekdays and cook another fresh batch on the following weekend.

A sample menu-planning guide (legume calendar) for incorporating and varying dals and whole legumes throughout the month, for vegetarian and non-vegetarian diets, is provided on page 38.

Drink 8-10 glasses of water on a daily basis. High fiber legumes alone cannot improve bowel movements and alleviate **constipation**. Water is an important facilitator of bowel movements, so be sure to stay well-hydrated.

Deal with flatulence, acidity, excess bile (pitta) or other discomforts associated with legumes. Follow fiber pairing ideas in this section to reduce flatulence associated with the consumption of whole legumes. For more ideas on reducing flatulence please refer to page 4.

Have some after-meal digestive or breath fresheners – fennel seeds or carom seeds. Mint leaves can help reduce acidity and excess bile secretion (pitta) very effectively while providing a cooling effect. Cumin and coriander powder can also help alleviate acidity and excess bile secretion. Healthy pairings with vitamin C rich fruits and vegetables can prevent acidity. Moderate the use of oil and spices, especially chili, red chili powder, black pepper, and garam masalas for reducing acidity. The amount of oil and spices used in the recipes may not cause any acidity; however, you may adjust them to your needs.

Grab some fresh or dry fruits, nuts, and seeds as snacks, or include them in your breakfast or main meals. They are an important source of phytochemicals, vitamins (B-complex, C, E, etc.) and some minerals. Fruits with the peel on (wherever applicable) and seeds can contribute to your fiber intake. Include a variety of seasonal fruits, at least 2-3 a day. When consumed fresh they can contirbute towards your daily vitamin C intake as well. Nuts and seeds are valued for their monounsaturated fatty acids that can increase HDL cholesterol and lower LDL cholesterol. Flaxssseds and walnuts are valued for their omega-3 fatty acids and the favorable ratio of omega-6 to omega-3 fatty acids, which can afford protection from inflammation. Chia seeds have a very high omega-3 fatty acid content. Almonds and sunflower seeds are an important source of vitamin E content, an important antioxidant. Flaxseeds and sesame seeds contain lignans that can help improve the hormone profile of those with PCOS.

Healthy food need not be low in oil or bland in taste. By learning to pair foods and cook with different ingredients, you can enjoy foods that you like in a way that it promotes health.

Every bit of effort can be a step forward in improving your health. Good health is a culmination of all your efforts not just in terms of healthy eating, but active lifestyle, ability to manage stress, genes, etc. I hope you find these diet-related tips useful!

Savor your food and enjoy good health!

LEGUME CALENDAR

DAY	MON	TUE	WED	THU	FRI	SAT	SUN
Legume	Whole	Split	Whole	Mixed	Split	Whole	Mixed
Week 1	Chickpeas (kabuli chana)	Green gram dal (mung dal)	Lentils (sabut masur)	Soy/ Poultry/ seafood/ mixed beans and dals	Pink lentils (masur dal)	Moth beans (matki)	Soy/ Poultry/ seafood/ dried peas
Week 2	Kidney beans (rajma)	Dried split peas (sukha vatana ki dal)	Lentils (sabut masur)	Soy/ Poultry/ seafood/ mixed beans or dals	Black gram (urad dal)	Green gram (sabut mung)	Soy/ Poultry/ seafood/ dried peas
Week 3	Black Chickpeas (black chana)	Red gram dal (toor dal)	Lentils (sabut masur)	Soy/ Poultry/ seafood/ mixed beans or dals	Pink lentils (masur dal)	Black gram (sabut urad)	Soy/ Poultry/ seafood/ dried peas
Week 4	Black beans	Pink lentils (masur)	Lentils (sabut masur)	Soy/ Poultry/ seafood/ mixed beans or dals	Black gram (urad dal)	Black-eyed peas (chawli)	Soy/ Poultry/ seafood/ dried peas

LET'S GET
started

SPICES, HERBS & AROMATICS

Spices can remarkably enhance the flavor and taste of your dish. They are also valued for their medicinal effect. Spice powders are now available in mainstream supermarkets in the US but may be expensive. However, you need to use only a small amount at a time. Ethnic Indian stores are also becoming popular and can be a good resource to check out different spice powders. Except for the use of garam masala and an occasional dash of Kitchen King masala, I am less inclined to use pre-mixed curry powders and prefer to play with the original ingredients to see how they impact the taste and flavor of my dish. Instead of curry powders, try buying some of the following ingredients and adding them in varying amounts in your recipes to create new flavors.

Chili (lal mirch) powders are available in different varieties depending on the type of chili pepper used. If you are not accustomed to eating hot or spicy foods, you may opt for paprika or Kashmiri red chili powder as they are not hot and only impart a natural red color to your dish. If you enjoy food with a little extra kick then go for the hot chili powder. Alternatively, use crushed red chili flakes, or dried chilies for tempering or making a hot sauce. Since chili powder is required in larger quantities than other spices in the spice box, I like to have an extra container with red chili powder so that I don't have to refill it often. Adjust the use of chili powder if you experience acidity.

Turmeric powder or ground turmeric (haldi) contributes a beautiful yellow color to your dish. Only a small amount is required – excessive amounts can turn the dish bright yellow in color and bitter in taste. It is highly valued for its anti-infective properties.

Coriander (dhania) powder or ground coriander imparts a fragrant and delicious flavor to your dish. However, if roasted for a longer time, it can make a dish taste bitter. Some may have a preference for cumin powder over coriander powder. However, I tend to use ground coriander more often.

Cumin (jeera) powder or ground cumin produces a cooling effect in your body, so go ahead and add some cumin powder to your buttermilk or beverages, especially in the summer. It is commonly used along with coriander powder in most Indian curries. Its flavor is very different from that of ground coriander, and is darker in color.

Garam masala of is a flavor-packed mix of roasted spices ground to a powder. The proportion of ingredients varies with the brand but generally includes cloves, cinnamon, peppercorn, bay leaf, cumin seeds, mace, caraway seeds, nutmeg, cardamom, star anise, etc. It makes for a convenient spice mix, as purchasing packets of the individual ingredients of the spice powder can be very expensive. Even a small amount of garam masala can significantly enhance the flavor of the dish. Each spice has a unique medicinal property but when used in excess, this masala may cause discomfort for some. Whole spices can be added to the tempering to enhance the flavor of the curry, biryani, or pulao. **Kitchen King masala** is another generic spice blend that is so flavorful that you can use it instead of garam masala or

exclusively (without any other spice powders).

Green cardamom can be used in savory and sweet dishes. Whole green cardamom can be tempered or the seeds can be lightly toasted and ground for using in desserts, whereas the black cardamom is generally used in savory dishes. In fact, cardamom shells, when added to boiling tea, create a beautiful aroma. Tea masala contains cardamom and some spices like cinnamon, fennel, black pepper, etc.

Curry leaves (kadi patta), cumin (jeera) seeds, black, red or yellow mustard (sarson) seeds and other

spices need to be tempered for maximum flavor extraction. Most seeds only sizzle in heated oil, however, mustard seeds and curry leaves crackle quite a bit. So, if you are experimenting with tempering for the first time, then start with seeds like cumin that do not crackle, before you learn to temper mustard seeds. A safe way to temper mustard seeds is to cover the pot or pan once the seeds or curry leaves are added, or allow the hot oil to cool a bit before adding them. Dehusked, split mustard seeds make for a great addition in spicy Indian pickles, while ground mustard can be used to make mustard sauce.

Asafetida (hing) is a cream to light yellow-colored spice powder. It has a fetid smell but when added to a tempering, it makes the tempering very aromatic. It is used in small amounts because of its strong flavor and it is also believed to relieve gas. However, you can add a generous amount for an intense flavor. Turn off the heat before you add it, as it burns easily.

Caraway (shah jeera, Persian cumin) looks like cumin or fennel seeds but has a distinct flavor. It is usually used in garam masala powders, specialty spice powders, or added to biryanis and rye bread.

Fennel seeds (saunf) are sweet and very aromatic, similar to cumin seeds, but light green in color. Add them to your tempering, kebabs, and crepes to create great flavor variations. They tend to have a cooling effect and can be used in the summer. They are believed to aid digestion. It is a common Indian practice to serve fennel seeds as a breath freshener after a meal.

Carom seeds (ajwain, ova) are used in small amounts, more often in the cold months as they generate heat in the body. Add them to flavored flat breads (theplas, parathas) or stir-fries. They also tend to alleviate flatulence and are believed to facilitate digestion.

Nigella seeds (onion seeds, kalonji) are black in color and resemble black sesame seeds. They impart a beautiful aroma that will make your pulaos or any curry all the more appealing, even if they are used in a small quantity. Add them to your tempering and simmering stews, or just sprinkle some as a garnish on your naans or flat breads.

Panch Phoron is a 5-spice mixture containing a combination of mustard, cumin, fenugreek, fennel and nigella seeds, and is popular in the eastern and some northern states of India. This mixture can be used for tempering to produce a unique mix of aromatic, sweet and bitter taste.

Fenugreek seeds (methi) are bitter, brown seeds that are used in small quantities in tempering or fermented batters. They are added to beans or dals at the time of soaking to make ground fermented batters that are used to make idlis (lens shaped steamed cakes), appes (puffs) or dosas (crepes).

Dry fenugreek leaves (kasuri methi) are a special ingredient that you can toss into your curries, flatbreads, or stir-fries to get a restaurant-like flavor. They are dried fenugreek leaves.

Dals such as chana dal and urad dal are also used for tempering. They usually turn pink when tempered and brown when burnt, so keep the heat on low to medium while tempering these dals. Make sure they are well toasted before you add other ingredients.

The spice pantry can be an adventure to explore… as such, I will not divulge the mystery of all the spices and leave it to you to experience their flavors.

Aromatics and herbs like onion, ginger, garlic, mint, cilantro (coriander leaves), curry leaves, chili peppers, lemon, lime, galangal, kaffir lime leaves, parsley, rosemary, thyme, basil, oregano, tarragon, etc. when added to your dish can take your dish to a whole new level. You can slice, chop, grate, grind to a paste, temper, juice, or purée to create a celebration of aroma and flavors. Using fresh aromatics can help you replace some of the processed curry pastes or sauces you may be tempted to buy. Homemade sauces and pastes can last for a few months in the freezer or for a few weeks in the refrigerator, depending on the ingredients used.

Besides fresh aromatics, dry herbs can also be used – dried rosemary, oregano, thyme, etc. – or you can purchase a jar of mixed herbs for common Mediterranean flavors. My favorite herb is cilantro (coriander leaves) and I have an irresistible urge to garnish every dish with chopped cilantro. Naturally, my go-to spice powder is coriander powder. But, I also love the aroma and flavor of fresh mint, basil, cardamom, cinnamon, cardamom, fennel and nigella seeds. What is your favorite herb, spice or spice powder that you use almost every day?

Like spices, herbs also have medicinal properties – ginger is great for sore throats, coughs and colds, and mint relieves acidity, excess bile production or indigestion. Garlic may have a cholesterol lowering effect, while curry leaves and lemon juice may help lower blood pressure. Onion, tomatoes, rosemary, oregano, parsley, etc. are packed with antioxidants.

It is easy to grow herbs such as mint, curry leaves, basil, oregano, thyme, rosemary, etc. even in a small space. Harvesting fresh herbs and spreading the blooms or seeds to grow new plants can be a rewarding experience. So, grab a potted plant or buy some fresh herbs for adding the finishing touch to your dish.

TEMPERING

Tempering spices, also known as vaghar or chaunk in Hindi, is an important element in Indian cooking. It involves adding whole spices, asafetida, seeds, herbs, aromatics and/or certain split legumes such as chana dal or urad dal, to hot oil. Tempering enhances the flavor because spices and aromatics contain fat-soluble flavor compounds that are released during tempering. For tempering, the oil needs to be hot, but not smoking. A good way to judge the right temperature for tempering is to move your palm over the pot or pan, high above the oil. If you feel some warmth, that's when you can add the tempering ingredients. Heat can then be turned off to prevent the tempering ingredients from getting burnt.

Mustard seeds and curry leaves are the only tempering ingredients that splatter when added to hot oil; most other ingredients just sizzle or their color changes. Mustard seeds will not crackle in warm oil; the oil needs to be hot. One can cover the pot with a lid once these ingredients are added, then turn off the heat. It is a common practice to temper whole spices such as spice seeds (cumin, mustard, fenugreek, etc.), bay leaves, cinnamon sticks, cloves, cardamom, peppercorns, dried chilies to extract maximum flavor. The color of turmeric and red chili powder, and the flavor of spice powders also intensifies in oil.

You can skip the tempering, if you prefer, and use only spice powders in your cooking. Sautéing the spices in oil along with the main ingredients is another way to infuse more flavor.

Tempering can be poured over a cooked dal, beaten yogurt, chutneys or a fresh salad of shredded vegetables. This technique is called tadka, and the dal prepared this way is called dal tadka or tadka dal. In such dishes, the tempering becomes the highlight of the dish. The tempering is varied to create interesting flavors. So feel free to use any of your favorite spices or herbs to temper your dals.

Tempering offers a minimalist way to season a cooked dal. Even if you do not sauté onion or tomato, you can still make a plain cooked dal interesting with a tempering of spices. Throw in some tangy lemon juice, sliced mangoes (unripe), or tamarind pulp along with jaggery, grated coconut, honey, or sugar and you will have a great sweet and sour dal ready in no time. Do not forget to garnish with cilantro and serve hot.

HOW TO CUSTOMIZE THESE RECIPES

Adjust the spice amounts per your family's preferences; reduce or increase the amount of chili powder for your threshold of heat and feel free to increase the ground spice powders to appeal to your standards. The spice powder quantities used here are only recommended amounts for creating a flavorful and delicious dish. Skip the garam masala and red chili powder if you are accustomed to eating less intense flavors, or if you prefer to avoid spicy food.

Substitute the beans or dals in these recipes for any variety of your choice. You may use ginger powder or garlic powder if you do not purchase them fresh on a regular basis. The powders can be very intense and should be used in smaller amounts and increased gradually. You may use commercially prepared ginger-garlic paste, if that works better for you. Alternatively, you can make ginger-garlic paste at home and refrigerate or freeze it. Replace whole spices with spice powders if you do not have easy access to whole spices. For example, instead of cumin seeds you may add cumin powder.

Experiment with different spice powders. Instead of garam masala, you may use a dash of cinnamon powder, clove powder, black pepper powder, and temper with bay leaf.

Adapt by using some tips and ideas from these recipes to your traditional dishes. Use herbs, spices, vegetables, and beans that are more commonly used in your culture.

Serve these versatile dishes for any meal. For example, black beans kebabs can be served as an appetizer or a main course burger, chana dal appe can be served for breakfast or at tea-time, dosas can be served for breakfast or main course, etc.

EASY WAYS TO ADAPT RECIPES TO YOUR PALATE

INDIAN CURRY	THAI CURRY	CHINESE STIR-FRY / SOUP	MEXICAN BOWL / PLATE	ITALIAN / SPANISH SAUCE	MEDITERRANEAN PLATE
temper regional **spices** in oil (optional)	sauté onion	sizzle **garlic & ginger** in a wok	prepare **salsa**	sizzle **garlic** in oil	pita bread
sauté onion and tomatoes	add vegetables, tofu	add vegetables, tofu	prepare **guacamole**	sauté onion and **tomatoes**	**hummus / tahini / baba ganoush**
ginger, garlic (optional)	fresh **curry paste** (galangal, garlic, shallots, chilies, coriander, cumin, lime juice, kefir lime)	**soy sauce**	sauté vegetables (fajitas)	add vegetables, beans, and cheese (optional)	add vegetables, beans
add vegetables, beans / tofu	**coconut milk**	black pepper / red chili flakes	add cooked beans	dried / fresh **herbs**	dried / fresh **herbs**, **paprika**
spice powders	sugar, lime juice		**cumin, pepper / jalapeño**		
& cook	& cook	& cook		& cook	
serve with whole grain roti, rice or dosas	serve with brown rice	serve with brown rice	serve with brown rice / whole grain tortilla / salad greens	serve with whole grain pasta / on pizza	

HIGHLIGHTS OF THE RECIPES

Most of the recipes presented here are carefully crafted to pack each serving with **enough protein and fiber along with other important nutrients,** without going overboard on the calories. In addition, **healthy pairing ideas** included here will ensure that you have well-balanced meals to serve your family.

Legume-based dishes are **gluten-free** unless paired with wheat based flatbreads or blended together with gluten containing flour. Most recipes are **nut-free and dairy-free** as well.

The majority of the recipes can be **cooked within 30 minutes,** and even less **(within 15 minutes)** if the legumes are cooked in advance.

Adjust the spice powders and chili powder per your preference. **Substitutions and variations** can help you create a diversity of flavors from just one recipe.

The recipes are quite **versatile,** as they can be used for different dals and beans, served as a side dish or main dish, cooked in one pot or two pots, transformed from a soup to a stir-fry for use as filling in wraps, sandwiches or toppings on salads, pizzas, etc.

Tips for cooking or preparing in advance have been provided to make the recipes more convenient. Although I like to use fresh herbs or aromatic pastes, you can make ginger paste, garlic paste or other ground aromatics at home in advance and store in the refrigerator. I chop or grate some herbs and aromatics, mash in a mortar pestle, or use a hassle-free, small size blender to make a ground paste in a minute to create delicious flavors. For more tips on efficient, space-saving and economical gadgets, check out the **SHOP section of my website (http://quicklydelicious.com).**

Standardized measuring cups and spoons were used for developing these recipes. **Medium-sized vegetables or fruits** were used unless specified.

Abbreviations and measurement units that you may come across are:

Abbreviations & Conversions	
tsp – teaspoon	1 tsp ~ 5 mL
Tbsp – tablespoon	1 tbsp ~ 3 tsp ~ 15 mL
oz. – ounce	1 cup ~ 240 mL
Kg – kilogram	1 cup ~ 8 oz.
g – grams	1 oz. ~ 30mL or 30 g
L – Liter	1 Tbsp ~ 3 tsp
mL – milliliter	1 kg ~ 2 lbs
lb – pound	1 lb ~ ½ kg
mins – minutes	½" ginger = 1 tsp ginger paste
~ – approximately	

STAY CONNECTED

These are just a few of my favorite recipes on legumes. There are a lot more recipes that I could not include in this book. I will continue to post them on my website. You can subscribe to my website **http://quicklydelicious.com** via email or social media to receive articles, ideas and resources on health and nutrition, and not miss out any delicious, healthy recipes with meal-balancing tips. Feel free to share your feedback on the website, Amazon, or on the Facebook page. Do not hesitate to send me your questions or requests for recipes or nutrition topics of interest to you; I will be more than happy to assist. In this book, I have made references to some recipes on my website. The website offers healthy recipes with nutrition snippets so you can learn about the ingredients used and tips for healthful pairings to create balanced meals. I also share tips and ideas for healthy food shopping and lifestyle-related resources and articles. If you would like to read more about the **budget-friendly, efficient and space-saving appliances and cookware** I have used in this book, please refer to the **SHOP section of the website for reviews and details about the products**.

Wishing you all a happy and healthy life!

Bubbling
CURRIES & STEWS

Curries and stews are easy to make and can be served as a main course, appetizer, or all-in-one soup. A well-balanced bean and vegetable stew can also be a delicious yet convenient lunch box meal.

You can serve your traditional dals and bean curries as soups and enjoy them plain, and pair the roti or rice with vegetables. This way, vegetarians can increase their protein and fiber intake without adding the extra calories from the additional roti or rice typically consumed with the dal or beans. You may feel full sooner than you normally would. If you don't, then have some yogurt or fruit.

Main course stews can be a great way to combine beans and vegetables. Make sure to include lots of vegetables. If adding vegetables to your stew throws the recipe off-balance, then serve them as a fresh salad, quick stir-fry or simple subzi, which can be prepared while the beans stew is cooking. Legumes do not preclude the need for vegetables or fruits in your diet. The goal of this cookbook is to assist you increase the intake of legumes by substituting some of your grains (bread, roti, rice, millet flatbreads, tortilla) or animal proteins. However, this does not imply that carbohydrates are bad for you, or that you should start a zero carb diet. Substituting part of your grains (cereals or millets) with legumes helps balance your diet by adding more protein and fiber without increasing overall calories. This may provide greater health benefits, especially if you have diabetes, pre-diabetes, hypertension, polycystic ovary syndrome, or need to lose weight while you make other lifestyle changes.

Adding a small amount of sweetener or coconut to some dishes can make the dish more palatable without making it unhealthy. Keep in mind the right perspective of evaluating the meal as a whole. Whole legumes are very high in fiber, especially soluble fiber, which can help counteract the impact of coconut and sugar on blood cholesterol and glucose, respectively.

Now, let's implement some of these ideas!

RESTAURANT-STYLE DAL MAKHANI / BLACK GRAM CURRY
a North Indian dish and global favorite

This lip-smacking, creamy dal is typically made with whole black gram (mungo bean, sabut urad) with or without kidney beans (rajma), simmered for several hours in a mélange of spices, and generous amounts of cream or butter. My healthier, quick version is equally delicious and uses moderate amounts of ghee (clarified, unsalted butter) which can be replaced by oil, if preferred. Skip the cream to limit the calories but not the deliciousness. Enjoy this no-soak recipe, packed with nutrients that could be otherwise lost by long hours of cooking.

Per serving: 140 Cal | 7g protein | 5g total fat | 5g fiber

Servings: 6 **Cooking Time: 30 mins**

Main ingredients
¾ cup whole black gram (sabut urad)
½ medium onion, chopped
2 large tomatoes, puréed
1½" ginger, chopped and mashed
2 large cloves of garlic, chopped
A few sprigs of cilantro, chopped

Spices
1 bay leaf
½ tsp cumin seeds
⅛ tsp turmeric powder
¾ tsp red chili powder
½ tsp kasuri methi
½ tsp garam masala

Staples
1 tsp sugar – read tip
2 tbsp ghee or oil
Salt to taste

Overnight soak is not required. Just wash the whole urad, add 1½ cups water and pressure cook for 5 minutes on low heat after the first whistle or after the pressure regulator begins to rock. Then, turn off the heat and wait until the pressure is released. You can cook the urad ahead and store in the refrigerator for up to one week.

While the urad is cooking, prepare the gravy. Heat the oil or ghee (clarified, unsalted butter) in a steel pot. Add the bay leaf and cumin seeds after the ghee melts. Allow the cumin seeds to sizzle a bit and then add the onion and garlic. Sauté on medium heat until the onion becomes light brown.

When the onion turns light brown, add the tomato purée and sauté until it thickens. Add the remaining spice powders and sauté for a minute. If you are still waiting for the pressure to release, prepare a fresh salad or raita, a yogurt dip with vegetables, preferably choosing those rich in vitamin C (cabbage, bell peppers, radish, tomato, etc.) to enhance the absorption of iron. Season the salad or raita with salt and black pepper.

Once the pressure is released, transfer the cooked urad to the steel pot (along with the cooking liquid) and mix well. Add salt, sugar, mashed ginger, and 1 cup of water, and bring it to a boil. Cover the pot and let it simmer for 3-4 minutes on low heat so that all the flavors get infused into the dal. Garnish with chopped cilantro and some ghee or butter, enjoy it with whole grain rotis and salad or raita.

Tip: The amount of sugar used is very small (<1g per serving) and does not alter the calories or glycemic index.

Note: Making chutneys, batters, smoothies, and purées became so quick and convenient with this small blender, that I tend to use it almost everyday. Visit the SHOP section of my website (quicklydelicious.com) to check out this appliance.

ZHATPAT MASUR / NO FUSS LENTILS CURRY
it couldn't get easier than this

This is a hassle-free curry that I learned from my mom after my marriage, when I was exploring easy and healthy recipes so that I could cook 2-3 dishes at a time. You can cook this curry in the pressure cooker while you prepare a vegetable subzi (stir-fry). Lentils are high in iron and folate, making them important for those with low blood hemoglobin. They do not require soaking, so add these to your weekly menu. You can serve this curry with roti or rice, or enjoy it as a side soup. You can also add vegetables of your choice such as carrots, bell peppers, zucchini, squash, etc. to make it a low-carb, main course soup.

Per serving: 150 Cal | 6g protein | 5g total fat | 7g fiber

Servings: 3 **Cooking Time: 30 mins**

Main ingredients
½ cup whole lentils (sabut masur)
¼ onion, chopped
½ tomato, chopped
1½" ginger, grated or mashed
2 garlic cloves, grated or mashed
1 green chili, chopped
A few sprigs of cilantro, chopped

Spices
⅛ tsp turmeric powder
¼ tsp red chili powder
¼ tsp coriander powder
½" cinnamon stick
2 peppercorns (kali mirch)
A pinch of asafetida, optional

Staples
1 tbsp oil or ghee
Salt as needed

Wash the lentils, transfer them to a steel container that can fit in your pressure cooker and add double the amount of water (1 cup of water for ½ cup lentils). Add the onion, tomato, ginger, garlic, chili, asafetida, turmeric, and chili powder to the lentils and mix well. Pressure cook for 5 minutes on low heat after the first whistle or after the pressure regulator begins to rock, and turn off the heat. Let the pressure cooker cool down. If you prefer to boil over the stove, cook until the lentils are tender.

In a steel pot, heat the oil or ghee and add the cinnamon stick and peppercorns (tempering) and let them sizzle a bit. Transfer the cooked lentils to the tempering. Sprinkle salt and coriander powder, and mix well, and let it boil for 2 minutes.

Add additional chili powder if you like it spicy. Garnish with cilantro and serve with whole grain roti or rice. Pair this curry with vitamin C rich cabbage and green beans subzi (stir-fry) from my website (quicklydelicious.com).

Variations: Transform this curry into **LENTILS VEGETABLE SOUP** by sautéing diced carrots, zucchini, squash, and bell peppers over the cinnamon and peppercorn tempering and adding the cooked lentils.
For the one-pot method, prepare the tempering in the pressure cooker and proceed with the recipe.

KALA CHANA CURRY / BLACK CHICKPEAS CURRY
curry with a meaty flavor

Kala chana (black chickpea) is important because it is one of the few legumes that contains omega-3 fatty acids, although in small amounts. It also contains more soluble fiber than the small, whole beans. This dish has a meaty flavor, which may appeal to meat lovers. This recipe has two versions – one is the dry version (stir-fry) and the other one is with curry. I grew up eating the dry version that my mom would make. I loved it so much that I would even grab some as an after-school snack. **Note:** Recipe contains dairy.

Per serving: 160 Cal | 8g protein | 5g total fat | 9g fiber

Servings: 6   **Soak time: 8-10 hours**   **Cooking Time: 30 mins**

Main ingredients
1 cup black chickpeas (kala chana)
1 large onion, chopped
1" ginger
2 large garlic cloves
2 tbsp yogurt, optional

Spices
⅛ tsp turmeric powder
½ tsp red chili powder
½ tsp garam masala

Staples
2 tbsp oil
Salt as needed

Soak the chana for 8-10 hours with 2 cups of water. Pressure cook it along with the soaking liquid for 10 minutes on low heat after the first whistle or after the pressure regulator starts to rock, and then turn off the heat. You can also cook it ahead and store in the refrigerator for up to one week. Rice can be pressure cooked along with the chana by using a stackable container.

While the chana is cooking, chop the onion and grate the ginger and garlic, or prepare fresh ginger-garlic paste. Heat the oil in a non-stick pot and add the chopped onion. Sauté the onion on medium heat for a few minutes until caramelized. Then add the ginger-garlic paste and spice powders, and mix well for a minute or two. Enjoy the aroma that develops from roasting the spice powders over the sautéed onion. Set this aside.

When the chana is done, add it with the cooking liquid to the pot. Add more water for desired consistency. Simmer for about 5 minutes on medium heat so the chana absorbs the flavors. The longer the chana steeps in the spices, the more flavorful it becomes! This curry tastes even better the next day!

Add salt and let the chana cool down a bit before adding the yogurt. The yogurt changes the color to a nice light brown curry, while also reducing the heat of the red chili powder and garam masala. Serve with whole grain phulkas, roti or even rice since this dish is very high in fiber. Pair with a fresh salad or quick stir-fry (subzi) of cabbage and green bell pepper (capsicum).

Variation: KALA CHANA SUBZI (BLACK CHICKPEAS STIR-FRY) – To make the dry version, skip the yogurt and additional water that was added to make the curry. Sauté the chickpeas until the cooking liquid dries out or reserve the cooking liquid for another stew or curry. My mom makes this subzi in an iron wok which gives it a darker color and an amazing flavor, while increasing the iron content.

ADRAKWALI MUNG DAL / GINGER-INFUSED MUNG DAL
for those who love ginger

I learned this dish from my husband – the hallmark of this dish is the generous use of freshly mashed ginger. Those who love ginger are sure to love this dish. It took me several tries to get the right proportion of ginger, onion, and tomato. In this dish, grated ginger may not yield the same flavor as well-mashed ginger. Therefore, I recommend that you mash the ginger well with a mortar and pestle to extract maximum flavor – a technique shared by my husband.

Per serving: 150 Cal | 7g protein | 5g total fat | 5g fiber

Servings: 3   **Cooking Time: 30 mins**

Main ingredients
½ cup mung dal with skin (chilkawali mung dal)
½ onion, chopped
1 medium tomato, chopped
1-1½" ginger piece, mashed
4-5 curry leaves, washed and patted dry
A few sprigs of cilantro, chopped

Spices
⅛ tsp mustard seeds
¼ tsp cumin seeds
2 pinches of asafetida
⅛ tsp turmeric powder
¼ tsp red chili powder

Staples
1 tbsp ghee
Salt to taste

Wash the mung dal. Add double the amount of water (1 cup of water) and pressure cook up to the first whistle or until the pressure regulator starts to rock. Then turn off the heat and allow it to cool down.

In the meantime, dice the onion and tomato, and mash the ginger. Heat the ghee in a steel pot and when it is hot add the mustard seeds. Turn off the heat when the mustard seeds begin to crackle. Cover the pot if you are not accustomed to tempering. Then add the cumin seeds, asafetida, curry leaves, and chopped onion. Turn on the heat to high and sauté the onion until it turns light brown.

Add the tomatoes, turmeric, and red chili powder, and sauté on medium heat until the tomatoes have softened. Turn off the heat and rest until the mung dal is ready.

Transfer the cooked mung dal from the pressure cooker to the steel pot and turn on the heat to medium. Add 1 cup of water, mashed ginger, salt and mix well. Let the dal or soup simmer for 2-3 minutes to infuse the flavor of ginger.

Adjust salt, red chili powder, or ginger per your preference. There are regional and seasonal variations in the taste and flavor of ginger, so adjust accordingly. You should be able to smell and taste ginger!

Garnish with chopped cilantro and serve with rice or whole wheat roti or enjoy it plain as a side soup. Pair with a fresh salad of grated beetroot and carrot seasoned with lemon juice and salt, or pumpkin stir-fry (subzi).

DAL HARYALI / DAL WITH SPINACH
spinach and black gram dal

This dal combines the goodness of urad dal (split black gram with skin) and spinach. Urad dal with the skin (chilkawali urad dal) has more fiber and other nutrients than the dehusked dal. Adding spinach or other leafy greens to a dal is a great way to eat more greens and makes your legume-based dishes more interesting.

Per serving: 150 Cal | 7g protein | 5g total fat | 5g fiber

Servings: 6 **Cooking Time: 30 mins**

Main ingredients
¾ cup urad dal with skin (chilkawali urad dal)
2 cups frozen chopped spinach or 1 bunch of fresh spinach, chopped
1 tomato, chopped
2 large garlic cloves, mashed
1-1 ½" ginger, mashed

Spices
½ - ¾ tsp red chili powder
½ tsp garam masala
½ tsp cumin powder, optional

Staples
2 tbsp ghee or oil
1 tsp crushed jaggery (<1g sugar per serving)
Salt to taste

Wash the urad dal and set it aside. Heat the oil in a pressure pan or a small pressure cooker and add the mashed garlic and ginger.

Wait for a few seconds and then add the dal, spice powders, and 1½ cups of water and pressure cook up to the first whistle or until the pressure regulator starts to rock. Turn off the cooker and let it cool down.

Once the dal is cooked, mash it lightly with the ladle. Add the chopped spinach, tomato, salt, and jaggery, and mix well. Then add water as needed and simmer for about 2 minutes on medium heat.

Serve the dal with whole grain roti or bhakri (jowar, bajra, mixed grain, etc.). Pair with a refreshing salad of grated radish, carrot, and beetroot seasoned with salt, black pepper, and lemon juice. Garnish with a few peanuts and raisins.

Variations: You can substitute urad dal with mung dal (with skin) for this recipe.
You may add a tadka – temper cumin, mustard or fenugreek seeds and then pour it over the dal.
Add a bay leaf, some caraway (shah jeera), or other whole spices to the ginger-garlic tempering, and sauté chopped onion to infuse more flavor.
Substitute spinach with any other greens – fenugreek, colocassia, mustard leaves, etc.
You may also cook some chicken along with the dal.

Tip: Keep in mind the amount of sugar is very small (<1g per serving) and only balances the taste.

ROJANA MASUR DAL / EVERYDAY PINK LENTILS SOUP
simply delicious pink lentils dal

The flavor of garlic, fenugreek seeds, and coriander powder used to create this delicious dal, will certainly leave you wanting more. You will believe me after you have tried it. Masur dal or pink lentils are rich in iron and do not increase in volume like other dals, so you can consume more protein in your usual portions. It also cooks in the shortest amount of time. Try to alternate your staple mung dal, chana, or toor dal (split pigeon peas) with this dal.

Per serving: 120 Cal | 6g protein | 4g total fat | 3g fiber

Servings: 6   **Cooking Time: 30 mins**

Main ingredients
¾ cup pink lentils (masur dal)
½ onion, chopped
1 tomato, chopped
2 large cloves of garlic, mashed
A few sprigs of cilantro, chopped

Spices
½ tsp fenugreek (methi) seeds
A pinch of asafetida, optional
⅛ tsp turmeric powder
½ tsp red chili powder
½ tsp coriander powder

Staples
1½ tbsp ghee or oil
Salt to taste

Pressure cook the masur dal with double the amount of water (1½ cups) up to the first whistle or until the pressure regulator begins to rock. Then turn off the heat and wait until the pressure is released. If you prefer to boil the dal on the stove, do not add salt and cook it with 3-4 times the water, until it is soft enough to mash. You can either cook it ahead and refrigerate for up to a week, or prepare it fresh.

Heat the ghee in a pot and add the methi seeds when it is hot. Lower the heat and let them sizzle a bit before you add the mashed garlic and asafetida. When the garlic becomes light brown, turn up the heat to high and add the chopped onion and sauté until it is translucent.

Add the tomato, spice powders, and salt and sauté for a minute or two. When the tomatoes soften and the ghee separates, add the cooked dal and mix well. Then add some water for the desired consistency and bring it to a boil.

Garnish with chopped cilantro and serve hot with whole grain roti or phulkas or serve as a side soup. Pair with a quick subzi (stir-fry) made with okra or green beans, as they are high in fiber and can balance the lower fiber content of dals.

Variation: Use this recipe for any other split beans (dals) such as mung dal with skin, chana dal (yellow split peas), toor dal (split pigeon peas), or mixed dals (mung, urad, masur, toor, chana).

SIMPLY CHOLE / CHICKPEAS CURRY
a simplified chole recipe

There are various recipes for making Chole, a chickpeas curry traditionally prepared in northern India, but popular all over the world. It may be referred to as chana masala as well. Chickpeas, also known as garbanzo beans or kabuli chana, are typically used in this recipe, but you can use this recipe for black chickpeas or the green variety. Here is a very simple yet flavorful recipe. If you want to make the elaborate version, please refer to the **PUNJABI CHANA MASALA** on page 96.

Per serving: 180 Cal | 7g protein | 7g total fat | 7g fiber

Servings: 6   **Soak time: 8-10 hours**   **Cooking Time: 30 mins**

Main ingredients
1 cup chickpeas (kabuli chana)
1 onion, finely chopped
2 tomatoes, finely chopped or puréed
1" ginger, mashed
1 green chili, sliced (optional)
A few sprigs of cilantro, chopped

Spices
½ tsp cumin seeds
A few pinches of asafetida, optional
⅛ tsp turmeric powder
¾ tsp red chili powder
¼ tsp garam masala
1 tbsp kasuri methi, optional

Staples
2 tbsp oil
1 tsp jaggery, honey or sugar (if tomatoes are sour) – read tip
Salt as needed

Soak 1 cup chickpeas for 8-10 hours with 2 cups of water. Pressure cook them along with the soaking liquid for 10 minutes on low heat after the first whistle or after the pressure regulator starts to rock. Turn off the heat and wait until the pressure is released. You can cook the chickpeas in advance and store in the refrigerator for up to one week.

While the chickpeas are cooking, prepare the curry. Heat the oil in a steel pot and add the cumin seeds. After they sizzle, turn off the heat and add the green chili, if you like it spicy. Then add the asafetida and chopped onions. Sauté the onion until it turns light brown on medium heat.

Then add the tomatoes and rest of the spices and allow the tomatoes to cook on medium heat. When the oil begins to separate, add the cooked chickpeas (along with the cooking liquid) and mix well.

Add an additional 1 cup of water, some salt, and ginger. Let the chickpeas boil on medium heat for about 5 mins. Taste to see if the curry is tangy. Add a little bit of sugar to balance the taste. Garnish with cilantro and serve with rice, fresh whole wheat phulkas or rotis. Pair with minty cucumber yogurt dip (raita), fresh salad of sliced vegetables, or add leafy greens (spinach, kale, fenugreek, etc.) to your chole.

Variations: You can vary this Chole recipe by using ginger-garlic paste. Throw in a bay leaf, cinnamon stick, and 1-2 cloves while sautéing onions for a more aromatic flavor. You may use ready-made chole masalas, tandoori masala, or chana masala to create delicious variations. Add green bell pepper, or paneer cubes, spinach, kale, etc. to transform your chole into a wholesome soup.

SINDHI CHOLE – temper cumin seeds, sauté onion and cooked chickpeas with ¼ tsp turmeric powder, ½ tsp each of red chili powder, coriander powder and cumin powder. Add water as needed, simmer for a few minutes and serve.

Tip: Do not add any tea extract to Chole or any legume recipes as it can impair the absorption of iron and other nutrients in the chickpeas. The amount of sugar used is very small (<1g per serving).

SAMBAR / SOUTH INDIAN VEGETABLE STEW
delicious vegetable stew infused with flavors of the South

South Indian delicacies such as idli (steamed cakes), dosas (crepes), or uttapams (thick dosas with toppings), that are made with fermented legume batters, are generally served with this flavorful vegetable stew and a few colorful chutneys. Preparing the whole meal can be a somewhat elaborate affair. However, you can prepare the sambar and chutneys in advance and then serve them with freshly cooked idlis or dosas. Sambar can be enjoyed with parboiled or brown rice as well. Although sambar is regularly cooked in a South Indian household, and the recipe may vary to highlight regional produce and spices, today it has found a place in every Indian household. Here is my mom's sambar recipe, that has been greatly appreciated by our family and friends.

Per serving: 160 Cal | 6g protein | 5g total fat | 5g fiber

Servings: 6 **Cooking Time: 30 mins**

Main ingredients
¾ cup split pigeon peas (toor dal)
½ onion, diced
2 tomatoes, diced
1 green bell pepper (capsicum), diced
1 carrot, peeled and diced
1 cup diced (1" pieces) drumsticks (pods of moringa oleifera) or eggplant
1 cup peeled and diced bottle gourd or red pumpkin
A few sprigs of cilantro, chopped
5-8 curry leaves, washed and patted dry

Spices
¼ tsp fenugreek (methi) seeds
¼ tsp mustard seeds
⅛ tsp turmeric powder
¾ tsp red chili powder
1 ½ tsp coriander powder
¾ tsp garam masala
A few pinches of asafetida
¼ tsp tamarind paste or 2 tsp tamarind pulp (dry tamarind rehydrated in warm water)

Staples
2 tbsp oil
Salt to taste

Wash the toor dal, add 1½ cups water, pumpkin, and drumsticks to the dal and pressure cook up to the first whistle or until the pressure regulator starts to rock. Turn off the heat and wait until it cools.

In the meantime, heat the oil in a steel pot and add mustard seeds when the oil is hot (but not smoking). Turn off the heat after the seeds begin to crackle and then add fenugreek seeds, asafetida, and curry leaves; cover the pot after you add the seeds if you are not accustomed to tempering.

Add the remaining vegetables and spice powders (turmeric, red chili, coriander, garam masala) and sauté for a minute on high heat. Pour in 1 cup of water, cover with a lid and let the vegetables cook on medium heat. Turn off the heat when the vegetables are lightly cooked.

Once the dal, pumpkin, and drumsticks are cooked, add them to the spiced vegetables. Add salt and water for desired consistency, and boil it for 2-3 minutes. Mix in the tamarind pulp slowly, otherwise the sambar may become very dark or very sour. Serve with idlis, dosa, uttapam, or parboiled rice, or enjoy as a main course soup.

Variation: Use cumin seeds, fresh coconut, freshly ground spices, or commercial sambar masala.

Tip: Include at least 6 cups of vegetables with ¾ cup of dal for a well-balanced dish. Otherwise, pair it with a generous portion of fresh salad or a mixed vegetable pachadi (vegetables lightly tempered with seeds, curry leaves, asafetida, chili, and coconut).

RAJMA MASALA / KIDNEY BEANS IN A SILKY CURRY
a quick kidney beans curry

This is another north Indian dish that is a global favorite. You can prepare restaurant-style rajma masala by using the same recipe as the restaurant-style dal makhani (page 50). But try this delicious and simpler recipe as well. Rich in soluble fiber, potassium, iron and B-complex vitamins, kidney beans can help improve control over blood glucose and high blood pressure, while also improving blood hemoglobin levels.

Per serving: 160 Cal | 8g protein | 5g total fat | 9g fiber

Servings: 6   **Soak time: 8-10 hours**   **Cooking Time: 30 mins**

Main ingredients
1 cup kidney beans (rajma)
1 onion, finely chopped
2-2½ large tomatoes, puréed
A few sprigs of cilantro, chopped

Spices
⅛ tsp turmeric powder
¾ tsp red chili powder
½ tsp garam masala
1 tsp kasuri methi, optional

Staples
2 tbsp oil
1 tsp jaggery or sugar, optional (if tomatoes are sour) – read tip
Salt as needed

Rinse and soak rajma for 8-10 hours with 2 cups of water. Pressure cook along with the soaking liquid for 10 minutes on low heat after the first whistle or after the pressure regulator starts to rock. Then turn off the heat.

Meanwhile, heat the oil in a steel pot and add the chopped onion. Sauté the onion on medium heat until light brown. If you want to add ginger-garlic paste, then you can add now, but trust me, this recipe tastes good even without ginger-garlic paste. Purée the tomatoes – I have a small blender that is very convenient to use and clean. It makes puréeing and grinding quick and easy. Check out the SHOP section of my website (quicklydelicious.com) for reviews on kitchen-friendly and time-saving appliances.

Add the tomato purée to the onion along with rest of the dry ingredients. Cook the tomatoes on medium heat. When the oil begins to separate add the cooked rajma (along with the cooking liquid). Add salt and additional water as needed, and let the rajma boil on medium heat for a minute or two. Taste to see if the curry is tangy. Add a small amount of sugar to balance the taste. Garnish with cilantro and serve with whole grain phulkas or vegetable pulao. Pair with a side of fresh salad with vitamin C rich vegetables (radish, cabbage, bell peppers, etc.).

Variations: You can vary this recipe by using ginger-garlic paste. Throw in a bay leaf and other whole spices like cinnamon, cardamom, cloves, etc. while sautéing onions for a more aromatic flavor.
You may use ready-made rajma masala, tandoori masala, pav bhaji masala or chana masala to create delicious variations.
Add any leafy greens to this curry.

Tip: The amount of sugar used is very small (<1g per serving), and only makes the dish more palatable. It does not alter the overall calories or glycemic index per serving.

RAGDA PATTIES / POTATO PATTIES WITH DRIED PEAS CURRY
yummy dried peas curry with potato patties

A popular street food in Mumbai and other metropolitan cities of India, this white or green peas curry is served with potato patties, and topped with colorful chutneys and a garnish of chopped tomato and onion. My mother's flavored patties will obviate the need for any chutneys, saving you some time and effort. However, if you make plain potato patties with just salt and no other flavoring, then cilantro chutney and tamarind chutneys are needed to add the extra zing.

Per serving of ragda: 160 Cal | 8g protein | 5g total fat | 9g fiber
Per serving of patties (2 patties): 110 Cal | 2g protein | 4g total fat | 2g fiber

Servings: 4 | **Soak time: 8-10 hours** | **Cooking Time: 30 mins + 30 mins**

Main ingredients
- 1 cup white or green dried peas (sukha safed ya hara vatana)
- 1 onion, diced
- 2 tomatoes, diced or puréed
- 1" ginger
- 2 large cloves garlic
- 1 green chili
- A few sprigs of cilantro, chopped

Spices
- ½ tsp cumin seeds
- A pinch of asafetida, optional
- ¼ tsp turmeric powder
- ¾ tsp red chili powder
- ¾ tsp coriander powder
- ½ tsp garam masala
- 1" cinnamon stick
- 1 bay leaf

Staples
- 2 tbsp oil
- Salt to taste

Flavored Patties
- 1 large Russet potato (~¼ kg, ½ lb)
- 1 slice whole wheat bread, toasted
- 1" ginger or 2 tsp ginger paste
- 1 green chili
- A few mint leaves, chopped (optional)
- 1 tbsp oil
- Salt to taste

Soak the dried peas for 8-10 hours in 2 cups of water.

Wash the potato well. Pressure cook the dried peas (along with the soaking liquid) and the potato in stackable containers for 10 mins on low heat after the first whistle or after the pressure regulator starts to rock. Turn off the heat. Once the pressure is released, take out the potato; cut it to let it cool. **Note:** Potato can be pressure cooked whole without any water to reduce nutrients from leaching away.

In the meantime, grind the ginger-garlic-chili into a coarse paste for the ragda. Grind the ginger and chili into a fine paste for the patties.

Heat the oil in a steel pot and add cumin seeds. Allow them to sizzle before you add the asafetida, cinnamon, and bay leaf. Then add the chopped onion and coarse paste, and sauté on medium heat until the onion is light brown. Add the chopped tomatoes and spice powders and sauté until the oil begins to separate.

Add the cooked peas when ready, along with some salt and mix well. Pour ½ to 1 cup of water depending on the consistency you prefer and let it simmer for a few minutes, then turn off the heat.

For the patties, peel and mash the potato after it has cooled. Blitz a slice of whole wheat toast into crumbs. Add the bread crumbs, salt, and ginger-chili paste to the mashed potato. Make equal-sized round balls and flatten them lightly. Heat the oil in a non-stick pan and pan-fry the patties until brown on both sides.

Serve the patties with the ragda, garnished with chopped cilantro, onion, and tomatoes. Ragda can be eaten with rice, whole grain bread or chapati if you prefer to skip the patties. Prepare the patties ahead to save some time. You can also stuff the patties with leftover ragda (by drying it out in a pan) to serve as an appetizer or a snack with chutneys.

HARA VATANA SHORBA / DRIED GREEN PEAS SOUP
a delectable soup

Dried green or white peas require soaking, however, if you prefer something instant then substitute with green split peas. They are rich in zinc, which is important for immunity or building resistance to infection. The split variety has lower fiber, vitamin, and mineral content than the whole dried peas, but can be a good substitute for animal protein. So try this recipe with whole or green split peas.

Per serving: 160 Cal | 8g protein | 5g total fat | 9g fiber

Servings: 6   **Soak time: 8-10 hours**   **Cooking Time: 30 mins**

Main ingredients
1 cup dried white or green peas (sukha hara ya safed vatana)
½ onion, diced, optional
1" ginger, grated or chopped and mashed
A few sprigs of cilantro, chopped

Spices
¼ tsp cumin seeds
½ tsp red chili powder
1 bay leaf
A few pinches of asafetida, optional

Staples
2 tbsp oil
Salt as needed

Wash 1 cup of white or green dried peas, and soak for 8-10 hours in 2 cups of water.

Pressure cook along with the soaking liquid for about 10 minutes on low heat after the first whistle or after the pressure regulator starts to rock. Turn off the heat and wait until the pressure is released. You can cook in advance and store in the refrigerator for up to one week.

In the meantime, heat the oil in a steel pot and when it's warm, add the cumin seeds along with a bay leaf. When the cumin seeds sizzle, add the asafetida.

Then add the chopped onion and sauté until light brown on medium heat. Sprinkle red chili powder and sauté for a minute. By now, your dried peas might be ready. Transfer them to the pot and add the mashed ginger, additional water, some salt, and chopped cilantro. Mix well and bring it to a boil.

Simmer for 2-3 minutes to infuse the ginger flavor. If you add ginger early on, it will lose some of its flavor. Adjust the red chili powder per your liking. Serve with a fresh garnish of cilantro and/or a dollop of yogurt. Pair with a generous portion of lightly sautéed kale, broccoli, or spinach, or grilled vegetables (zucchini, bell pepper, carrot, mushrooms, etc).

Variation: You can use ¾ cup green split peas for this recipe. No soaking is required for split peas and they can be directly cooked in a pressure cooker for 10 minutes on low heat after the first whistle or after the pressure regulator starts to rock. You can boil them on the stove as well, so cook per your preference. The whole dried peas, however, have more fiber and need to be soaked.

LASOONI PALAK CHANA / SPINACH & CHICKPEAS STEW
garlic infused spinach and chickpeas stew

I adapted my lasooni palak (garlicky spinach stir-fry) recipe to include chickpeas and make this quick and delicious stew. Spinach and chickpeas have a very subtle taste and seamlessly take on the bold flavor of garlic.

Per serving: 200 Cal | 9g protein | 9g total fat | 8g fiber

Servings: 2 **Cooking Time: 15 mins**

Main ingredients
4 cups fresh spinach, chopped coarsely
1 cup cooked chickpeas
2 large cloves of garlic or 4 small cloves

Spices
¼ tsp cumin seeds
½ tsp red chili powder
¾ tsp coriander powder

Staples
1 tbsp oil, ghee, or butter
Salt to taste

Cook ahead: Soak ⅓ cup of chickpeas in double the amount of water for 8-10 hours to yield about 1 cup of cooked chickpeas. Pressure cook along with the soaking liquid, for 10 minutes on low heat after the first whistle or after the pressure regulator starts to rock. Then turn off the heat. Store the cooked chickpeas in the refrigerator for up to one week.

Wash and chop the spinach.

Heat the oil in a pan and add the garlic and cumin seeds. Let the seeds sizzle and then add the chickpeas (along with the cooking liquid) and spice powders. Sauté for a minute so that the chickpeas are coated with the spices.

Add the spinach and let it cook for 2-3 minutes. Cover with the lid. Add water if you want to make a stew, or you can serve this dish as a stir-fry.

Add salt and adjust the spice level and serve with a **HEALTHY GRILLED CHEESE OPEN TOAST.** Combine chopped onion and tomato or bell pepper with grated cheese, season with salt and black pepper, and spread on a slice of whole grain bread. Grill this toast on both sides in a pan using oil.

Variation: Substitute spinach with other leafy greens such as kale, collard greens, mustard, fenugreek, etc.

MATKI CHI AMTI / SIMPLE MOTH BEANS CURRY
a simple yet delicious Maharashtrian curry

Moth beans weren't my favorite beans until my mom shared a couple of recipes to transform moth beans into tasty curries. Some of these Maharashtrian recipes are simple, while others might be a bit elaborate. Here is a simple one to enjoy moth beans. Moth beans are also rich in iron, folate and magnesium. Note: Recipe contains coconut.

Per serving: 140 Cal | 7g protein | 5g total fat | 5g fiber

Servings: 6 **Cooking Time: 30 mins**

Main ingredients
¾ cup moth beans
½ onion, finely chopped
¼ cup coconut milk – read tip
A few sprigs of cilantro, chopped

Spices
⅛ tsp mustard seeds
2-3 pinches of asafetida, optional
⅛ tsp turmeric powder
½ tsp red chili powder
½ tsp garam masala

Staples
2 tbsp oil
1 tsp powdered jaggery (unrefined sugar) – read tip
Salt to taste

Wash the moth beans and set aside.

Heat the oil in a small pressure cooker or pressure pan . Add mustard seeds when the oil is hot but not smoking. Turn off the heat after the seeds begin to crackle.

Then add the asafetida, onion, moth beans, and spice powders, and sauté on high heat for a minute. Pour 1½ cups water and pressure cook for 2-3 minutes after the first whistle or after the pressure regulator starts to rock steadily. Turn off the heat. This way, the moth beans are undercooked and we can cook them in the coconut milk later, for enhanced flavor.

After the pressure is released, season with salt and jaggery, and stir in the coconut milk. Add more water, if needed, and simmer until the beans are cooked. Garnish with cilantro, and serve with roti or rice and a side salad or koshimbir, as the Maharashtrians say. I made a **carrot-red bell pepper salad** with lemon juice, salt, black pepper and cilantro to go with it. Bell peppers are rich in vitamin C that can enhance iron absorption.

Variations: This recipe goes very well with whole mung as well.
Make an **MATKI CHI USAL** (Maharashtrian stir-fry) by pressure cooking the beans with ¾ cup of water and not adding water after the beans are pressure cooked. Substitute coconut milk with dry coconut powder (dessicated coconut).
Substitute garam masala with any specialty or regional masala such as goda masala, CKP talla masala, etc.
Add ginger-garlic paste to the onion to boost the flavors.

Tip: Since the whole beans are high in fiber, especially soluble fiber, using a small amount of coconut or coconut milk and jaggery, may not impact your blood cholesterol and sugar.

DHABA DAL / ROADSIDE EATERY DAL
simple and delicious

This dal recipe is my all-time favorite. Quick and flavorful, I assure you it takes hardly 10 minutes if you have cooked the mung dal in advance. I call it the dhaba dal because it reminds me of the dal I have tried at a few roadside eateries, that specialize in serving food quickly to travelers on the go. Whenever you cook dal, cook an extra amount so that you can refrigerate a portion for using later in the week. Just jazz it up with the spices and aromatics you like over ghee or oil, toss in some onion and/or tomato, and you have a nourishing side soup ready within minutes.

Per serving: 120 Cal | 7g protein | 5g total fat | 2g fiber

Servings: 3   **Cooking Time: 30 mins**

Main ingredients
½ cup mung dal or mung dal with skin (split mung beans or split green gram)
½ onion, finely chopped
1 tomato, finely chopped
2 cloves garlic, coarsely chopped
½ green chili, sliced, optional
4-5 curry leaves, wash and pat dry
A few sprigs of cilantro, chopped

Spices
¼ tsp cumin seeds
A few pinches of asafetida
¼ tsp turmeric powder
½ tsp red chili powder

Staples
1 tbsp ghee
Salt to taste

Wash the mung dal and add double (1 cup) of water. Pressure cook the dal up to the first whistle or until the pressure regulator starts to rock. Turn off the heat and wait until the pressure is released. You may boil the dal on stove but it will take longer and may taste slightly different. Cook a few varieties of dals in advance using stackable containers and refrigerate for up to a week in order to save time on weeknights.

Melt the ghee in a pot and add the garlic, chili, and cumin seeds. When the seeds begin to sizzle, add the asafetida, chopped onion, some chopped cilantro, and curry leaves. Sauté on high heat until the onion becomes translucent.

Then add the chopped tomato, turmeric and red chili powder, and sauté on high heat until the tomato softens a bit. Turn off the heat. The onion and tomato should be a bit undercooked as they impart a characteristic taste and texture to the dhaba dal. Pour the cooked dal into the pot. Add additional water, salt and chopped cilantro, and bring it to a boil. Serve the dal as a side soup or enjoy with whole grain rotis and a high-fiber subzi (stir-fry). Pair with the quick and easy, high fiber, cabbage-green beans stir-fry from my website (quicklydelicious.com).

Variation: You can use this recipe for any dal – toor dal (split pigeon peas), urad dal, mung dal with skin, chana dal (split chickpeas, yellow split peas), or mixed dals. Vary the tempering with different spices.

Tip: Mung dal is low in fiber and increases considerably in volume when cooked. As such, one may consume less protein and fiber in the usual serving size of a dal, especially if it is runny. Consider making it thick, mixing in different dals or having extra servings of the runny dal.

BENGALI GHUGNI / BENGALI WHITE PEAS SOUP
street-side flavors of the east

This recipe is my attempt to replicate the street-side Bengali ghugni, or white peas curry, that I tasted in a street stall in Mumbai. It is similar to Mumbai's ragda (page 64) but the panch phoron spice mix imparts a unique flavor. It contains mustard seeds, cumin seeds, nigella seeds (kalonji), fenugreek seeds (methi), and fennel seeds (saunf). This spice blend is typically used in the northern and eastern states of India, and some parts of Nepal. You can create this spice blend at home by mixing equal parts of the individual spices.

Per serving: 160 Cal | 8g protein | 5g total fat | 9g fiber

Servings: 6   **Soak time: 8-10 hours**   **Cooking Time: 30 mins**

Main ingredients
1 cup dried white peas (sukha safed vatana)
½ onion, finely chopped
1" ginger piece
2 cloves garlic
1 green chili
4-5 curry leaves, washed and patted dry
½ cup cilantro leaves and stems

Spices
½ tsp panch phoron (5-spice mix)
½ tsp garam masala
2-3 pinches of asafetida, optional

Staples
2 tbsp ghee
Salt to taste

Wash and soak the white peas for 8-10 hours in 2 cups of water.

Make a coarse paste of ginger, garlic, chili, curry leaves, and cilantro or just chop them coarsely.

Heat the oil in a pressure pan or small pressure cooker. Add the panch phoron and allow the seeds to crackle. Then add the asafetida, chopped onion, and garam masala, followed by the coarse paste. Sauté on high heat until the onion becomes light brown, and then add the white peas along with the soaking liquid.

Seal the cooker and pressure cook the peas for 10 minutes on low heat after the first whistle or after the pressure regulator starts to rock. Then turn off the heat and allow the cooker to cool down. Add salt, garnish with freshly ground black pepper, and serve.

Variations: You can use mixed beans for this recipe – white, green dried peas, black eyed peas, moth beans, black chickpeas, etc. Instead of garam masala, you may season with whole spices such as ½" cinnamon, 2-3 peppercorns, 1 bay leaf, 2 cloves and black cardamom (masala elaichi). Add some amchur powder (dry mango powder) for a different flavor.

Tip: Try a fusion meal to cut back some calories and serve it as a side soup with a salad of your choice. I paired it with one of my favorite salads – diced apple, strawberries, and almonds over a bed of salad greens topped with some crumbled paneer and dressed with a simple honey vinaigrette (page 97).

LASOONI MUNG DAL / LEMON GARLICK MUNG DAL SOUP
with refreshing pickled onion

I believe that the simplest way to bump up the aroma and flavor of any dish is to add some sizzling garlic. This soup highlights the simplicity and flavor of garlic, while the pickled onion adds a refreshing touch to the creaminess of the mung dal.

Per serving: 120 Cal | 7g protein | 5g total fat | 2g fiber

Servings: 3 **Cooking Time: 30 mins**

Main ingredients
½ cup mung dal
2-3 large cloves garlic, mashed
1-2 tsp lemon juice
½ onion, cut into thin slices
1 tbsp fresh coconut, optional
A few sprigs of cilantro, chopped

Staples
1 tbsp ghee
Salt to taste

Wash the mung dal and set it aside. Pickle some sliced onion in lemon juice and set it aside. Pickled onion makes this thick soup very refreshing. Mung dal when cooked becomes quite voluminous, and so in order to consume enough protein, it is recommended that you either make the dal thick or consume an extra serving of the runny dal.

Heat the ghee in a steel pot. When the ghee is warm enough add the garlic and let it sizzle. Add the washed mung dal, 1 cup of water and bring it to a boil. Let it simmer on medium heat until tender. Add more water if needed.

Season with salt and black pepper, and enjoy with a garnish of cilantro and pickled onion or fresh coconut. Pair with a high-fiber stir-fry of okra, eggplant, cluster or green beans as mung dal is low in fiber.

DHANSHAK DAL / MIXED DAL & VEGETABLE STEW
a Parsi specialty dal

Please refer to the **CHICKEN DHANSHAK** recipe (page 112). Exclude the chicken and follow the same instructions and proportions.

PALAK CHOLE / CHICKPEAS IN SPINACH SAUCE
creamy and lip-smacking

Please refer to the **TOFU PAKORAS IN SILKY SPINACH GRAVY** recipe (page 166). Instead of making tofu pakoras, add cooked chickpeas. Soak 1 cup chickpeas for 8-10 hours in 2 cups of water. Pressure cook them along with the soaking liquid for 10 minutes on low heat after the first whistle or after the pressure regulator starts to rock. Then turn off the heat. Add the cooked chickpeas to the spinach gravy.

CHAWLI CHI AMTI / BLACK-EYED PEAS CURRY
versatile recipe for crispy stir-fry or comforting curry

Black-eyed peas (chawli), also referred to as cowpeas, are great for weeknights as they do not require soaking. Just pressure cook and enjoy a delicious curry (amti) as a side soup or as a stir-fry (usal) for a wrap or salad. Amti is the Maharashtrian term for curry, while Usal refers to stir-fry (subzi). My mom turns the left-over curry into a stir-fry by sautéing it in a cast iron wok so that the cowpeas darken and become crisp. As kids, we loved eating the crispy peas as a snack.

Per serving: 150 Cal | 7g protein | 5g total fat | 3g fiber

Servings: 6 **Cooking Time: 30 mins**

Main ingredients
1 cup black-eyed peas (chawli, cowpeas)
½ onion, diced
1" ginger, mashed
2 garlic cloves, mashed
A few curry leaves
A few sprigs of cilantro, chopped

Spices
A pinch of asafetida, optional
⅛ tsp mustard seeds
½ tsp red chili powder
⅛ tsp turmeric powder

Staples
2 tbsp oil or (1 tbsp oil + 1 tbsp ghee)
1 tsp jaggery, powdered (<1g sugar per serving)
Salt to taste

Wash the cowpeas and set aside. No soaking necessary.

Heat the oil in a pressure cooker or pressure pan. Add the mustard seeds and let them crackle. Then add asafetida, curry leaves, diced onion, ginger and garlic, spice powders, and sauté for a minute on high heat.

Then add the cowpeas with 2 cups of water and jaggery, and pressure cook the cowpeas for about 10 minutes after the first whistle or after the pressure regulator starts to rock. Turn off the heat and let the pressure subside. Add salt to the cooked cowpeas, garnish with cilantro and serve. Pair with whole grain roti and a fresh salad or any leafy vegetable stir-fry.

Variations: You can use this recipe not just for any small beans, but you can soak and cook the large beans in the same manner.
Add any specialty or regional masala such as goda masala, CKP talla masala, etc. for more flavor.
Transform this into a **CRISPY COWPEAS SNACK** by sautéing the leftover curry in a cast iron pan on medium heat until the cowpeas darken a bit and crisp up. Add some oil to prevent sticking.
My mother-in-law makes a similar curry but tempers cumin seeds, adds chopped tomato, and does not add any garlic.

Note: Cowpeas are the only large beans that do not require soaking. However, they do not have as much fiber as most whole beans. Cowpeas contain omega-3 fatty acids, although in small amounts.

Tip: The amount of sugar used is very small (<1g per serving).

JAIN LAUKI CHANA DAL / SIMPLE SPLIT PEAS & CALABASH SOUP

a simple dal with no onion or garlic

Most of the dals can be tailor-made for the Jain community by excluding onion, ginger, and garlic, except in the recipes that are characterized by garlic and ginger flavors. Jain recipes can be quick to prepare. However, you may need to add some sweetener and increase the spices in order to compensate for the sweetness typically imparted by the onion or the flavor imparted by ginger and garlic. **Note:** Recipe contains dairy.

Per serving: 160 Cal | 7g protein | 7g total fat | 7g fiber

Servings: 4	Soak time: 1 hour	Cooking Time: 30 mins

Main ingredients
½ cup chana dal (split yellow pea, split chickpeas)
2 cups bottle gourd (lauki), peeled and diced
1½ tomato, diced
A few sprigs of cilantro, chopped

Spices
½ tsp cumin seeds
2-3 pinches asafetida, optional
¼ tsp turmeric powder
¾ tsp red chili powder

Staples
2 tbsp oil
1 tsp sugar, honey, or jaggery (powdered) – read tip
Salt to taste

Wash the chana dal and soak in 1 cup of water for 1 hour.

Heat oil in a pressure pan or small pressure cooker and temper cumin seeds. When the seeds sizzle, add asafetida, spice powders, bottle gourd, and chana dal with the soaking liquid. Mix well and pressure cook for 5 minutes on low heat after the first whistle or after the pressure regulator starts to rock steadily. Turn off the heat and let it cool down.

Add the tomatoes, salt, jaggery, and additional water, if needed. Bring it to a boil and then serve with a garnish of chopped cilantro. Enjoy this dal with whole wheat rotis, a quick stir-fry of leafy greens (fenugreek, mustard, kale, etc.) along with some refreshing Indian buttermilk (chaas).

Variations: Use ¾ toor dal (split pigeon pea) instead of chana dal when you need to cook something quick. Toor dal does not require soaking and can be pressure cooked up to the first whistle or until the pressure regulator starts to rock.

Substitute bottle gourd with peeled and diced red pumpkin or diced drumsticks (pods of moringa oleifera) and temper with mustard seeds.

Make **KASHMIRI DAL** by replacing bottle gourd with 1 cup diced paneer. Include 1" mashed ginger and 1½ tsp of coarsely ground fennel seeds in the tempering with rest of the spice powders. Add the paneer after the dal is ready.

You can also make **MUGA CHI AMTI (MUNG BEANS CURRY)** without onion, ginger, and garlic. Temper mustard seeds and curry leaves, and use the same proportion of rest of the ingredients. Pressure cook ½ cup whole mung beans with 1 cup of water (without soaking) for 5 minutes on low heat after the first whistle or after the pressure regulator starts to rock. Then turn off the heat, and wait until pressure is released. Add 1 puréed tomato along with salt, jaggery, and chopped cilantro. Add additional water if needed, and bring it to a boil. Serve with whole grain rotis and a fresh salad.

Tip: The amount of sugar used is very small (<1g per serving).

DAL METHI / FENUGREEK & PIGEON PEAS SOUP
splendid and aromatic

Fenugreek leaves are a tad bitter, but very aromatic. This dal does not taste bitter and highlights the flavor of fenugreek leaves. Although picking of fenugreek leaves is time consuming, you may pick, wash and freeze an extra bunch so that you can add some leaves to any of your dals, any time of the year.

Per serving: 150 Cal | 7g protein | 5g total fat | 7g fiber

Servings: 3 **Cooking Time: 30 mins**

Main ingredients
½ cup split pigeon peas (toor dal)
4 cups fenugreek leaves
½ onion, finely chopped, optional
1 large garlic clove, grated or mashed
1" ginger piece, grated or mashed

Spices
½ tsp fenugreek (methi) seeds
½ tsp red chili powder
½ tsp coriander powder
⅛ tsp turmeric powder
1-2 tsp lemon juice or tamarind pulp

Staples
4 tsp ghee or oil
1 tsp powdered jaggery, honey, or sugar (<1g sugar per serving)
Salt to taste

Wash and rinse the dal and set it aside.

Heat the oil in a pressure pan or cooker and add fenugreek seeds. When they sizzle, add mashed or grated garlic and ginger. Then add the onion and sauté for a minute.

Add the spice powders along with the dal and mix. Add 1 cup of water and pressure cook up to the first whistle or until the pressure regulator starts to rock. Turn off the heat and let it cool down.

Add fenugreek leaves, lemon juice, salt, and jaggery to the cooked dal and mix well. Adjust the consistency per your liking and simmer for 2-3 minutes.

Serve with whole grain roti and a raita of sliced radish and beetroot.

Tip: Add leafy greens at the end of cooking in order to retain maximum nutrients. Avoid pressure cooking any leafy vegetables, or cooking them for a long time or in excess water.

Note: Toor dal (split pigeon pea) and chana dal (split chickpeas, yellow split peas) look similar, but toor dal is the flatter variety (left bowl). It cooks quickly and does not require soaking if pressure cooked.

ZHATPAT MISAL PAV / QUICK MIXED BEANS SPICY CURRY
a delicious Maharashtrian spicy curry

Misal is one of the most popular dishes from my home state of Maharashtra, in the western region of India. It is a spicy curry made with sprouted beans, topped with farsaan (fried Indian snacks) along with chopped onion and tomato, and served with soft pav (Indian bun). This is my quick yet healthy misal recipe, made with beans that do not require soaking and cook quickly. However, you can use this recipe for dried white or green peas or mixed soaked beans. Anyway, it is very delicious. Remind yourself to eat more of this delicious misal and less pav, so that you can consume more protein and fiber. Top it with 1 tablespoon of farsaan per serving, if you must add. And, do not forget the generous serving of fresh salad on the side or as a garnish.

Per serving: 140 Cal | 7g protein | 5g total fat | 5g fiber

Servings: 6 **Cooking Time: 30 mins**

Main ingredients
1 cup mixed small beans (mung, moth bean, lentils, black-eyed peas)
½ large onion, chopped
2 garlic cloves, mashed
1" ginger, mashed, optional

Spices
¼ tsp mustard seeds
5-6 curry leaves
2-3 pinches asafetida
⅛ tsp turmeric powder
¾ tsp red chili powder
½ tsp Kashmiri red chili powder for red colored curry, optional
¾ tsp garam masala
¾ tsp cumin powder
¾ tsp coriander powder
¼ tsp tamarind concentrate or
2 tsp rehydrated tamarind pulp
2 tbsp dry coconut powder, optional

Staples
2 tbsp oil
Salt to taste

Salad
1 onion, finely chopped
2 tomatoes, finely chopped
A few sprigs of cilantro, chopped
Salt and lemon juice to taste

Wash the beans and pressure cook with 2 cups of water for 2-3 minutes after the first whistle or after the pressure regulator starts to rock. The beans will be slightly undercooked, as the misal tastes better when the beans are cooked in the curry with all the spices.

Prepare the curry by tempering the mustard seeds in oil. Once they crackle, turn off the heat and add the curry leaves, mashed garlic and asafetida. Turn on the heat and let the garlic become golden before you add the onion. Then sauté the onion on medium heat until it turns brown.

Add the spice powders and coconut powder, and sauté on medium heat until aromatic. Transfer the beans with the cooking liquid and let them boil until done. Add water as needed. Season with salt and tamarind pulp, and mix well.

Prepare the salad by combining all the salad ingredients. Top each serving of curry with 1-2 tbsp of the salad and 1 tbsp of farsaan. Serve additional salad on the side. Toast the pav (preferably whole grain) lightly with or without some ghee or butter and enjoy. You may also inlcude a side of tempered yogurt (page 142).

Variation: Substitute mixed small beans with mixed large beans such as black chickpeas, or dried peas. Soak 1 cup large beans in 2 cups of water for 8-10 hours. Then pressure cook along with the soaking liquid for 10 minutes on low heat after the first whistle or after the pressure regulator starts to rock. Turn off the heat and wait until the pressure is released. Use the cooked beans with the cooking liquid in this recipe.

PANEER DAL FRY / DAL WITH INDIAN COTTAGE CHEESE
paneer in a simmering dal

My mom makes this scrumptious dal and serves it with crispy paneer, which is one of my weaknesses. This dal is made with chana dal. It is the only dal that requires soaking, even if you are pressure cooking. While paneer is a good source of protein, calcium, B-complex vitamins, and vitamin A, it is also calorie-dense and contains a high amount of saturated fat. It is a good idea to pair paneer with legumes and plenty of vegetables, so that you do not over-indulge in paneer. For example, you can add green peas, bell peppers, carrot, green beans, broccoli, etc. to your paneer dishes or pair with a generous serving of fresh salad. **Note:** Recipe contains dairy.

Per serving: 150 Cal | 8g protein | 7g total fat | 5g fiber

Servings: 6 **Soak time: 30 mins** **Cooking Time: 30 mins**

Main ingredients
½ cup chana dal (split chickpeas, yellow split peas)
1 cup diced paneer (~100 gms)
½ onion, chopped
1" ginger piece, mashed
2 large garlic cloves, mashed
1 tomato, puréed
A few sprigs of cilantro, chopped

Spices
½ tsp caraway seeds (shah jeera)
A pinch of asafetida
1 bay leaf
½" cinnamon stick
1 large black cardamom (masala elaichi), optional
2 cloves
¼ tsp turmeric powder
½ tsp red chili powder

Staples
1 tbsp oil
Salt to taste

Wash and soak the chana dal with 1 cup of water for 30 minutes. Meanwhile, pan-fry the paneer on a non-stick pan on high heat to make a crisp brown outer crust with a soft interior. Flip the paneer cubes quickly, otherwise they can toughen and become dry. Transfer to a plate, cover and set aside. You can pat the cubes with a paper towel to absorb a bit of the fat.

In a pressure cooker, heat the oil and temper with caraway seeds. When they sizzle, add asafetida, onion, whole spices, and mashed ginger and garlic. Sauté the onion on high heat until it turns light brown. Then add the spice powders and sauté on high heat until aromatic.

Transfer the chana dal to the pressure cooker along with the soaking liquid, and pressure cook for about 5 minutes after the first whistle or after the pressure regulator starts to rock steadily. Then turn off the heat and wait until the pressure is released.

Add the tomato purée, salt, and some water for desired consistency, and bring it to a boil. Garnish with paneer cubes and cilantro, and serve with whole grain rotis. Pair with a generous side of **RAINBOW SALAD** (juliennes of onion, tomato, green and yellow bell peppers, carrot, cabbage, and beetroot seasoned with salt and pepper or chaat masala).

Variations: MIXED DAL FRY – Make dal fry with 1 cup of mixed dals (use some dals with skin) and cook it in 2 tbsp ghee if you do not add paneer. Sprinkle kasur methi for a restaurant-style flavor.
SOYBEANS CURRY – Use the mixed dal fry recipe to make a soybeans curry. Soak 1 cup soybeans in 2 cups of water for 8-10 hours. Pressure cook with the soaking liquid for 10 minutes after the first whistle or after the pressure regulator starts to rock. Turn off the heat. Use the cooked soybeans and cooking liquid in the recipe.

BLACK BEANS CURRY
a basic curry recipe

This is a basic curry recipe that can be used for cooking any beans – pinto, fava, navy, black chickpeas, whole mung, black-eyed peas, etc. Just pressure cook the smaller beans and black-eyed peas for a shorter length of time. Every bean has a unique taste; the curries will not taste the same even if you use the same recipe. Give this idea a try and see if you like the outcome.

Per serving: 170 Cal | 8g protein | 5g total fat | 6g fiber

Servings: 6   **Soak time: 8-10 hours**   **Cooking Time: 30 mins**

Main ingredients
1 cup black beans
1 onion, chopped finely
2 tomatoes, chopped finely
1" ginger piece, chopped and mashed, or grated
A few sprigs of cilantro, chopped

Spices
½ tsp red chili powder
½ tsp garam masala, optional
½ tsp cumin powder or coriander powder

Staples
2 tbsp oil
1 tsp sugar (if tomatoes are sour) – read tip
Salt as needed

Soak the black beans in 2 cups of water for 8-10 hours. Pressure cook along with the soaking liquid for 10 minutes after the first whistle or after the pressure regulator starts to rock. Then turn off the heat and wait until the pressure is released.

In the meantime, heat the oil in a steel pot and add the chopped onion. Sauté the onion on medium heat until it turns light brown. Now, add the tomatoes and the spice powders and allow the tomatoes to cook on medium heat.

When the oil begins to separate, add the cooked black beans. You may discard part of the dark-colored cooking liquid, as it can make the curry unappealing.

Add a cup of water, some salt, and ginger. Mix well and bring it to a boil on medium heat. Let it simmer for about 5 minutes. If the curry is too tangy for your preference, add a small amount of sugar to improve the palatability.

Garnish with cilantro and serve with rice or whole grain tortillas, salsa and guacamole (page 132) for a Mexican plate. For an Indian thali (plate), serve with roti, fresh salad and sautéed kale or kale subzi from my website (quicklydelicious.com).

Tip: The amount of sugar used is very small (<1g per serving), and only balances the taste. It does not alter the calories or glycemic index per serving.

MEXICAN BEANS SOUP
a hearty soup

Just like the black beans curry, this is also a delectable soup. The vegetables added make it a more wholesome meal. Bean and vegetable soups or stews are a great way to pack a well-balanced lunch for yourself or your family. Serve this soup with whole grain crackers (optional) and a bowl of diced fruits.

Per serving: 340 Cal | 16g protein | 10g total fat | 12g fiber

Servings: 3 **Soak time: 8-10 hours** **Cooking Time: 30 mins**

Main ingredients
1 cup black beans, kidney beans, or mixed large beans (fava, navy, pinto, etc.)
1 onion, diced
1 tomato, diced
2 large garlic cloves, chopped
1 carrot, diced
1 red bell pepper, diced
1 broccoli head, cut into florets or ½ bunch kale leaves, coarsely chopped
A few sprigs of cilantro, chopped

Spices
½ tsp cumin powder
½ tsp red chili powder

Staples
2 tbsp oil
1 tsp sugar, optional – read tip
Salt as needed

Soak the beans in 2 cups of water for 8-10 hours. Pressure cook along with the soaking liquid for 10 minutes after the first whistle or after the pressure regulator starts to rock. Turn off the heat and wait until the pressure is released.

In the meantime, heat the oil in a steel pot and add the chopped garlic. Sauté the garlic on medium heat until golden and then add the onion. Sauté the onion until it turns light brown.

Add the rest of the vegetables and spice powders, and sauté for around 2 minutes on medium heat. Transfer the cooked beans (with the cooking liquid), additional water, and some salt. Mix well and bring it to a boil. Let it simmer for a minute.

Add the sugar, if necessary, to balance the taste of the soup. Garnish with chopped cilantro and serve with whole grain crackers and a bowl of diced fruits.

Variation: Add some chicken or cheese to this soup.

Tip: The amount of sugar used is very small (~1g per serving), and only balances the taste. It does not alter the calories or glycemic index per serving.

TURKISH CARROT & PINK LENTILS SOUP
comforting soup with a hint of mint

This is my take on the Turkish Mercimek Çorbası, which is prepared with pink lentils (split lentils or masur dal), potato, carrots, and dried mint leaves. You have to try this gorgeous and delicious soup the next time you find some beautiful carrots in the farmer's market.

Per serving: 130 Cal | 7g protein | 3g total fat | 4g fiber

Servings: 4   **Cooking Time: 30 mins**

Main ingredients
- ½ cup pink lentils (masur dal)
- ½ onion, diced
- 1 tomato, diced
- 1 carrot, peeled and diced
- 2 cloves garlic, diced
- A few fresh mint leaves, reserve the stalks

Spices
- ½ tsp cumin powder
- ½ tsp red chili powder, optional

Staples
- 1 tbsp olive oil
- Salt to taste

Wash the lentils and set aside.

Heat the oil in a pot and add the garlic. After it turns golden, toss in the diced vegetables, lentils, and mint stalks, and add 2 cups of water. The mint stalks will impart a strong mint flavor to the soup. Bring the water to a boil and let it simmer until the lentils are cooked (15 minutes or so).

Turn off the heat and allow the mixture to cool. Discard the mint stalk and purée the vegetables along with the diced tomatoes. Adding tomatoes to the lentils at the time of cooking can increase the cooking time.

Transfer the puréed soup to the pot and boil it after adding the desired amount of water. Sprinkle with salt, cumin powder, and freshly chopped mint leaves. Do not cut the mint leaves in advance, as they discolor. You may add red chili powder, however, this soup tastes great even without the heat of the chili. Enjoy this soup as a side and pair with a salad or a whole grain toast topped with spiced eggplant (recipe on the website – quicklydelicious.com).

Variation: Try this recipe without the garlic.

Tip: I use mint stalks along with the leaves for my masala chai. The stalks of most herbs, including cilantro, are packed with flavor. Add them to your stocks and stews for some zest.

ITALIAN HEARTY BEANS SOUP
a great soup that celebrates whole beans

Throw in all the beans you can get your hands on and prepare this comforting soup to keep you warm in the fall or winter. Add seasonal vegetables and any fresh herbs to customize.

Per serving: 420 Cal | 24g protein | 12g total fat | 20g fiber

Servings: 2 **Soak time: 8-10 hours** **Cooking Time: 30 mins**

Main ingredients
¾ cup mixed beans (lima, pinto, black, kidney, etc.)
2 cloves garlic, chopped
½ onion, diced
2 tomatoes, puréed
1 zucchini, diced
1 orange bell pepper, diced
1 cup mushrooms, sliced
1 cube or ¼ cup shredded cheese, optional
Chopped parsley for garnish

Spices
½ tsp red chili flakes
½ tsp dried oregano or mixed dried herbs, or 1-2 tsp fresh oregano leaves

Staples
1 tbsp olive oil
1 tsp honey or maple syrup, optional
Salt and ground black pepper to taste

Soak the beans in 1½ cups of water for 8-10 hours. Pressure cook along with the soaking liquid for 10 minutes after the first whistle or after the pressure regulator starts to rock. Turn off the heat and wait until the pressure is released.

In the meantime, heat the oil in a steel pot and add garlic. When it turns light brown add all the vegetables except tomatoes, and sauté on high heat until the zuchini is slightly tender.

Pour the tomato purée and let it boil for a minute on high heat. Sprinkle chili flakes, oregano or mixed herbs, and salt. Mix well and turn off the heat.

Add the cooked beans along with the cooking liquid and bring the soup to a boil. Add more water, if needed. Stir in the shredded cheese, but reserve some for garnishing. Adjust the salt and add honey if necessary to balance the taste.

Serve hot with a garnish of chopped parsley. Pair with **GARLIC-HERB CROUTONS** (page 88) or a bowl of fruits. Alternatively, you can add 1 cup of cooked regular pasta or 1½ cups of whole grain pasta to this soup.

FRENCH FUSION LENTILS SOUP
a fusion of French and Indian flavors

French flavors of classic mirepoix (carrots, celery, and onion) are infused with some Indian spices to take this soup to a whole new level. This soup does not use any store-bought stock. The flavorful spice powders and vegetables obviate the need for a stock. Store-bought stocks can be high in sodium, and are not recommended for those with high blood pressure.

Per serving: 270 Cal | 13g protein | 8g total fat | 16g fiber
Per serving of croutons: 100 Cal | 3g protein | 5g total fat | 4g fiber

Servings: 3　　　　　　　　　　　　　　　　　　　　　　　　**Cooking Time: 30 mins**

Main ingredients
¾ cup lentils
1 onion, chopped
1 large carrot, chopped
1 cup finely chopped celery stalk
1" ginger, grated
½ tsp red chili powder
1 tsp coriander powder
¼ tsp cinnamon powder
2 tbsp olive oil or butter
4 tbsp shredded cheese, optional

Garlic-herb croutons
2 whole grain bread slices
1 tbsp butter
2 garlic clove, grated
A few sprigs of cilantro, chopped
2-3 pinches dried herbs
Salt, ground black pepper to taste

Wash the lentils. Add double the amount of water (1½ cups) and pressure cook for 5 minutes after the first whistle or after the pressure regulator begins to rock steadily. Then turn off the heat and wait until it cools down.

Meanwhile, melt the butter (or heat the oil) in a pot and sauté the onion, carrot, and celery on medium heat until the carrot is cooked; cover the pot if needed. Add the spice powders and salt, and sauté for a minute on medium heat. Then, turn off the heat.

Add the cooked lentils and mix well. Adjust the salt, and alter the consistency of the soup by adding more water and boiling it for a minute. Garnish with some shredded cheese and serve hot with whole grain, garlic-herb croutons, a side salad, and a glass of wine.

GARLIC-HERB BUTTER: In a microwave-safe bowl, melt the butter. Add rest of the ingredients and mix well. Your garlic-herb butter is ready. **GARLIC-HERB CROUTONS:** Toast the bread until brown and crisp. Then spread the garlic-herb butter evenly, and cut the toast into croutons.

Variations: Add ½ tsp of oregano leaves instead of coriander powder.
Use this recipe to prepare a soup with any beans.
Add any vegetables of your choice.

SIZZLING STIR-FRIES & KEBABS
for salads, wraps, & sandwiches

Cooked whole beans can be stir-fried with any of your favorite spice powders, herbs, or aromatics. These stir-fries or subzi can be used as a topping on salads, pizza, stuffed into a sandwich or a wrap, or served on the side.

If you are concerned about your carbohydrate intake or wish to lose weight, a salad with lots of vegetables, stir-fried legume toppings and a yogurt-based dressing makes a delicious low-carb lunch.

Wraps are an easy way to pack lunch. They can also help you consume more vegetables and beans per bite if you pack them well! Instead of two slices of bread for a sandwich or two rotis, you could eat more vegetables and beans in a single wrap. You can choose a whole grain flatbread that won't fall apart and pack it up with lots of vegetables and some seasoned beans. Or, use plain vegetables and legumes and simply dress them up with a tasty homemade sauce or chutney. Pack the sauce or chutney separately if it is runny. Don't find wraps filling? No worries – add a side of diced fruit in yogurt or a fruit for dessert.

Wraps can also be a creative way of consuming your regular roti, subzi and dal meal. Wrap your subzi in a roti, and pack the dal as a side soup! These wraps can not only help you eat more vegetables, but also encourage you to enjoy dals or whole legumes by themselves. For kids, try serving stir-fries as toppings on pizza, or as a stuffing in mini-sandwiches.

Kebabs made with whole mung, black beans, chickpeas, kidney beans or other legumes can be served as an appetizer or as patties for a main course salad or burger.

CHOLE CHAAT / CURRIED CHICKPEAS SALAD
curry flavored chickpeas salad

Chickpeas or garbanzo beans (kabuli chana) are popularly used to make Chole in India. However, they are very versatile and can be used in several ways and in different cuisines. Here is one quick salad that you have got to try. Sauté the chickpeas over olive oil with some ground spices and voilà – you have a delightful salad protein ready in no time. Add them as a topping to a bed of greens and diced vegetables. A few nuts or homemade croutons for some extra crunch, and you have a balanced meal to go. Did I forget the salad dressing? Well, you will be surprised how lemon juice, spices, and juicy vegetables bring it all together.

Per serving: 320 Cal | 12g protein | 13g total fat | 12g fiber

Servings: 2   **Cooking time: 15 mins***

Chole chaat
½ cup chickpeas (or 1½ cups cooked chickpeas)
½ tsp red chili powder
½ tsp coriander powder
½ tsp cumin powder
1 tsp freshly squeezed lemon juice
1½ tbsp oil
Salt to taste

Salad ingredients
1 yellow bell pepper, diced
1 tomato, diced
1 cucumber diced
½ onion, diced
2 cups lettuce, baby spinach, or mixed greens

Cook ahead: wash and soak the chickpeas overnight in double the amount of water. Pressure cook them along with the soaking liquid for 10 mins on low heat after the first whistle or after the pressure regulator starts to rock steadily. Turn off the heat. You can cook over the weekend and refrigerate for up to one week.

Heat the oil in a pan and add the cooked chickpeas, dry powders, salt, and lemon juice. Sauté for 1-2 minutes on medium heat until the chickpeas become dry and toasted. If you like it tangier, feel free to add more lemon juice. Similarly, if you prefer more heat and flavor – chatpata as Indians say – then sprinkle additional chili powder and coriander powder.

Dice the salad vegetables and transfer them to a bowl. Sprinkle with salt and ground pepper. Add the curried chickpeas to the bowl and mix. Serve as a side salad or a light meal.

Variations: Use different spice powders to make variations in flavors – garam masala, amchur powder, tandoori masala, chaat masala, etc.
Instead of salad, you can also serve the curried chickpeas as a snack or a side to add a protein to your meal.
Add roasted nuts (peanuts, cashew, almonds, etc.) for some crunch.
Add cilantro-mint chutney, tamarind chutney, or hot sauce for variations.
Turn this salad into a wrap, and pair with Indian buttermilk.

* 15 minutes if chickpeas are cooked in advance

SPROUTS CHAAT SALAD
healthy chaat

Here is your favorite roadside chaat made healthy. May this chaat remind you of Mumbai's seaside stalls where you once enjoyed these chaats in the salty mist. **Note:** Recipe contains dairy, gluten and/or nuts.

Per serving: 350 Cal | 14g protein | 12g total fat | 9g fiber

Servings: 2   **Soaking and Germination: 24-36 hours**   **Cooking Time: 15 mins**

Main ingredients
½ cup mung beans, moth beans, lentils combined (or 2 cups mung sprouts, or mixed sprouts)
1 cup yogurt
½ onion, chopped
1 tomato or red bell pepper, chopped
1 cooked and diced potato or sweet potato (3"), or 2 cups grated carrot
½ cup fresh pomegranate seeds, optional
1 cup diced unripe mango, whole cherries, or any seasonal fruit
4 homemade fried or 8 baked small puris or whole grain crackers or ¼ cup roasted peanuts

Dressings
4 tsp mint-cilantro chutney
4 tsp tamarind chutney

Wash and soak ½ cup mixed beans (mung bean, moth beans, and lentils) in 1 cup of water for 8-10 hours. Drain and use the soaking liquid for cooking rice, vegetables, or stews. Transfer the legumes to a colander, and place it over a small bowl, so that the holes are ventilated. You may wrap the legumes in a cheese cloth or muslin cloth before placing in a colander. Cover the colander and leave it in a cool and dark place for 12-36 hours depending on the desired length of sprouts. Aerate the legumes by shuffling them every 12 hours. Then store the legumes in the refrigerator or use right away.

Transfer the sprouts to a bowl. Add the diced vegetables and mix.

Prepare the chutneys (page 93).

Mix in the desired amount of yogurt and chutney, and garnish with pomegranate seeds, diced cherries, or unripe mango. For the missing crisp element and to include some fat in the meal, add crushed homemade fried or baked puris or roasted peanuts. Skip the sev and farsaan (gram flour-based fried snacks) that are typically added to most chaats. You can also substitute puris with whole grain crackers.

Variations: If you do not like raw sprouts, then steam them in a small amount of water in a steamer or microwave; however, be careful not to overcook. Use the cooking liquid, if any, in your salad dressing.
Use any seasonal fruits in this chaat.
Make **SPROUTS BHEL** by adding 1 cup puffed rice or ½ cup toasted rice flakes to this recipe.

5-MINUTE DRESSINGS & CHUTNEYS
the important finishing touch

These chutneys and dressings are ready in 5 minutes and can make any dish all the more interesting. They can be poured over salads, spread in sandwiches, used plain, or mixed in with yogurt to be served on the side as a dip. **Note:** Some recipes contain dairy, coconut, or nuts.

Tamarind Yogurt Chutney

Tamarind date chutney
½ tsp tamarind paste or 2 tbsp rehydrated tamarind pulp
¼ cup dates (~5-6 dates)
¼ tsp red chili powder
½ tsp cumin powder
Black or pink salt to taste

Tamarind yogurt dressing
⅔ cup yogurt, beat lightly
1-2 tsp of tamarind chutney

Soak the dates and dry tamarind in warm water until they soften (5-10 minutes) and squeeze the tamarind to extract the pulp. Blend the tamarind pulp, dates, and dry powders to make a smooth and thick **TAMARIND DATE CHUTNEY**, adding small amount of water at a time. Add salt to the chutney and use as a dressing in salads and chaats, or as a dip.

To make tamarind yogurt dressing, lightly beat the yogurt, add 3-4 tsp of tamarind date chutney and mix well. Store the unused tamarind date chutney in the refrigerator.

Cilantro Coconut Chutney

Ingredients
½ cup fresh grated coconut
1 cup cilantro
1 green chili
1 tsp rehydrated tamarind pulp
1 tsp grated jaggery or sugar
Salt to taste

Grind all the ingredients to a coarse chutney using a small amount of water. Serve this chutney with idli, dosa, uttapam, or appe. Apply as a spread in your sandwiches.

Variations: Substitute part of the coconut with peanuts or roasted chana dal.
Skip the cilantro to make **PLAIN COCONUT CHUTNEY.** Temper mustard seeds, asafetida, curry leaves, and red chilies in oil, and add to the chutney for extra flavor.
Substitute tamarind pulp with lemon juice.

Mint Cilantro Chutney

Ingredients
½ cup mint leaves
1 cup cilantro
1 green chili
¼ onion, diced
1 garlic clove
1 tsp lemon juice
1 tsp sugar. honey or jaggery
Salt to taste

Blend all the ingredients to a fine paste using a small amount of water. Serve this chutney as a dip for idlis, dosas, uttapam, appe, as a spread in sandwiches, or as a dressing for salads.

Variation: Add this chutney to lightly beaten yogurt to make **YOGURT-MINT CHUTNEY.**

KACHORI-INSPIRED MUNG CHAAT SALAD
with tamarind yogurt dressing

This main course salad is quite filling and has bold flavors. The fennel-infused mung beans dressed with the sweet and tangy, tamarind yogurt dressing, will remind you of kachori chaat (a popular fried street food enjoyed in the northern and western states of India). The warm and cold elements make the salad more interesting. **Note:** Recipe contains dairy and/or nuts.

Per serving: 350 Cal | 15g protein | 13g total fat | 9g fiber

Servings: 2 **Cooking time: 15 mins***

Spiced mung bean
½ cup mung beans
⅛ tsp turmeric powder
½ tsp red chili powder
½ tsp coriander powder
¼ tsp garam masala, optional
½ tsp fennel seeds (saunf)
1½ tbsp oil
Salt to taste

Salad ingredients
4 cups lettuce, mixed greens, baby spinach, or shredded cabbage
1 carrot, shredded
10 cherry tomatoes (or 1 cup diced tomatoes) or 1 bell pepper, sliced
½ red onion, sliced, optional
A few raisins or 1-2 dried figs, chopped
A few roasted cashew nuts or peanuts, optional

Wash and pressure cook the mung beans in ½ cup of water for 5 mins on low heat after the first whistle or after the regulator starts to rock steadily. Then turn off the heat. You can cook in advance over the weekend and refrigerate for up to one week. The beans need to be slightly undercooked or intact, as they will be cooked in the spice powders to infuse more flavor.

In the meantime, prepare the vegetables and the tamarind yogurt dressing (page 93). Wash, pat-dry, and dice the lettuce leaves. Peel and shred the carrot, and cut the onion and tomatoes.

When the pressure cooker has cooled, heat the oil in a pan and add the mung beans along with the spices and sauté for a few minutes or until the mixture becomes slightly dry and the beans are cooked.

Combine the salad vegetables, dried fruits, and nuts in a bowl, add the spiced mung beans and dress with yogurt and tamarind chutney separately or as a tamarind yogurt dressing.

Variations: Use the spiced mung beans as a filling for baked or pan-fried samosas or kachoris (recipe on page 106).
The salad dressing is so flavorful that you can add plain boiled mung beans instead of spiced mung. Include a generous serving of nuts to add some fat to the salad, to help absorb the fat-soluble nutrients and phytochemicals or add some olive oil to the dressing.
Serve the spiced mung beans as a protein side for main course or enjoy as a snack.
Just use the tamarind date chutney or as a dressing to make the salad dairy-free. Add a tbsp of olive oil to the chutney to incorporate some fat in the meal.
Substitute tamarind date chutney with mint cilantro chutney (page 3).

* 15 minutes if beans are cooked in advance

PUNJABI CHANA MASALA SALAD
Super flavorful chana masala

Salad is a great way to enjoy Punjabi chana masala, chickpeas coated in freshly roasted and ground whole spices. Instead of serving it with fried puffy breads (puris or bhaturas) generally made with all-purpose wheat flour (maida) – why not serve it in the form of a delicious salad?

Per serving: 320 Cal | 12g protein | 13g total fat | 12g fiber

Servings: 2 **Cooking time: 15 mins***

Stir-fry ingredients
½ cup black chickpeas (kala chana) (or 1½ cups cooked)
½ onion, chopped, optional
½" ginger
½ tbsp coriander seeds
½ tbsp cumin seeds
½ tbsp dried pomegranate seeds (anar dana)
½ tsp red chili powder
¼ tsp garam masala or cinnamon powder
1½ tbsp oil
Salt as needed

Salad ingredients
½ onion, thinly sliced
4 cups shredded cabbage
1 green bell pepper (capsicum), thinly sliced
1 tomato, sliced
1-2 tsp lemon juice
Salt and black pepper to taste

Wash and soak the chana overnight in double the amount of water. Pressure cook the chana along with the soaking liquid for 10 minutes on low heat after the first whistle or after the regulator starts to rock steadily. Then turn off the heat. You can cook in advance over the weekend and refrigerate for up to one week.

In the meantime, chop the onion. Then, lightly roast the three seeds in a pan, on medium heat while stirring occasionally. Roast the seeds until they are aromatic and transfer them to a plate to cool down. Grind them together with the ginger to create a coarse mixture.

Heat the oil in a pot and add the chopped onion, spice powders, and ground seeds. Sauté for a few minutes on medium heat. Add the cooked chana and salt, and mix well. Reserve the cooking liquid for a soup or curry.

Prepare the salad base by combining the salad ingredients. Add a generous serving of chana masala to the salad and mix well.

Variation: Serve the chana masala as a protein side with roti and a light vegetable soup, or in a wrap or chaat.

* 15 minutes if chickpeas are cooked in advance

MEDITERRANEAN BEANS & PASTA SALAD
eating light with pasta

Pasta can be eaten as part of a healthy diet by modifying the amount, type, and frequency of consumption and, more importantly, changing the way it is paired. Whole grain pasta is a healthier alternative to regular pasta. However, if it is consumed in large portions or paired with few vegetables and generous amounts of cheese and butter, then the healthfulness of the dish is reduced. It is important to use moderate amounts of olive oil, butter or cheese, and pair your pasta with more vegetables and beans. For example, for every 1 cup of cooked pasta, combine 2-3 cups of vegetables and at least ½ cup of cooked beans, for a more balanced, healthy meal. **Note:** Recipe contains gluten.

Per serving: 440 Cal | 16g protein | 16g total fat | 13g fiber

Servings: 2 **Cooking time: 15 mins***

Main ingredients
1½ cups cooked kidney beans or any large beans of your preference
1½ cups cooked whole grain or 1 cup regular pasta (penne, macaroni, farfalle, etc.)
1 zucchini, diced
1 cup mushrooms, sliced
1 red bell pepper, diced
1 cup chopped broccoli
1-2 tbsp chopped cilantro, parsley, or basil
A few black olives, sliced
1 tbsp oil
Salt to taste

Honey vinaigrette
½ cup honey
½ cup olive oil
½ cup vinegar
¼ tsp ground black pepper
¼ tsp dried herbs or dried oregno
Salt, if needed

Cook ahead: wash and soak ½ cup beans overnight in equal amount of water. Pressure cook the beans along with the soaking liquid for 10 minutes on low heat after the first whistle or after the regulator starts to rock steadily. Then turn off the heat. Cook the pasta of your choice per instructions on the packet. Make sure it is cooked *al dente* (firm to the bite).

Heat oil in a pan and stir-fry the zucchini, mushrooms, bell pepper, broccoli, and beans lightly. Season with salt and black pepper, and transfer them to a salad bowl. Add the cooked pasta and olives.

Prepare the dressing by combining the ingredients in a jar and shaking well. Use 2 tbsp dressing for the recipe and store the remainder in the refrigerator. Shake well before each use. Olive oil may solidify in the refrigerator, but you can leave it out for some time to melt.

Pour 2 tbsp of the dressing over the salad and toss. Garnish with the chopped fresh herbs and olives, and enjoy.

Variations: Use different bean and vegetable combinations with other salad dressings. You can add 1-2 tbsp of feta cheese or boiled egg as well.
Skip the pasta for a lower carb or lower calorie salad.

* 15 minutes if beans and pasta are cooked in advance

PERUVIAN SPROUTS CEVICHE
an amazing appetizer

Inspired by the Peruvian seafood ceviche where the seafood is "cooked" in lemon juice for several hours, I decided to play with the flavors of ceviche and pair them with sprouts. Ceviche can be very tangy with the generous use of lemon or lime juice. For a little sweetness, I added some freshly squeezed orange juice to create a great recipe for a fun cocktail party.

Per serving: 80 Cal | 4g protein | 0g total fat | 3g fiber

Servings: 4 **Marinating time: 1 hour** **Cooking time: 10 mins**

Main ingredients
1 tightly packed cup mixed sprouts (mung beans, moth beans, lentils, etc.)
½ onion, finely chopped
1 tomato, finely chopped
½ green chili or more, chopped
150 mL (a little more than ½ cup) freshly squeezed orange juice
4 tsp lemon juice
A few sprigs of cilantro, chopped

Staples
Salt to taste

Combine the sprouts and orange juice in a jar and refrigerate for an hour. When ready to serve, add rest of the ingredients and shake well.

Transfer the sprouts to individual glasses and pour equal portions of the juice over each serving. Enjoy!

SWADISHTA MATKI USAL / DELICIOUS MOTH BEANS STIR-FRY
a quick and delicious moth beans side

This moth beans stir-fry recipe is influenced by my sister-in-law's recipe and makes for a great side. You can substitute the moth beans with mung beans. **Note:** Recipe contains coconut.

Per serving: 150 Cal | 9g protein | 3g total fat | 2g fiber

Servings: 6 **Cooking time: 15 mins***

Main ingredients
1 cup moth beans
½ onion, chopped, optional
A few curry leaves
1 tbsp dry coconut powder (desiccated coconut)
A few sprigs of cilantro, chopped

Spices
¼ tsp mustard seeds
½ tsp red chili powder
½ tsp garam masala

Staples
2 tbsp ghee or oil
Salt to taste

Cook ahead: wash and pressure cook the beans in 1 cup of water for 5 minutes on low heat after the first whistle, or after the regulator starts to rock steadily. Then turn off the heat. You can cook over the weekend and refrigerate for up to one week.

Heat the oil in a pan and season with mustard seeds until they crackle. Then add the curry leaves and onion, and sauté for 2 minutes on high heat. Now, add the spice powders and coconut, along with the cooked moth beans and pan-fry for a few minutes. Add salt and garnish with chopped cilantro and serve.

Serve this high fiber beans stir-fry with whole grain phulkas or rotis. You can even pair some lower fiber foods like vermicelli, semolina, jowar roti, or bajra roti with this stir-fry to bump up the nutritive value of the meal. Add a side of mixed vegetable soup, spinach, or carrot soup that can be ready while the moth beans are cooking.

Variations: Grate 2 large garlic cloves at the end and mix well for an absolutely great finish!
Substitute garam masala with any Indian regional specialty masalas such as goda masala, CKP talla masala, etc.

* 15 minutes if beans are cooked in advance

PAN-FRIED PAKORAS WRAP WITH KADHI
pan-fried fritters wrap served with a soulful yogurt soup

This is my modern take on serving pakoras in a wrap and the Gujarati kadhi as a side. Kadhi is a yogurt soup thickened with gram flour and tempered with different spices, popular in the western states of India. Pakoras are deep-fried fritters of vegetables, flavored with spice powders and coated in gram flour. What can be a healthier way to enjoy pakoras than pan-frying them? We get to enjoy the texture and taste of the fried pakoras in this healthier version without having to deal with excess intake of calories, oxidation or smoking of oil, storage of leftover oil, and loss of important nutrients. So, grab your pan and vegetables from your refrigerator and let's get started. **Note:** Recipe contains gluten.

Per serving (without roti or wrap): 200 Cal | 8g protein | 9g total fat | 7g fiber
Per serving with 1 whole grain roti: 330 Cal | 11g protein | 3g total fat | 10g fiber

Servings: 2 **Cooking time: 30 mins**

Main ingredients
½ cup gram flour
1 zucchini, cut into round slices
2 baby eggplants, cut into round slices
A few sprigs of cilantro, chopped
2 whole grain wraps or rotis

Spices
½ - ¾ tsp red chili powder
½ - 1 tsp coriander powder or
1 tbsp coriander seeds, coarsely ground
⅛ tsp turmeric powder
⅛ tsp carom seeds (ajwain)

Staples
Salt to taste
1½ tbsp olive oil or ghee

Salad filling
½ onion, sliced
1 red bell pepper, sliced
Salt and black pepper to taste, or chaat masala

Make a thick paste by combining the gram flour, cilantro, salt, and spices. Add water gradually to avoid any lumps. Pat-dry the slices so that the batter can cling well to the slices.

Heat the oil in a small to medium size pan and add only half the amount of oil or ghee. Use the other half for the 2nd batch.

Dip the vegetable slices in the batter to coat them well and pan fry on medium heat. Flip them over only when the first side has turned brown.

Transfer the pakoras to a plate when both sides are done. Turn up the heat for a few seconds, if you want them crispier. Add the remainder oil and repeat for the next batch.

Keep your wraps or roti ready. Spread some mint chutney (page 93) and hot and sweet sauce or ketchup on one half. Combine the sliced onion and bell pepper and sprinkle with salt and pepper or chaat masala to make the salad filling. Place the pakoras on the wrap, add the salad filling, and roll it up. Serve with kadhi (picture on page 105, recipe page 104) as a side soup.

Variations: Use any vegetables of your choice – sliced onion, radish or shredded mixed vegetables – cabbage, carrot, beetroot, etc., and serve these pakoras as appetizers.
For a gluten-free version, use whole grain maize tortilla, jowar or bajra bhakris, etc.

Tip: Use a generous amount of ajwain (carom seeds) in the winter, as they tend to generate heat in our bodies.

KADHI / SOULFUL YOGURT SOUP
a soup made with yogurt and gram flour

A warm and comforting yogurt based side that goes very well with khichadis or pulaos. Now try it with my pakora wraps (page 102). **Note:** Recipe contains dairy.

Per serving: 90 Cal | 3g protein | 5 total fat | 1g fiber

Servings: 2 **Cooking time: 15 mins**

Main ingredients
¼ cup gram flour
1 cup yogurt (preferably fresh)
A few curry leaves
1" ginger piece, lightly mashed (keep the piece intact)
A few sprigs of cilantro, chopped

Spices
½ tsp red chili powder
¼ tsp fenugreek (methi) seeds
¼ tsp cumin or mustard seeds
¼ tsp turmeric powder
2 pinches of asafetida

Staples
Salt to taste
2 tsp ghee
~2 tsp sugar, jaggery, or honey if yogurt is sour, optional

Lightly whisk the yogurt in a bowl. Add all the dry spice powders, ginger, and cilantro and mix well.

Make a thick paste of the gram flour with water and add it to the yogurt. Add 1 cup of water and mix well to avoid lumps.

Heat the oil in a steel pot and add cumin or mustard seeds. After they sizzle or crackle, turn off the heat and add methi seeds and curry leaves. Allow the tempering to cool down.

Add the yogurt mixture and let it simmer on medium heat. Stir occasionally otherwise the yogurt may curdle. Turn off the heat when the kadhi becomes thick.

Add salt and sugar (in case the yogurt is not fresh and tastes sour). Remove the ginger piece and serve.

Variations: Skip the turmeric if you prefer cream colored kadhi. Add a bay leaf, 2" cinnamon stick, and 2-3 peppercorns to the tempering for varying the taste of the kadhi. This kadhi is especially soothing in the winter. Feel free to add any leafy greens to your kadhi.

KADHI PAKODI / YOGURT SOUP WITH FRITTERS
pan-fried pakoras in soulful yogurt soup

Per serving: 160 Cal | 5g protein | 8 total fat | 3g fiber

Servings: 4 **Cooking time: 30 mins**

Ingredients
1 cup gram flour (besan)
1 cup mixed grated vegetables (cabbage, onion, capsicum, carrot, beetroot, radish, etc.)
A few sprigs of cilantro, chopped
½ tsp red chili powder
1 tbsp coarsely ground coriander seeds
2 tbsp oil
Salt to taste

Prepare the pakoras by combining the ingredients in a bowl. Then, fry them in a pan per instructions on page 102.

Make kadhi as described above.

Add the pakoras to the kadhi and serve with whole grain rotis and a fresh salad.

PAN-FRIED / BAKED SAMOSA WITH SPICED CARROT LENTILS
delicious lentils filling for samosas, tacos, wraps, etc.

This spiced lentils and carrot filling is so yummy that you can use it any way you like. Bake the samosas when you feel adventurous or pan-fry when you are impatiently hungry. Roll the filling into a wrap and serve with a side of minty yogurt dip (mint raita), any chutney or ketchup, or just enjoy them plain. **Note:** Recipe contains gluten.

Per serving (3 samosas): 300 Cal | 12g protein | 11g total fat | 13g fiber

Servings: 2 (6 samosas) **Cooking time: 1 hour***

Samosa filling
⅓ cup dry lentils (1 cup cooked)
½ onion, chopped
½ large carrot, chopped
½" ginger, grated
⅛ tsp turmeric powder
½ tsp red chili powder
½ tsp coriander powder
¼ tsp garam masala
1 tbsp oil
Salt to taste

Samosa cover or pastry
½ cup whole wheat flour
A pinch of carom seeds (ajwain), optional
2 tsp ghee
¼ tsp salt

Staples
Oil for greasing baking dish and coating the samosas, optional

Make semi-hard dough using the ingredients for the samosa cover (samosa pastry) by adding water slowly. The amount of water needed might be a little less than ¼ cup. Cover the dough and set it aside. If you would rather use the spiced lentils as a filling for a taco or wrap rather than samosas, you can skip this step.

Wash the lentils. Add ⅓ cup of water and pressure cook them for 5 minutes on low heat after the first whistle or after the pressure regulator begins to rock. Turn off the heat.

While the lentils are cooking, heat the oil in a pot and sauté the onions and carrots on medium heat until the carrot is cooked. Add the spice powders and salt, and sauté for a minute on medium heat. Turn off the heat and keep it aside. When the lentils are cooked, add the lentils along with the cooking liquid and mix well. Sauté until the water dries out. Turn off the heat and allow the mixture to cool down.

Divide the dough into 3 parts. Roll out each part into a thin roti (flatbread), without using any flour. The dough may be less pliable, so do not worry about the shape and let the samosas look rustic. If you are particular about the shape, then use a knife to get the shape right. You can create ravioli or turnover shapes as well.

Portion out the lentils into six servings, and place two servings on one side of the roti, leaving a gap between the fillings as shown in photos on page 107. Try to make a triangular shape. Now, fold the roti to cover up the filing and seal the sides by pressing gently. Moisten the joints if they do not seal all the way.

Cut with a knife to separate the two samosas and make sure they are sealed properly. Repeat these steps for the remaining samosas.

Lightly coat the samosas with oil and pan-fry on both sides.

Continued on next page.

Alternatively, preheat the oven at 350° F and bake the samosas on a greased pan for 20-25 minutes, flipping over halfway through. (Baked samosas in the picture collage)

Serve with ketchup and spinach or broccoli soup or stir-fry.

Variations: Use the filling to stuff parathas or tacos.
Instead of making samosas, serve the filling as a protein side.
You may use filo sheets or patti samosa wrappers, but they may not be as healthy.

* spiced carrot lentils can be ready in 15 minutes if the lentils are cooked in advance, otherwise 30 minutes.

CHATPATA CHANA SALAD / BLACK CHICKPEAS SALAD
Spicy and meaty

Black chickpeas have a meaty flavor and when dressed with spice powders they can be very flavorful. You can use any spice powders such as chaat masala, tandoori masala, Kitchen King masala, etc. Black chickpeas stir-fry or subzi makes a delicious addition to main course salads.

Per serving: 350 Cal | 12g protein | 13g total fat | 12g fiber

Servings: 2   **Cooking time: 15 mins***

Stir-fry ingredients
½ cup black chickpeas
(or 1½ cups cooked black chickpeas)
½ tsp garam masala
½ tsp red chili powder
1½ tbsp oil
Salt to taste

Salad ingredients
4 cups salad greens (lettuce, spinach, kale, chard, arugula, etc.)
1 beetroot, sliced
½ onion, sliced
1 carrot, shredded
1 orange or mandarin, slices or segments, or any seasonal fruit
¼ cup peanuts or any nuts, optional
1½ tbsp lemon juice
Cilantro, chopped
Salt to taste

Cook ahead: wash and soak the beans overnight in double the amount of water. Pressure cook the beans along with the soaking liquid for 10 mins on low heat after the first whistle or after the regulator starts to rock steadily. Turn off the heat. You can cook over the weekend and refrigerate for up to one week.

Heat the oil in a pan and sauté the cooked chickpeas and peanuts. Reserve the cooking liquid for a soup or curry. Add the spice powders and season with salt. After the chickpeas are well coated and become toasty, turn off the heat.

In a bowl, combine the salad ingredients and add the seasoned chickpeas and peanuts. Sprinkle salt and pepper, and drizzle some lemon juice. Mix well and serve.

Variation: Use different bean and vegetables combinations of your choice and experiment with spice powders such as tandoori masala, chaat masala, etc.

* 15 minutes if beans are cooked in advance

BLACK BEANS KEBABS / BURGER PATTIES
delicious meat-patty replacer

This is one of my favorite recipes – I love the meaty flavor of black beans. You have to try this recipe to really taste what I mean. Delicious and versatile, these kebabs can be served with a pasta or salad, or used to make a black beans burger. **Note:** Recipe contains gluten.

Per large patty with cheese: 250 Cal | 12g protein | 10g total fat | 11g fiber
Per large patty, no cheese: 225 Cal | 10g protein | 8g total fat | 11g fiber

Servings: 2 (2 large or 5 small burger patties)   **Cooking time: 15 mins***

Main ingredients
1 cup cooked black beans or
⅓ cup dry black beans
1 slice whole grain, high fiber bread
¼ big red or yellow onion, minced
2 large garlic cloves, grated
A few sprigs of cilantro, chopped
1 cube or 3 tbsp of grated cheese, optional

Spices
¼ - ½ tsp red chili powder
¼ tsp garam masala

Staples
1½ tbsp oil
Salt to taste

Cook ahead: soak ⅓ cup black beans in double the amount of water for 8-10 hours and then pressure cook along with the soaking liquid for 10 minutes after the first whistle or after the pressure regulator starts to rock steadily. Then turn off the heat and wait until the pressure is released.

Drain the cooked beans as it will make the final dish quite dark and mushy. Then mash the cooked beans while retaining some whole beans to create an uneven texture. Toast a slice of whole grain, high fiber bread and grind it to make crumbs.

In a bowl, combine the beans, crumbs, and rest of the ingredients, except oil, and make 4-5 balls. Flatten them into patties. If you want to make burgers, then make 2 large patties.

Heat a pan and add oil. Once the oil is hot, transfer the patties to the pan and fry on medium heat until both sides turn brown. I like them crisp, so I prefer to leave them on the pan for a bit longer to crisp up.

Serve the kebabs over a bed of salad greens and diced vegetables, and dress with any vinaigrette to create a main course salad. Or, serve as an appetizer with ketchup, hot and sweet sauce, or mustard.

Make burgers with whole grain buns, sliced vegetables (tomato, cucumber, caramelized red bell pepper and onion), spinach and condiments of your choice (mustard, ketchup or a small amount of mayo).

Variations: You can substitute black beans with kidney beans, black gram, or black chickpeas as they also have a meaty flavor.

For other **KEBAB, KOFTA,** or **APPE** recipes please refer to page 138 (Cheese and Whole Mung Kebabs), page 137 (Whole Mung Koftas), page 136 (Chana Dal Appe) and page 134 (Mung Dal Appe). These can be used in a salad, sandwich, or wrap along with chutneys and salad vegetables.

* 15 minutes if beans are cooked in advance

NON-VEGETARIAN
& sort of non-vegetarian

You are probably wondering what I mean by "sort of non-vegetarian". The term non-vegetarian refers to meat, seafood and poultry. The sort of non-vegetarian dishes include soy nuggets and soy granules, also known as textured vegetable protein (TVP), that develop the texture of meat when cooked. They may not have the flavor of meat but their texture and their ability to take on flavors of the curry, gravy or marinades, etc. can make them appealing to those who wish to transition to a vegetarian diet or for those who are considering reducing their consumption of meat. They do not contain added sodium, are low in fat, and may afford some of the beneficial effects associated with the soybean. Adding some soy nuggets or soy granules can help vegetarians to increase their protein intake, while helping non-vegetarians to replace some of the animal protein in their diet.

Substituting part of your animal protein intake with legumes can considerably improve the nutritive of your meal. Whole beans can add fiber to help you feel full sooner, thereby reducing your overall intake. Soluble fiber, B-complex vitamins and potassium in legumes can offer some cardio-vascular protection as well.

Here are some ideas to pair animal proteins with vegetarian proteins: consider adding some cooked chickpeas or mung beans to your chicken curries or stews, lentils or soy chunks to your mutton curry or meat stews, kidney beans or soy granules to your chili con carne (American chili), tofu to your seafood dishes, make legume based crepes (dosas) to pair with any of your non-vegetarian curries or stir-fries, make kebabs by combining beans and ground meat or poultry, make tofu scramble instead of egg or paneer scrambles, etc.

CHICKEN DHANSHAK / CHICKEN CURRY WITH VEGETABLES
a lip-smacking Parsi specialty

Mutton dhanshak is a flavor-packed mutton and legume stew, traditionally prepared by the Parsi community, using seasonal vegetables and a unique blend of freshly ground spices. It is an exotic curry that makes you crave it all the more, since it is not easy to find in Indian restaurants here in the US. I have cooked this recipe with chicken, instead of mutton, and I can say that it is really worth trying. You can also follow this recipe to make vegetarian dhanshak dal by simply omitting the chicken.

Per serving: 200 Cal | 19g protein | 7g total fat | 7g fiber

Servings: 6 **Cooking time: 30 mins**

Main ingredients
1½ lb chicken drumsticks (¾ kg, 6 pieces.), skinless
½ large onion, chopped
1 cup red pumpkin, peeled and diced
1 cup diced eggplant
¼ cup mung or urad dal with skin (chilkawali dal)
¼ cup pink lentils (masur dal)
¼ cup black gram (urad) dal or green split peas (hara vatana ki dal)

Dhankshak masala
1" ginger
2 large cloves of garlic
2 Kashmiri red chilies
2 spicy red chilies or ½ tsp red chili powder
3-4 peppercorns
½" cinnamon stick
3-4 cloves
1 star anise

Other spices
1 bay leaf
⅛ tsp turmeric powder
1 tbsp kasuri methi
2 tsp tamarind pulp

Staples
2 tbsp oil or ghee
Salt to taste

Clean the drumsticks and set them aside. Make the Dhanshak masala by grinding the Dhanshak masala ingredients to a coarse paste. There is no need to dry roast these spices, since we will be roasting the paste later, to make it more fragrant.

Chop and dice the vegetables and wash the dals.

Heat the oil in a pressure cooker or pressure pan and add the chicken drumsticks, onion, bay leaf, turmeric powder, kasuri methi, and salt. Sauté on high heat until the drumsticks become slightly caramelized.

Then add the vegetables, dals, and Dhanshak masala and sauté on medium heat until aromatic.

Add about 1½ cups water, mix well, and pressure cook for about 10 minutes on low heat after the first whistle or after the pressure regulator starts to rock. Then turn off the heat and let it cool.

Once the pressure is released, add tamarind pulp and salt.

Mix well and garnish with caramelized onion (page 114). Pair with my cabbage mint salad (Dhanshak salad on page 114) and brown rice.

Variations: Omit the chicken for the **VEGETARIAN DHANSHAK DAL.** and cook the dals up to the first whistle or until the pressure regulator starts to rock. Then turn off the heat.
You can add 1 cup fresh fenugreek leaves or spinach as well – just add them after the dals are cooked, and boil for 1-2 minutes before serving.

Tip: Avoid pressure cooking leafy vegetables as the nutritive value will be considerably reduced.

DHANSHAK SALAD / CABBAGE WITH CARAMELIZED ONION
a refreshing salad with some vitamin C

This salad goes very well with dhanshak, whether it is chicken or mutton dhanshak, or even the vegetarian version. The sweet and tangy dressing and the fresh cabbage provide a good balance to the thick dhanshak gravy.

Per serving: 50 Cal | 1g protein | 2g total fat | 1g fiber

Servings: 6 **Cooking time: 10 mins**

Main ingredients
6 cups cabbage, shredded
1½ onion, sliced
12-18 mint leaves
1-2 tbsp lemon juice

Staples
1 tbsp oil
1-2 tsp honey or maple syrup
Salt and black pepper to taste

Heat the oil in a pan and caramelize the sliced onion on medium heat. Use a portion of this **CARAMELIZED ONION** for garnishing the chicken dhanshak and remainder for this salad.

Combine the cabbage, caramelized onion, freshly chopped mint leaves, lemon juice, honey, salt, and black pepper. Mix well and serve immediately, as the mint leaves will turn black. Alternatively, use whole mint leaves.

Tip: To make the caramelized onion crispy, turn up the heat to high for a few seconds towards the end. Keep a close watch as it could burn.

TURKEY CHILI WITH SOY GRANULES
so delicious and aromatic

Chili in the US refers to a stew prepared with ground (minced) beef. I often crave my mother's delicious mutton kheema (minced mutton). So, I adapted her recipe using minced turkey in my attempt to replicate the taste. Turkey meat may not be as flavorful as mutton, but you can bump up the spices to make it taste good. While it does come close to the taste I reminisce, it also brings back memories of us dining together.

Per serving: 130 Cal | 12g protein | 6g total fat | 3g fiber

Servings: 8 **Cooking time: 30 mins**

Main ingredients
½ lb (¼ kg) minced turkey
1 cup dry soy granules
1 large onion, finely chopped
2 tomatoes, finely chopped
3 large cloves of garlic + 2" ginger, ground to paste
¼ cup cilantro leaves and stalks, chopped

Spices
1 tsp red chili powder (adjust to your palate)
½ tsp garam masala
1 tsp coriander powder
1 tsp cumin powder
1 tsp kasuri methi
1 bayleaf
2-3 green cardamoms

Staples
2 tbsp olive oil + 1 tbsp ghee or butter

Wash the granules lightly to remove any soy dust and set aside. Cut the vegetables and prepare the paste.

Heat the oil and ghee in a pot and add the bay leaf and cardamoms along with the chopped onion. Sauté until the onion has caramelized to dark brown, but not burnt. This gives the curry a slightly darker color to resemble the mutton dish.

Now add the minced turkey, soy granules, tomato, ginger-garlic paste, cilantro, spice powders and salt, and mix well. Sauté for a minute or two on high heat and then add some water. Bring it to a boil on high heat and then cover to let the turkey cook on medium heat.

When the turkey is cooked, serve the chili with whole grain bread and a generous helping of colorful salad.

Variations: You can add 1 cup frozen green peas or a diced green capsicum (green bell pepper) to this dish. Add the peas half-way through the cooking, and capsicum at the end. This will retain the color and flavor, and prevent them from overcooking.

Use this recipe to make **CHILI CON CARNE** by using ½ lb minced meat and 1½ cups cooked beans.

Note: The soy granules absorb the curry (liquid) even after cooking. You may need to add water and adjust salt and spices when reheating leftovers.

FENNEL-INFUSED CHICKEN MUNG BEANS STEW
a delicious stew with fennel seeds

This aromatic stew or curry is loaded with nutrients. The colorful vegetables, chicken, mung beans, and yogurt make for a great way to enjoy this wholesome stew.

Per serving: 190 Cal | 22g protein | 4g total fat | 4g fiber

Servings: 6   **Soak time: 8-10 hours**   **Cooking time: 30 mins**

Main ingredients
1 lb (~500 g, ½ kg) chicken thighs, diced into 1" pieces
½ cup mung beans soaked overnight
½ cup yogurt, optional
½ onion, diced
1 tomato, diced
2-3 cups spinach
1 green bell pepper, diced
1" ginger piece, grated
2 large cloves of garlic, grated

Spices
1 tbsp fennel seeds
1 tsp coriander powder
½ tsp red chili powder
¼ tsp garam masala or cinnamon powder
⅛ tsp turmeric powder
1 bay leaf, optional

Staples
2 tbsp oil
Salt to taste

Wash the mung beans and soak overnight for 8-10 hours with 1 cup of water.

Clean and cut the chicken thigh pieces and vegetables. Use separate chopping boards for vegetables and chicken, and wash them thoroughly after use.

Heat the oil in a pot and add the diced onion and bay leaf. Let the onion cook on high heat for a minute or so and then add the chicken and soaked mung beans (retain the soaking liquid). Add the ginger, garlic and spices, and sauté on medium heat until aromatic.

Then add the soaking liquid and some water, cover the pot and let the chicken and mung beans cook on medium heat. When the chicken is cooked, stir in the yogurt and rest of the vegetables and mix well. Cook for 2 minutes on medium heat and serve with whole grain bread or cooked steel-cut oats. Oats seasoned with salt and pepper taste fantastic with this stew and provide additional fiber.

Variations: I have prepared this stew with carrots, broccoli, and kale and it tastes great as well. Use vegetables of your preference or those in season.

If you haven't soaked the mung bean, then cook this dish in the pressure cooker. Pressure cook for 5 minutes after the first whistle or after the pressure regulator starts to rock. Add the green vegetables after the pressure is released and let them cook in the stew for a minute or two, and then serve. If the chicken is undercooked after pressure cooking, simmer until it is done.

Make **CARDAMOM-INFUSED CHICKEN & CHICKPEAS STEW** by substituting fennel seeds with 3-4 partially crushed whole green cardamom. Add 1½ cups of cooked chickpeas to the stew towards the end, along with 1 cup diced mushrooms and 3-4 cups of chopped kale. Omit the yogurt, and bring it to a boil before serving. Serve with brown rice or whole grain pasta.

SOY KHEEMA / VEGETARIAN MINCED MEAT
minced soy for vegetarians

Soybean granules, also known as textured vegetable protein, make for an instant protein-packed food to add to your meals. Kheema means "minced" in Hindi. My mother makes several delicious dishes with soy granules and chunks (nuggets), and this is one of them. I believe you will not miss minced meat as much after you taste this dish. If you still crave some meat, then add some minced meat to this recipe. Substituting some of the meat with soy granules can help you include some plant protein in your diet. You can enjoy this dish in a wrap or sandwich, as a protein side, or as a topping for your pasta.

Per serving: 160 Cal | 13g protein | 7g total fat | 5g fiber

Servings: 4 **Cooking time: 30 mins**

Main ingredients
- 1 cup dry soy granules
- 1 onion, finely chopped
- 2 tomatoes, puréed
- 1 cup green peas
- 2 large cloves of garlic and 1½" ginger, ground to paste
- ¼ cup mint leaves
- ¼ cup cilantro, chopped

Spices
- ½ tsp red chili powder
- ½ tsp garam masala
- ½ tsp kasuri methi
- 2 cloves
- 2 pepper corns
- 1 bayleaf
- 1" flat cinnamon stick
- 1 large black cardamom (masala elaichi)

Staples
- 1 tbsp olive oil + 1 tbsp ghee
- Salt to taste

Wash the granules lightly to remove any soy dust. Transfer the granules to a pot, add 1 cup of water and bring it to a boil. Turn off the heat and drain the water using a colander. This is a processed food like pasta, so discarding the water in which soy granules are briefly cooked will not lead to a significant loss of nutrients.

Heat the oil and ghee in a pan. Add the whole spices and chopped onion, and sauté until the onion has caramelized to a dark brown color (but not burnt).

Now add the ginger-garlic paste and cooked soy granules, green peas, spice powders, cilantro, salt and tomato purée and mix well.

Cook until the tomato purée thickens a bit. Set it aside for a few minutes for the kheema to absorb the flavors. This dish does not have any gravy or curry. Mix in the mint leaves and serve as a filling for wraps, whole grain burgers, and sandwiches, or add as a topping on pasta or pizza.

Variations: Prepare a delicious biryani with this kheema, by mixing in with cooked Basmati rice. Serve with a vegetable raita (yogurt dip with chopped vegetables).
You can use this recipe for cooking dal wadis or soy chunks.
Make your tofu scramble (bhurjee) with this recipe.
Add 1 cup minced meat, chicken, or turkey to this recipe.

MEDITERRANEAN CHICKEN HUMMUS WRAP
a great combination of chicken and chickpeas

This is a great way to discreetly include chickpeas in your wrap. Grill some chicken the way you like and toss in a wrap after spreading a generous helping of hummus and veggies.

Per serving: 340 Cal | 23g protein | 13g total fat | 11g fiber
With wrap: 440 Cal | 26g protein | 15g total fat | 14g fiber

Servings: 2   **Cooking time: 30 mins**

Main ingredients
2 whole grain wraps (100-150 Cal each)
1 cup chicken pieces (thigh or breast)
2 cups diced or shredded vegetables (carrots, onion, cucumber, bell peppers, beetroot, celery, etc.)
2 cups salad greens (mixed greens, spinach, arugula, etc.)
1 zucchini, sliced (optional)
4 tbsp hummus (page 192)

Marinade
2 garlic cloves
¼ cup cilantro or parsley
½ tsp paprika or red chili powder
A few pinches of mixed dried herbs
1 tbsp olive oil
Salt and black pepper to taste

Prepare the chicken marinade by grinding the cilantro and garlic, or parsley and garlic to a paste – use very little water. Mix in the remaining marinade ingredients and coat the chicken well. Cover and set aside for at least 10 minutes – the longer the better. For a longer marination, keep the marinated chicken in the refrigerator.

Wash and prepare the salad vegetables while the chicken is marinating. Sprinkle salt and black pepper on the vegetables just before serving.

Heat a pan or grill and cook the chicken on medium heat until it is tender and slightly browned. When done, transfer it to a plate. Grill the zucchini on the same pan on medium heat until it is slightly soft and browned. Season with salt and pepper and set it aside.

Warm the wraps and assemble the ingredients – spread some hummus on one side of the wrap, transfer the chicken pieces, and then the shredded vegetables and salad greens. Season with salt and pepper. Roll, wrap, or fold and enjoy with the grilled zucchini on the side.

Variation: Use hummus to make meat or veggie wraps.

SPANISH CHICKPEAS BRAVAS
chicken bravas to chickpeas bravas

Spanish tapas are small plates of appetizers served with drinks at a bar. Just like the patata bravas, a popular Spanish tapa made with potatoes and tomato paste, I tried the recipe with chickpeas and *si, que resultó ser genial* (yes, it turned out great)! Check out more tapas recipes on my website (quicklydelicious.com). The original recipe calls for tomato paste, which is tomato pulp concentrate; however, you can use fresh tomato purée and cook it until it thickens. Use this recipe for boiled potatoes and chicken and serve as bravas platter.

Per serving: 150 Cal | 6g protein | 6g total fat | 4g fiber

Servings: 2 **Cooking time: 10 mins**

Main ingredients
1 cup cooked chickpeas
½ tomato, puréed or 1 tsp tomato paste
1 large clove of garlic, grated
2 tbsp shredded cheese
2-3 pinches of mixed dried herbs or fresh oregano

Spices & Staples
¼ tsp paprika or red chili powder
2 tsp olive oil
½ tsp honey
Salt and black pepper to taste

Heat the oil in a pan and add garlic and chickpeas. Sauté the chickpeas for a minute on medium heat, and then add rest of the ingredients. Cook until the tomato purée thickens. If you use tomato paste then you can add some water, but do not make it runny. Garnish with some cheese and crushed oregano. Serve chickpeas bravas as a tapa (an appetizer).

Use this recipe with 1 cup chicken pieces and 1 cooked large potato (250g, ½ lb) to make **CHICKEN BRAVAS** and **POTATO BRAVAS.** Serve these tapas as bravas platter. Try other quick tapas recipes from my website (quicklydelicious.com).

TURKEY / CHICKEN KEBABS
super delicious kebabs for burgers, hot dogs, pasta, or salads

We were quite fond of the chicken kebabs that we regularly purchased from a non-vegetarian specialty store in Ahmedabad. They were good enough to pacify our hunger for kebabs from our favorite restaurants in Mumbai. I tried to replicate the taste of those kebabs, and this recipe does bring back memories of enjoying kebabs with our pasta and salad dinners on Friday nights. You can serve these kebabs as an appetizer, or add them to your salad, pasta, burger, or hot dog buns.

Per serving: 130 Cal | 12g protein | 6g total fat | 3g fiber

Servings: 4 **Cooking time: 30 mins**

Main ingredients
½ lb (¼ kg) minced (ground) turkey or chicken
¼ cup chana dal (split chickpeas, yellow split peas)
½" ginger piece
2 garlic cloves
¼ cup cilantro leaves, chopped

Spices
½ tsp red chili powder (adjust to your palate)
½ tsp fenugreek seeds
½ tsp garam masala
½ tbsp fennel seeds

Staples
1 tbsp olive oil
Salt to taste

Wash and soak chana dal and fenugreek seeds in a little less than ½ cup of water for 4 hours or overnight, whatever is convenient for you.

Grind the soaked dal with ginger, garlic, cilantro and fennel seeds, along with the soaking liquid to make a smooth paste.

Rinse the minced turkey or chicken, if necessary, and drain well. Pat the minced turkey dry with paper towel. I do not wash the packaged minced or ground turkey available here in the US, but in India, the meat is coarsely minced and needs to be rinsed.

Add the chana dal paste to the minced turkey, add salt and spices and mix well. Make 12 balls and flatten them so that they are not too thick. This will allow the turkey to cook all the way through. Otherwise, you may need to cook the sides of the kebabs.

Heat the oil in a pan and fry the kebabs. Cover and cook each side on low heat until they turn crisp and brown before flipping them over. Serve with yogurt mint chutney (page 93) as an appetizer or add them to a main course salad.

Make a large batch of these kebabs, pan-fry, and freeze them for quick weeknight dinners.

Variations: Make burgers using this recipe and serve over whole wheat buns, sliced onion, tomato, or bell pepper, spinach or kale, with mustard or mint chutney, and ketchup.

Make **ITALIAN PATTIES** by omitting the ginger and spices, and adding dried herbs, red chili flakes and some grated cheese to the chana dal and minced turkey or meat. Substitute cilantro with parsley, but retain the garlic. Serve these patties as a substitute for meatballs over pasta or to replace sausages in your hot dogs.

for the
LOVE OF RICE

White rice is a staple food common in many coastal cuisines – parts of India, Thailand, Mexico, and other countries. Rather than associating a negative label with rice, it would be more helpful to understand one's diet and other lifestyle factors in totality and alter them accordingly. The type of rice used, what you pair it with in your meals, how much and how often you consume are some of the dietary factors that can influence your weight gain or your blood sugar levels. Parboiled rice, brown rice, and unpolished rice are healthier choices over long grain white rice, which in turn is better than short grain, sticky white rice, because of higher fiber, B-complex vitamins, iron, and magnesium content.

Brown rice makes for a great side for non-vegetarian meals or curries that do not contain much fiber. However, it may not be palatably substituted in all traditional recipes that call for white rice. Also, a meal that contains more servings of brown rice and fewer servings of protein and vegetables, may not qualify as a healthy, well-balanced meal, even if it substitutes white rice with brown rice. One way to enjoy any kind of rice or rice based recipes is to pair each serving of rice with equal or more servings or amounts of cooked whole beans or high fiber vegetables (list on page 35).

The proportion of rice to other meal components or recipe ingredients is a more important aspect that just the type of rice consumed. When preparing recipes with dal and rice combinations, such as idli or dosa batters, consider using 1 part dal and 2 parts rice, rather than the usual 1 part dal and 3 or more parts rice. A more favorable alternative would be to pair rice with whole beans or dals with skin, as they have much more fiber than any type of rice. When you serve rice with dal or beans curry or cook khichadis, consider a much healthier 1:1 proportion (1 part dal or beans and 1 part rice). This way you add more fiber, protein, vitamins, and minerals to the meal and reduce the spike in blood glucose associated with rice. Alternatively, try serving dal and rice combinations with high fiber vegetables such as okra (lady's fingers), eggplant (brinjal), green beans, etc. to better control the blood glucose spike or to feel full earlier, thereby cutting back on some calories.

Now, we do have a lot of ideas to implement. So, let's enjoy rice with healthy pairings to make the meal more balanced.

BROWN RICE & LENTILS PULAO
delicious and nutritious

This is a wholesome dish that makes for a well-balanced meal with cereal, legumes, and vegetables, even though it uses just a few ingredients. Brown rice requires more water than white rice, and takes longer to cook on the stove top. Try the pressure cooker method for quick and healthy dinners.

Per serving: 240 Cal | 9g protein | 8g total fat | 8g fiber

Servings: 4 **Cooking time: 30 mins**

Main ingredients
- ½ cup lentils (sabut masur)
- ½ cup brown rice
- ½ medium onion, chopped
- 1 large red bell pepper, diced
- ½ cup cilantro, leaves and stalks, chopped
- 1" ginger, grated
- 3 large cloves of garlic, chopped

Spices
- ½ tsp red chili powder
- ⅛ tsp cinnamon powder

Staples
- 2 tbsp oil
- Salt to taste

Combine the lentils and brown rice, wash and pressure cook them together in about 1¾ cups water for about 10 minutes on low heat after the first whistle or after the pressure regulator starts to rock. Then turn off the heat and wait until the pressure is released.

Meanwhile, prepare the vegetables and herbs.

Heat the oil in a pot and add the chopped onion. Sauté the onion on medium heat until it becomes light brown. Then add the bell pepper, ginger and garlic, and sauté until the bell pepper softens a bit – do not make it mushy.

When ready, add the cooked lentils and rice, along with the spice powders and chopped cilantro. Mix well and sauté on high heat for 1-2 minutes or until aromatic. Remember to include chopped cilantro stalks as they are packed with flavor.

Add the salt and serve with a side salad or just enjoy it plain. Pack away the rest for your lunch.

Variations: You can use parboiled or unpolished white rice instead of brown rice, especially if high fiber causes discomfort. Lentils are high in fiber and nutrients and can balance those lacking in white rice.

Use this recipe to make **ITALIAN LENTILS & MUSHROOM RISOTTO**, by pan-frying 2 cups of sliced mushrooms instead of bell pepper, and omitting the spices and ginger. Sprinkle ¼ tsp dried herbs (Italian seasoning or *herbes de Provence*) and 4 tbsp of shredded cheese. Serve with a quick side of stir-fried kale, Brussels sprouts or broccoli (recipes on my website – quicklydelicious.com).

NUTRIENT-DENSE KHICHADI / NUTRIENT-DENSE PORRIDGE
high fiber and high protein khichadi

Indians love their khichadis – a comfort food just like the American mac and cheese. Khichadi is a traditional rice and dal dish that is minimally spiced and cooked to a soft porridge-like consistency. Generally, a khichadi may contain more rice than dal. One can make this one-pot comfort food more wholesome by using equal amounts of rice and dals, or using whole small beans or dals with skin, and pairing with vegetables.

Per serving: 250 Cal | 10g protein | 6g total fat | 6g fiber

Servings: 4 **Cooking time: 30 mins**

Main ingredients
½ cup rice
½ cup whole mung or mung dal with skin
1 cup frozen or fresh green peas or diced green beans
2 large cloves of garlic, mashed

Spices
½ tsp cumin seeds
A few pinches of asafetida, optional
½ tsp red chili powder
½ tsp Kitchen King Masala (special spice blend) or garam masala

Staples
2 tbsp ghee (clarified, unsalted butter)
Salt to taste

Wash rice and mung and set aside. Use brown rice, white, unpolished rice, or parboiled rice.

Heat a pressure pan or a small pressure cooker. Add ghee and when it melts add the mashed garlic and cumin seeds, and let the cumin sizzle.

Then add asafetida and rest of the ingredients along with salt. Sauté for a minute and add 2 cups of water (double the amount of rice and dal) or more if you like your khichadi to be runny. Taste to ensure that the water tastes slightly saltier because rice absorbs the salt and the khichadi will taste just right when done. Otherwise you may need to add salt at the table and could end up adding more than necessary.

Seal the pressure cooker and pressure cook the khichadi for 10 minutes after the first whistle or after the pressure regulator starts to rock. Turn off the heat and allow it to cool. Serve with yogurt and a fresh salad.

Variations: Add 1-2 cups of vegetables to your khichadis. Avoid adding leafy vegetables to khichadis as pressure cooking can reduce their nutritive value. Simply sauté the leafy vegetable and serve as a side. Alternatively, add the leafy vegetables after the khichadi is done and let them cook in the steam of the khichadi for a few minutes.
Substitute rice with barley or cracked wheat (dalia).

PROTEIN-PACKED KHICHADI / PROTEIN-PACKED PORRIDGE
Indian comfort food

This light khichadi is easy to digest and makes for a good meal, especially when you are recuperating. Otherwise, pair it with a high fiber okra stir-fry, that complements this khichadi very well. This khichadi is so delicious that you will be tempted to make it often. It is one of the first few recipes I learned from my mom. I once prepared this for my father-in-law, and he was so impressed that he said it was the best khichadi he ever had! You can make it with 1:2 proportion of dal and rice, or pack in more protein with equal amounts as used in this recipe.

Per serving: 230 Cal | 8g protein | 6g total fat | 5g fiber

Servings: 4 **Cooking time: 30 mins**

Main ingredients
½ cup rice
½ cup mung dal
½ onion, sliced
1 tomato, sliced
Cilantro for garnishing

Spices
½ tsp cumin seeds
½ tsp red chili powder
¼ tsp turmeric powder

Staples
2 tbsp ghee
Salt to taste

Wash the rice and mung dal and set aside.

Heat a pressure pan or small pressure cooker. Add ghee and when it melts add cumin seeds and let them sizzle.

Then add the onion and sauté for a minute. Add the tomatoes and spice powders, and continue to sauté for another minute. Add rest of the ingredients along with salt and 2 cups water (double the amount of rice and dal). Taste to ensure that the water tastes slightly saltier because once cooked, it will taste just right after the rice absorbs the salt. Else you may need to add salt at the table and could end up adding more than necessary.

Seal the pressure cooker and pressure cook the khichadi for 10 minutes after the first whistle or after the pressure regulator starts to rock. Turn off the heat and allow it to cool.

Garnish with chopped cilantro and some ghee. Pair with kadhi (recipe page 104) or plain yogurt, and a high fiber vegetable stir-fry (okra, eggplant, cabbage, green beans, cluster beans, etc.) to balance the meal.

Variations: Use this recipe to make **BARLEY KHICHADI** with 1 cup barley and ⅔ cup mung dal, and you will be impressed how delicious this khichadi turns out. Pressure cook with 3 cups of water for the same duration.
Vary the tempering of khichadis by using mustard seeds, fenugreek seeds, asafetida, garlic, green chili, whole spices such as cinnamon, peppercorns, cardamom, etc. for creating new flavors.
Use any other dal, dals with skin, small beans or black-eyed peas.
If you want to add leafy vegetables, then add them after the khichadi is cooked, in order to retain their nutritive value. Most leafy vegetables can cook in the residual heat, or simply sauté the leafy vegetables and serve as a side.

BISIBELE BATH / SOUTH INDIAN RICE STEW
an all-in-one flavorful rice stew

This is a very flavorful rice stew with dal and vegetables commonly prepared in the south of India. Spice combinations usually vary from state to state, but this stew tastes good with any combination. Keep in mind that the proportion of legumes and vegetables in relation to rice is important. And so, be sure to include plenty of vegetables or serve some on the side.

Per serving: 240 Cal | 8g protein | 6g total fat | 6g fiber

Servings: 4 **Cooking time: 30 mins**

Main ingredients
½ cup rice
½ split pigeon peas (toor dal)
1 cup diced pumpkin
1 cup diced eggplant (brinjal)
1 cup diced green beans
A few sprigs of cilantro, chopped

Spices
1 tbsp black gram dal (urad dal)
1 tbsp whole coriander seeds
1 tbsp dessicated coconut (dry coconut powder)
2 red chilies (hot variety)
3-4 black peppercorns
1" cinnamon stick
10-12 curry leaves
2 tsp rehydrated tamarind pulp

Staples
2 tbsp ghee or oil
Salt to taste

Wash the rice and dal and set aside. You can use parboiled or unpolished white rice.

Grind all the ingredients listed under spices (except tamarind) to a coarse paste. There is no need to dry roast these spices, since we will be roasting the paste over ghee, to make it more fragrant.

Heat the ghee in a pressure pan or a small pressure cooker. Add the ground mixture and roast for a minute on low heat.

Then add the vegetables, rice and dal, 2-3 cups of water, and salt. Mix well and taste to ensure that the water is slightly saltier. Once cooked, it will taste just right as the rice absorbs the salt. Else you may need to add salt at the table and could end up adding more than necessary.

Pressure cook for 10 minutes after the first whistle or after the pressure regulator starts to rock. Turn off the heat and allow it to cool.

Add the tamarind pulp to the stew and mix well. Garnish with cilantro and serve with yogurt. Sprinkle some chutney podi for added flavor (page 191).

Variations: Substitute toor dal with mixed dals, dals with skin, small beans, or black-eyed peas.
Use any vegetables of your choice.

VEGGIES & LENTILS PULAO
a high fiber pulao

This was one of my random, impromptu creations that I once prepared after returning home late. To my surprise, it tasted great and I thought I should share this recipe in my book. I love how aromatic this pulao becomes with just a few nigella seeds (kalonji). You should try them with all your pulaos!

Per serving: 250 Cal | 9g protein | 6g total fat | 9g fiber

Servings: 4 **Cooking time: 30 mins**

Main ingredients
½ cup rice
½ whole lentils (sabut masur)
½ onion, diced
1 cup frozen green peas and carrot
A few sprigs of cilantro, chopped

Spices
½ tsp cumin seeds
½ tsp red chili powder
½ tsp garam masala or Kitchen King Masala (special spice blend)
½ tsp nigella seeds (kalonji)

Staples
2 tbsp ghee or oil
Salt to taste

Wash the rice and lentils and set aside. Use brown rice, parboiled rice or white, unpolished rice.

Heat a pressure pan or a small pressure cooker. Add ghee and when it melts add cumin seeds and let them sizzle. Then add rest of the ingredients, and sauté for a minute.

Add salt and 2 cups water. Taste to ensure that the water is slightly saltier. It will taste just right after the pulao is cooked, as the rice absorbs the salt. Otherwise, you may need to add salt at the table and could end up adding more than necessary.

Seal the pressure cooker and pressure cook the khichadi for 10 minutes after the first whistle or after the pressure regulator starts to rock. Turn off the heat and allow it to cool.

Garnish and serve with yogurt and a fresh salad.

Variations: Add vegetables of your choice. Avoid adding leafy vegetables to khichadis as pressure cooking can reduce their nutritive value. Simply add them at the end of cooking and let them cook in the residual heat. Alternatively, sauté the leafy vegetables and serve as a side.
Use any biryani or pulao masalas in this recipe for added flavor.

BLACK CHICKPEAS FRIED RICE
a novel way to enjoy chickpeas

Here is another recipe to enjoy black chickpeas. You can substitute chickpeas with any other cooked beans. Whole beans cooked in advance come in handy to make quick and delicious stir-fries for salads or rice dishes. Whole beans have a lot of fiber and make them ideal for pairing with lower fiber grains such as rice, jowar, bajra, wheat semolina or vermicelli, etc.

Per serving: 260 Cal | 8g protein | 8g total fat | 7g fiber

Servings: 4 **Cooking time: 15 mins***

Main ingredients
½ cup Basmati rice
½ cup black chickpeas
½ large onion, sliced
3 cloves garlic, chopped
1 red or green bell pepper (capsicum), sliced
1 cup green beans, julienned
1 carrot, julienned
A few sprigs of cilantro, chopped
1 spring onion (scallion), choppped

Spices
1 star anise
1" cinnamon stick
2 cloves
½ tsp fennel seeds
½ tsp red chili flakes

Staples
2 tbsp ghee (or butter) + 1 tsp ghee (or butter) for cooking rice
Salt and black pepper to taste

Wash and soak chickpeas overnight in 1 cup of water.

Wash the rice and add ½ cup of water, salt, and 1 tsp ghee. Pressure cook the rice and the soaked chickpeas (with the soaking liquid) simultaneously using stackable containers. Pressure cook for 10 minutes after the first whistle, or after the pressure regulator starts to rock. Then turn off the heat. Cook these ahead and store in the refrigerator for up to one week.

Heat the ghee in a pan or wok and add the garlic and whole spices. When the garlic turns golden, add the vegetables, chili flakes, salt, and cooked chickpeas, and sauté on high heat. Cover and let them cook for about 2 minutes on medium heat. Keep the vegetables *al dente* (firm to the bite).

Add the cooked rice, adjust salt and mix well. Garnish with chopped scallions and serve.

Variations: Vary the vegetables – cabbage, mushrooms, sprouts, broccoli, Brussels sprouts, green peas, etc. will taste great in this recipe. Substitute black chickpeas with any cooked beans such as kidney beans, chickpeas, black beans, etc. Try with tofu and brown rice as well.
Grind the spices to a fine powder and then add this Chinese 5-spice blend to the fried rice.
Use oil instead of ghee or butter.
Add left-over **KALA CHANA SUBZI** (page 53) to this recipe for making a lip-smacking pulao.
Add any pulao or biryani masala to this recipe or throw some cooked black chickpeas or whole beans into your pulao or biryani.

* if the chickpeas and rice are cooked in advance.

MEXICAN RICE & BEANS BOWL
with refreshing pineapple salsa and simple guacamole

This is a very refreshing and filling bowl of rice and beans. It is packed with vitamin C and the heat of jalapeño is sweetly balanced by the pineapple salsa. Keep in mind the proportion of rice and beans used in this recipe.

Per serving: 300 Cal | 8g protein | 11g total fat | 11g fiber

Servings: 4   **Cooking time: 15 mins***

Rice and beans
½ cup rice
½ cup black beans
A few sprigs cilantro, chopped
½ tsp cumin powder
½ tsp red chili powder
1 tbsp oil + 1 tsp oil (for cooking rice)
Salt to taste

Vegetable Fajitas
1 onion, sliced
1 red bell pepper (red capsicum)
Salt and ground black pepper to taste
1 tbsp oil

Simple Guacamole
1 avocado, peeled and mashed
2 cloves garlic, grated
½ green chili or jalapeño, chopped
1-2 tsp lemon juice
1-2 sprigs cilantro, chopped
Salt to taste

Pineapple salsa
1 cup diced pineapple
½ green chili or ¼ jalapeño, finely chopped
1-2 sprigs cilantro, chopped
Salt to taste

Wash and soak beans overnight in 1 cup of water.

Wash the rice and add ½ cup of water, salt and 1 tsp oil. Pressure cook the rice and the soaked beans (along with the soaking liquid) simultaneously using stackable containers. Pressure cook them for 10 minutes after the first whistle or after the pressure regulator starts to rock. Then turn off the heat. Cook them ahead and store in the refrigerator for up to one week.

Heat 1 tbsp oil and sauté the onion and bell pepper on high heat until the onion begins to caramelize. Turn off the heat and transfer the vegetable fajitas to a plate. Season the fajitas with salt and black pepper.

Then sauté the cooked black beans in the same pan for 1-2 minutes on high heat. Discard the cooking liquid as it can make the dish unappealing. Season the beans with salt, cumin and chili powder and transfer them to a plate as well.

Prepare the guacamole by combining all the ingredients listed under guacamole. Get your pineapple salsa ready as well by combining the ingredients for salsa.

Assemble your bowl by serving equal amounts of rice and beans, some fajitas, guacamole and salsa, and wait no more.

Variations: Substitute the pineapple salsa with mango salsa or tomato salsa (on the website – quicklydelicious.com).
Grill some marinated chicken, fish or shrimp, and add to this bowl for the extra protein.

Tip: Avocado can make up for the nutrients lost when the cooking liquid is discarded.

* if rice and beans are cooked in advance.

ANYTIME MEALS
from idlis & appe to crepes & pancakes

In this section, you will find recipes that you can serve any time of the day – breakfast, snacks, lunch, or dinner.

Whole and split legumes batters make very nutritious breakfast dishes such as dosas (crepes), idlis (lens shaped, steamed mini-cakes), dhoklas (steamed savory cakes), and appe (pancake puffs). Legume flours can also be used to make an instant version of these batters. Ferment the batters to increase the nutrient content and to make them easy to digest.

Appe, dosas, and dhoklas made with whole beans or split beans with skin, can boost your efforts to lose weight, and gain better control over blood sugar, blood cholesterol, and blood pressure. Most of these recipes are kid-friendly (taper the use of spices as required). By including legume-based breakfast, you will not only increase your protein and fiber intake but also reduce your glycemic load, which is beneficial for diabetes or prediabetes. Follow healthy cooking practices covered in the educational portion of this book to maximize the health benefits.

Legume batters are very versatile. Idli batters can be used to make dosas, uttapam, or appe, and vice versa. Idlis and dosas can be served for breakfast or main course – so long as you use a higher proportion of legumes, thereby replacing some amount of grains (rice, wheat, ragi, etc.) with legumes. Similarly, including more whole legumes rather than split legumes (dals), or pairing dals with high fiber grains, vegetables, or fruits will help you plan well-balanced meals.

Whole legume, dal or flour dosas, omelets, or chillas can be easily packed for lunch with any stir-fry (subzi) or curry to make a lower carb, yet well-balanced meal. The legume-based crepes are perfect for weight loss and for diabetes, as you replace the grains (roti, rice, pasta, etc.) with more protein and fiber.

MUNG DAL APPE & DOSAS / MUNG DAL PUFFS & CREPES
a healthy breakfast or snack

Appe are very similar to the Danish aebleskives (aebeliskiver puffs, pancake puffs) – small puffed balls made in a pan with small wells, called an abeliskiver pan. Instead of using a pancake batter or a semolina and yogurt base, a legume-based batter can also be used to make appe. You can cook individual puffs in smaller amounts of oil in this type of pan, without having to deep-fry. Refer to pictures of appe pan on page 26.

Per serving: 240 Cal | 11g protein | 8g total fat | 7g fiber

Servings: 2 (24 balls)	Soak Time: 4 or 8-10 hours	Cooking Time: 30 mins

Main ingredients
¼ cup mung dal with skin (split mung bean with skin) or whole mung (mung beans)
¼ cup chana dal (yellow split peas)
1" ginger piece
1 green chili
½ cup cilantro, chopped

Spices & Staples
2 tsp flaxseeds (alsi) or 1 tsp fenugreek seeds (methi seeds)
1 tbsp oil
Salt to taste

Wash the dals and soak them along with the flaxseeds or fenugreek seeds in ¾ cup of water for 4 hours or 8-10 hours, whichever is convenient.

Grind the dals along with ginger and chili to make a thick, smooth batter by adding a small amount of the soaking liquid at a time. Reserve the remainder, nutrient-rich soaking liquid as a broth for making curries, dals, stews, rice, or dough. Add chopped cilantro and salt into the batter and mix well.

For making appe, heat an appe pan (aebeliskiver pan) and add 2-3 drops of oil in each well. Add a teaspoonful of batter in each well if it has 12 wells; add more batter if it has fewer, larger wells. Cover and let them cook on medium heat.

Check after about 2 minutes to see if the bottom surface of each puff has turned golden brown. Flip them over and cook the other side until golden brown. Add 1-2 drops of oil on each puff before flipping. Otherwise, they can become very dry.

Once both sides are done, transfer to a plate and repeat the process for rest of the batter. Serve them hot with chutney, ketchup, or any dip.

Variations: Make **DOSAS (CREPES)** with this recipe (process details on page 137).
You may even add the appe to your rasam, sambar, or kadhi.
Use this recipe with a combination of different dals and whole legumes – urad (black gram), toor dal (split pigeon peas), chana dal (yellow split peas, split chickpeas), mung, sabut masur (lentils), masur dal (pink lentils), etc. to make **MULTI-LEGUME APPE**.

Tip: For making **KOFTAS (DEEP-FRIED FRITTERS)**, soak dals for 4 hours only and keep the batter as coarse and dry as possible, so that the koftas will absorb less oil. Be mindful when you eat deep-fried items as they are high in calories. You may use an absorbent paper towel to remove some oil from the koftas. Then add these to your kofta curry.

CHANA DAL APPE / LIGHT FALAFEL
from pakoras to falafel

You can make appe (puffs), dosas (crepes), or pakoras (fritters) with this recipe. Mediterranean falafel are deep-fried balls made with a batter of whole chickpeas, cooked and ground with garlic and paprika, with cumin powder or herbs. This is a lower calorie version made with chana dal (yellow split peas). Use them as koftas in your kofta curry, or serve as a side for some extra protein. You can even enjoy these for breakfast or an evening snack. **Note:** Recipe is kid-friendly.

Per serving: 250 Cal | 11g protein | 10g total fat | 5g fiber

Servings: 2 (24 balls)	Soak Time: 4 or 8-10 hours	Cooking Time: 30 mins

Main ingredients
½ cup yellow split peas (chana dal)
1" ginger piece
2 garlic cloves, optional

Spices
½ tsp cumin seeds
½ tsp red chili powder or red chili flakes

Staples
1 tbsp oil
Salt to taste

Wash the dal and soak in ¾ cup of water for 4 hours or 8-10 hours, per your convenience.

Grind the dal along with the garlic (for **LIGHT FALAFEL**), or with the ginger, garlic and cumin seeds (for appe), to make a thick, coarse batter. Add a small amount of the soaking liquid at a time. Reserve the leftover soaking liquid, if any, as a broth for cooking curries, dals and stews, or for making dough.

Add red chili powder (or flakes) and salt to the batter and mix well. Heat an appe pan (aebeliskiver pan) and add 2-3 drops of oil in each well. Add a teaspoonful of batter in each well if it has 12 wells; add more batter if it has large wells. Cover and let them cook on medium heat.

Check after a few minutes to see if the bottom surface of each puff is cooked. Flip them over and cook the other side. Add 1-2 drops of oil on each puff before flipping. Otherwise, they can become very dry.

Once both sides are done, transfer to a plate and repeat the process with rest of the batter. Serve them hot with chutney, ketchup, or any hot and sweet sauce. Please see the section on Chutneys (page 93) for an understanding about the amazing world of these fresh sauces which can lift even the most ordinary dish to an extra-ordinary level.

Variations: You can make dosas (crepes) with this batter. Pack these crepes for lunch for a lower-carb meal along with a vegetable stir-fry. If you want to deep-fry the koftas, make sure the batter is as dry as possible to prevent excess absorption of oil at the time of frying. Combine equal amounts of a variety of dals and add ginger, garlic, and chili paste to make a different version of **MULTI-LEGUME APPE**. Add grated vegetables or some leafy greens to pack in more nutrients. Add these falafels to your salad or wrap with loads of vegetables. and dress with tahini (page 192) or mint chutney (page 93).

WHOLE MUNG DOSAS & KOFTAS
lip-smacking crepe or koftas

My mother often makes these protein-packed koftas or uses the batter to make dosas. I have grown to enjoy mung all the more because of this dish. You can even make dhokla with this recipe (without fruit salt to preserve more nutrients). **Note:** Recipe is kid-friendly.

Per serving: 250 Cal | 12g protein | 7g total fat | 9g fiber

Servings: 2	Soak Time: 4 or 8-10 hours	Cooking Time: 30 mins

Main ingredients
¼ cup whole mung (mung beans)
¼ cup split mung beans (mung dal with skin, chilkawali mung dal)
½ medium onion, finely chopped
2 large cloves garlic
1 green chili
1 cup cilantro, spinach, or any leafy greens, chopped

Spices
2 tsp flaxseeds (alsi) or
1 tsp fenugreek seeds (methi seeds)
A pinch of asafetida, optional

Staples
1 tbsp oil
Salt to taste

Wash the whole mung and mung dal, and soak them along with the flaxseeds or fenugreek seeds in ¾ cup of water for 4 hours or 8-10 hours, per your convenience.

Grind along with garlic and chili to make a smooth batter by adding a small amount of the soaking liquid at a time. Reserve the remainder of the nutrient-rich soaking liquid, if any, as a broth for making curries, dals, stews, rice or dough. Add chopped cilantro, onion, and salt to the batter, and mix well.

Heat some oil in a pan and swirl it around. When the pan is slightly warm, spread the batter to make dosas (crepes) of desired thickness. Cover and cook the first side on medium heat. Flip the dosa when it peels easily and is slightly brown. Cook the other side without the lid for a crispy texture. Drizzle a few drops of oil before flipping. Transfer the dosas to a plate when done and repeat the process for rest of the batter.

Serve the dosas with chutney, ketchup, or dips of your choice. These dosas are so flavorful that you can enjoy them as is. Pack a fiber and protein packed, lower-carb lunch by pairing this dosa with a vegetable stir-fry.

Variations: You can make koftas, appe, or kebabs in the appe pan and add them to your kofta curry.
Steam the batter (without adding any soda bicarb or fruit salt) for about 12 minutes to make dhoklas. Temper the dhoklas with mustard seeds, sesame seeds, asafetida, and curry leaves.
Make **VEGETABLE KOFTAS** by adding ginger, garlic and chili paste, along with some grated vegetables (shredded bottle gourd, carrot, zucchini, etc.)

Tip: This recipe uses mung dal with skin and whole mung, which have more fiber than the plain mung dal. If you are fond of fresh orange juice or any citrus juice, then this is a great dish to pair with your juice, because the high fiber of the dosa may prevent a big spike in blood glucose, the potassium in mung can help lower your blood pressure, while the vitamin C in the juice can improve the iron absorption of mung. Choose ½ cup (125 mL) serving of juice rather than a 1 cup serving. But, remember that a whole fruit is better than a fruit juice.

CHEESE & WHOLE MUNG KEBABS OR DOSAS
unbeatable taste

The advantage of eating whole mung or other whole legumes over dals or split legumes without the skin, is the higher fiber, vitamins, and minerals content. You can enjoy some cheese with this high potassium dish. If you pair 1 cube or slice (15-30 g) with at least ¼ cup raw or ¾ cup cooked whole legumes, then your meal is better balanced. Keep in mind healthful cooking practices as discussed earlier in the book. If you eat a few cubes or slices of cheese (or paneer) in one sitting and do not balance with good amounts of potassium and fiber rich foods, then it can adversely impact your blood pressure and blood lipids. **Note:** Recipe contains dairy. Recipe is kid-friendly.

Per serving: 160 Cal | 8g protein | 8g total fat | 4g fiber

Servings: 4 **Soak Time: 4 or 8-10 hours** **Cooking Time: 30 mins**

Main ingredients
½ cup whole mung (mung beans)
1 green chili
2 large cloves garlic
1½" ginger piece
½ cup cilantro, chopped
¼ cup shredded cheese
or 2 cubes cheese, grated

Spices
2 tsp flaxseeds (alsi) or 1 tsp fenugreek seeds (methi seeds)
1 tbsp fennel seeds

Staples
1½ tbsp oil
Salt to taste

Wash the whole mung and soak it along with the flaxseeds or fenugreek seeds in ¾ cup of water for 4 hours or 8-10 hours, per your convenience.

Grind along with ginger, garlic, chili and fennel seeds, to make a coarse batter by adding only a small amount of the soaking liquid at a time. Reserve the remainder of the nutrient-rich soaking liquid, if any, as a broth for making curries, dals, stews, rice, or dough.

Add salt, chopped cilantro, and cheese to the batter, and mix well. You will need lower than usual amounts of salt, as cheese contains salt.

You can make kebabs using an appe pan or prepare dosas on a pan. For kebabs or appe, follow steps on page 134, and for dosas (crepes) refer to page 137.

These dosas or kebabs taste so good, you can enjoy them as is, or serve with a chutney or ketchup, if you must. Pair with a berry smoothie for a nutritious and elegant Sunday brunch.

Variations: You can make this recipe without cheese.
Try these kebabs with a mix of mung beans, lentils (masur), and black gram (urad).
For sweet crepes, please refer to page 180 (Chocolate Crepes).

Tip: Pack these dosas for lunch with any vitamin C rich vegetable stir-fry. Vitamin C can help increase iron absorption.

DAHI VADA / BLACK GRAM PUFFS IN YOGURT
my favorite black gram puffs immersed in tempered yogurt

Like most Indians, dahi vadas are one of my favorite deep-fried foods. But, I eat fried foods only on a few occasions and go for the best. My mom's dahi vadas are inarguably the best I have ever had. I consider them as the gold standard. Once you have tasted those you will know what I mean. She has served most of our family and friends, who swear by them and lovingly demand for more. It's hard to ever find anything that even comes close to that standard. Prepared without any Eno or Soda, they fluff up so naturally in the pool of oil as you watch over the kadai (wok). My favorite way to enjoy is to contrast the hot vadas with the cold tempered yogurt, without any distracting chutneys. I remember how my mom would put those hot, yummy vadas right off the hot kadai (wok) and into my bowl of cold, tempered yogurt. The hot crisp cover and the soft insides of the vada melt in your mouth with a crunch. The cold yogurt then contrasts and soothes your palate, making the two a perfect pair. Seriously, one should enjoy and celebrate dahi vadas for their true taste rather than douse their identity with chutneys and fried farsaan. Alternatively, for health reasons, we can reserve the deep-frying for special occasions and use the appe pan or abeliskiver pan to make a quick and healthier version of the dish in order to enjoy these more often. **Note:** Recipe contains dairy. Recipe is kid-friendly.

Per serving: 130 Cal | 8g protein | 4g total fat | 4g fiber

Servings: 4 (24 vadas) **Soak Time: 4 or 8-10 hours** **Cooking Time: 30 mins**

Main ingredients
½ cup black gram dal (urad dal)
2 tbsp mung dal (split mung bean)

Spices & Staples
1 tbsp flaxseeds (alsi) or 1 tsp fenugreek seeds (methi seeds)
1 tbsp oil
Salt to taste

Wash the dals and soak them in 1 cup of water along with the flaxseeds or fenugreek seeds for 4 hours or 8-10 hours, per your convenience.

Grind the dals and seeds to make a smooth paste. Add a small amount of the soaking liquid at a time, while you grind. If you are unable to utilize all of the water, use the remainder as a broth for cooking rice, vegetables, beans, or soups. Add salt into the batter and mix well. Beat the batter a bit so that the vadas turn out fluffy without the addition of soda or fruit salt. Add only a small amount if you must.

Make appe style vadas. Heat an appe pan or abeliskiver pan and add 2-3 drops of oil in each well. Add teaspoonful of batter in each well if there are 12 wells; more batter if the pan has large wells. Cover and let them cook on medium heat.

Check after a few minutes to see if the bottom surface of each vada has turned golden brown. Flip them over to the other side and cook the other side until golden brown. Add additional oil before flipping. Transfer to a plate and or a bowl of tempered yogurt (page 142) to serve immediately. Repeat the process for rest of the batter.

Continued.

Tips: For deep-frying the vadas, use a small kadai or wok and fill it only ⅓ of its volume with oil, so that you do not have a lot of oil leftover after frying. It is best not to re-use that oil for cooking as it is oxidized. Pat the deep-fried vadas between layers of paper towel to remove some oil, before adding them to the tempered yogurt.

Add the vadas to the yogurt only at the time of serving. If you add them too early, they will absorb the water from the yogurt and the dish becomes dry. Some people immerse the vadas in water before adding them to the yogurt, but this reduces the flavor and charm of the vadas, which then need to be compensated by adding the chutneys.

Variations: Use the Dahi vada recipe to make **MEDU VADAS**, another South Indian delicacy that is served with sambar and chutneys. Add 1" ginger (finely chopped), a few curry leaves and 1-2 tsp of chopped, fresh coconut chunks. Instead of deep-frying you can make them in an appe pan and serve with sambar (page 61). **Note:** Recipe contains coconut.

DAHI TADKA / TEMPERED YOGURT
aromatic, seasoned yogurt to immerse the dahi vadas

This flavored yogurt is so delicious that you may devour it as is (photo on page 44). Enjoy as a side for extra protein and calcium or immerse the dahi vadas. **Note:** Recipe contains dairy.

Per serving: 100 Cal | 4g protein | 6 total fat | 0g fiber

Servings: 4 **Cooking Time: 5 mins**

Main ingredients
2 cups fresh yogurt (curd)
1 green chili, chopped
A few sprigs of cilantro, chopped
6-7 curry leaves, wash and pat dry

Spices
¼ tsp mustard seeds
2 pinches of asafetida
A few pinches of red chili powder, coriander and cumin powder, or chaat masala for garnishing, optional

Staples
2 tsp oil
2 tsp sugar, optional
Salt to taste

Add salt and sugar to the yogurt and beat it lightly. Sugar quantity can be adjusted per your needs and sourness of the yogurt, or omitted if you are serving with chutneys. Fresh homemade yogurt may not require any sugar. Incidentally, if the yogurt is sour you can add in a teaspoon or two of fresh milk to balance the taste.

Heat the oil in a tempering pot or a small steel pot. Add mustard seeds when the oil is hot and then turn off the heat as the mustard seeds crackle. Then add asafetida, curry leaves, and green chili. After the tempering has cooled down, pour it over the yogurt and mix well.

Refrigerate the tempered yogurt and add the hot dahi vadas just before serving, otherwise they will absorb the water from the yogurt.

For those who love dahi vadas with the various garnishes – go ahead and sprinkle some red chili powder, cumin powder and cilantro, and drizzle tamarind and mint chutneys (page 93).

INSTANT TOASTY IDLIS / INSTANT STEAMED CAKES
gluten-free steamed cakes

Idlis are steamed lens shaped mini-cakes served with chutneys or sambar. They are a South Indian specialty, but today they are popular all over the globe. Most instant idlis use a batter of semolina and curd which is steamed after adding fruit salt (soda bicarb) that makes the idlis light and spongy but it also reduces important vitamins. Here is my instant toasty idli version, that will actually taste like idlis that have been pan-fried after steaming. It contains more protein than regular idlis, and retains important nutrients as it does not involve the use of fruit salt or soda. After you make these, you still need to try my mom's idli recipe to enjoy the real deal – soft delicious idlis (page 145). **Note:** Recipe contains dairy. Recipe is kid-friendly.

Per serving: 350 Cal | 13g protein | 13 total fat | 3g fiber

Servings: 2 (24 mini idlis)   **Cooking Time: 30 mins**

Main ingredients
½ cup black gram flour (urad flour)
½ cup rice semolina, rice grits or idli rava
½ cup yogurt
1" ginger piece, grated

Spices & Staples
½ tsp red chili flakes
1 tbsp oil
Salt to taste

Prepare the batter using all the ingredients, except oil and salt. Add water as needed (~1-1¼ cups), mix and then add the salt. Whisk it lightly to incorporate some air. Set it aside.

Heat an appe pan (aebeliskiver pan) and add 2-3 drops of oil in each well. Whisk the batter again and then add a teaspoonful of batter in each well; more batter if the wells are large. Cover and cook them on medium heat.

Check on them after about 2 minutes to see if the bottom surface of each idli has turned golden brown. Flip them over to the other side and cook the other side until golden brown. Add 1-2 drops of oil on each idli before flipping.

Since this dish or similar dishes made with semolina are low in fiber, serve them with sambar (page 61) or curry leaves and chana dal chutney (page 190), to add more fiber and protein to the meal. You can also enjoy an apple, pear, or peach for some extra fiber.

Variations: You can substitute rice semolina with coarse wheat semolina. Include fresh herbs such as cilantro, mint, or leafy greens to make green Idlis. Make dosas or uttapam using this batter.
Add some shredded vegetables – calabash, carrot, etc. to make **VEGETABLE IDLIS**.
Instead of ginger and chili flakes, you can add 1-2 tbsp of chutney podi (page 191) for making **MASALA APPE** (picture on the left). Serve with peanut chutney (page 93).

PROTEIN-PACKED IDLIS & HIGH FIBER IDLIS
a more nutrient-dense recipe

Typically, idlis (steamed mini-cakes) are made with a greater proportion of rice (3 or 4 parts rice and 1 part urad dal). This is my mom's nutrient-dense recipe for idlis, that calls for more urad dal to make more nutritious idlis. The proportion of rice and dal used in this recipe (2 parts rice and 1 part urad dal) helps reduce carbohydrate load. Our friends and relatives frequently request my mother to make idlis, and she just loves treating them with her specialties for no special occasion. These idlis make for a balanced lunchbox meal when paired with sambar, a vegetable and legume stew (page 61). Also, check out my equally delicious and gorgeous, high fiber idlis. **Note:** Recipe is kid-friendly.

Per serving: 160 Cal | 8g protein | 1g total fat | 4g fiber

Servings: 6 **Soak: 4 hours, Ferment: 8-10 hours** **Cooking Time: 45 mins**

Protein-packed idlis
1 cup parboiled rice or rice semolina (rice grits, idli rava)
½ cup black gram dal (urad dal)
1 tbsp fenugreek seeds (methi seeds)
1 tbsp ghee (clarified, unsalted butter)
Salt to taste

High fiber idlis *
1 cup parboiled rice or rice semolina (rice grits, idli rava)
½ cup black gram dal with skin (chilkawali urad dal)
1-2 tbsp flaxseeds
1 tbsp ghee
Salt to taste

* you can make these idlis with brown rice instead of parboiled rice, but retain the same rice to dal proportion of 2:1, otherwise
it will still be loaded with carbohydrates. Black gram dal with skin has more fiber than brown rice.

Wash and soak the urad dal along with the seeds in 1 cup of water for about 4 hours. Wash and soak rice (or semolina) in 2 cups of water. Soak it alongside the urad dal for the same duration.

Grind them separately, adding the soaking liquid gradually. Make a smooth batter with the soaked urad dal and a slightly coarse batter with the rice or semolina. Utilize the excess soaking liquid for making chutney or sambar.

Now, combine both the batters into a large bowl, leaving enough room for the batter to leaven and to prevent the batter from overflowing during fermentation. Cover with a lid and let it ferment overnight, or for 8-10 hours in a warm place. If the batter does not leaven (rise) after 10 hours, then ferment it for a few more hours.

When you are ready to steam idlis, pull out your idli stand or use round pressure cooker containers to steam idlis in batches. Fill your steamer with the necessary amount of water, close the lid and turn on the heat to high. You can steam in a pressure cooker – fill the pressure cooker with water until the rack is submerged; seal the lid, remove the whistle or pressure regulator, and turn on the heat to high.

Continued.

In the meantime, grease the idli stand or containers lightly with ghee. Add salt to the batter and mix well. Add any flavors now, if you want to.

Fermented batters do not require fruit salt (soda bicarb) for leavening. Pour the batter in the idli slots or the steel container to make no more than ½" thick idlis.

Once the pressure is built up, you will see a steady stream of vapor. Turn off the heat and open the lid when safe. Transfer the idli stand to the steamer or pressure cooker and close the lid.

Steam the idlis for 12-15 minutes on medium heat. Then turn off the heat and release the lid when safe.

Remove the idli stand and scoop out the idlis gently with a knife when slightly cooled. Repeat the process for rest of the batter – grease the idli slots before starting a new batch.

Serve with chutneys (page 93, 190), sambar (page 61) or chutney podi (page 191). Batter can be refrigerated for a few days. Idlis can be stored in the refrigerator for a few days, or longer in the freezer.

IDLI VARIATIONS / STEAMED CAKE VARIATIONS
spice up, temper, or flavor them up

TOASTED IDLIS: Leftover idlis can be pan-fried in a pan with some ghee or oil and served with chutney or sambar. With a crispy exterior and soft interior, they make idlis all the more enticing.

Make interesting **IDLI UPMA** by tempering the leftover, diced idlis with mustard seeds, red or green chili, curry leaves, asafetida, and chopped cilantro. Sauté some onions and vegetables to pack in more nutrients and flavor. Vary the tempering to create new flavor combinations.

Add freshly chopped cilantro or spinach, or grated broccoli, along with grated ginger to make **GREEN IDLIS.** You may also use shredded carrot for orange colored idlis. When cut in different shapes, these colorful idlis can make for an alluring, healthy snack for your children.

Make **MASALA IDLIS/APPE** by adding ginger, chili, and some vegetables into the batter and cooking them in an appe pan.

You can also make dosas (thin crepes) or uttapam (thick crepes with toppings) using the same batter.

PROTEIN-PACKED DOSAS, UTTAPAM / PROTEIN-PACKED CREPES
a more nutrient-dense crepe

Enjoy these thin crepes (dosa) and thick crepes (uttapams), that can be easily made by using the fermented idli batter. Instead of steaming the batter to make idlis, spread the batter on a greased pan and fry on both sides to make dosas. This recipe uses more urad dal and a lower proportion of rice, rather than the usual 3 or 4 parts rice and 1 part urad dal. This makes the dosas more healthful with a higher protein, vitamins and minerals content, besides making them more delicious. Dosas can be served plain or stuffed with the popular boiled potatoes stir-fry. However, you can stuff the dosas with any stir-fry, minced meat, chicken, or turkey. Uttapams are thicker dosas and topped with chopped onion, tomato, cheese, and other toppings. **Note:** Recipe is kid-friendly.

Per uttapam: 180 Cal | 8g protein | 3g total fat | 4g fiber

Servings: 12 dosas, 6 uttapams **Soak: 4 hours, Ferment: 8-10 hours** **Cooking Time: 45 mins**

Protein-packed dosas / uttapams*
1 cup parboiled rice or rice semolina (rice grits, idli rava)
½ cup black gram dal or urad dal
1 tbsp flaxseeds or 1 tsp fenugreek seeds (methi seeds)
1½ tbsp ghee
Salt to taste

* you can make these dosas with brown rice instead of parboiled rice, but retain the same rice to dal proportion of 2:1, otherwise
it will still be loaded with carbohydrates

Uttapam toppings
2 red bell peppers, finely chopped
1 onion, finely chopped
2 green chilies, chopped
A few sprigs of cilantro, chopped
Salt and black pepper to taste

Soak and ferment the dosa batter the same way as the idli batter (page 145). But, grind the rice or rice semolina to a smooth batter rather than a coarse one.

Add salt to the batter and mix well. Add water if you think the batter is very thick.

Grease and heat a non-stick pan. Spread a ladleful of batter before the pan gets hot. You can add the batter to the center of the pan and make concentric circles with your ladle to make thin crepes or use a crepe spreader. Alternatively, add a ladleful to one side of the pan and swirl the pan to spread it. Cover with a lid and let it cook on medium heat.

Flip the dosa after 1-2 minutes when the dosa peels off easily. If it does not peel off easily with your spatula then it still needs some more time to cook. Try again in a short while. Flip and allow it to cook on the other side lightly (without lid) before serving.

If it is a super thin dosa (very runny batter), then the dosas crisp up and cook all the way through and can be served without flipping.

Repeat this process for rest of the batter, greasing the pan a bit each time to prevent sticking.

Continued.

Serve the dosas with chutney (page 93, 190), sambar (page 61), or chutney podi (page 191). Or pair them with vegetable, seafood, poultry or meat curries to take your meal to a whole new level. For example, dosas go well with mixed vegetable curry, shrimp, fish, chicken or meat curries, minced chicken, turkey or meat, or even soybean kheema.

Alternatively, add a side of quick vegetable stir-fry to balance the meal. For example, pachadis beautifully complement dosas. Make a **PACHADI** by tempering vegetables (shredded cabbage or chopped carrot, beetroot, etc.) with mustard seeds, asafetida, curry leaves, and green chili. Season with salt, and garnish with cilantro and fresh coconut (optional).

Variations: Use the high fiber idli recipe to make **HIGH FIBER DOSA** by combining black gram dal (with skin) and flaxseeds with rice (page 145).
Make **COLORFUL MINI-DOSAS** for children by using puréed or chopped spinach, shredded carrots, or beetroot to help them eat more vegetables as well as legumes.
Try **MASALA DOSA ROLLS** with potato peas stir-fry (subzi), paneer bhurji, or any other subzi that complements well with dosas, and pack for lunch. And, do not forget to add a fruit and some yogurt to the lunchbox.

UTTAPAM / INDIAN PIZZA
thick crepe with toppings

Note: Recipe is kid-friendly.

Prepare the topping of the uttapam by combining the ingredients listed under uttapam toppings (page 149).

For making Uttapam (thick crepes), do not add any water to the batter or make sure the batter is thick. Spread 2 ladles of batter on the greased pan to make one uttapam.

Add the topping, cover and let it cook on medium heat. When it is ready to flip, sprinkle a few drops of oil on the topping and then flip. Let it cook on low heat without the lid. Transfer to a plate when done. Serve with chutneys or sambar.

Variations: Add cheese or crumbled paneer to the toppings to make a **CHEESE UTTAPAM** or **PANEER UTTAPAM** (about ½ cube of cheese or ¼ cup of crumbled paneer per uttapam).
You can make **TOMATO UTTAMPAM** by using tomato instead of bell pepper.

MASALA DOSA FILLING
lip-smacking potato peas filling for dosas

Dosas can be served plain or stuffed with a mild or spicy boiled potatoes stir-fry (Classic Masala Dosa). You can also use mixed vegetable stir-fries, minced meat, chicken, etc. for more interesting fillings. The standard masala dosa can be flavored with different chutney podis (page 191) to create regional specialties, or served with some grated cheese for an irresistible cheese masala dosa. Check out this masala dosa filling that I have modified by adding peas to boost the flavors and nutrients.

Per serving: 160 Cal | 8g protein | 1g total fat | 4g fiber

Servings: 6   **Cooking time: 30 mins**

Main ingredients
½ lb (250 gms) medium potatoes
1 medium onion, sliced
1 cup frozen green peas, rinsed
1-2 tomatoes, diced
5-6 curry leaves

Spices
¼ tsp mustard seeds
2-3 pinches of asafetida
⅛ tsp turmeric powder
½- ¾ tsp red chili powder

Staples
2 tbsp oil
Salt to taste

Wash the potatoes and pressure cook them in a container without adding any water. If you are making sambar to go with the masala dosa, then stack the potatoes container over the toor dal. Pressure cook the two items at the same time, up to the first whistle or after the pressure regulator starts to rock steadily. Then, turn off the heat and wait until the pressure is released and it is safe to open. If the potatoes are very large, then cut them in half and then pressure cook. Do not add any water to the potatoes as the nutrients will leach into the water.

Remove the potatoes and allow them to cool down. Peel and then cut them along with onion and tomatoes. Rinse the peas.

Heat the oil in a pan and add the mustard seeds when it is hot. Turn off the heat when the seeds crackle. Let the oil cool a bit and then add the asafetida, curry leaves, vegetables, and spice powders. Sauté the vegetables on medium heat until the tomatoes soften a bit.

Prepare the dosas (page 149) and serve the potato peas stir-fry on the side or as a stuffing inside the dosa, along with sambar (page 61).

Variations: Mix the chutney podi (page 191) in some ghee and spread it over the dosa before adding the filling, to make **MYSORE MASALA DOSA.** Grate some cheese to make a **CHEESE MASALA DOSA**. More ideas on page 151.

FLAVORED DOSA & PANEER UTTAPAM
gluten-based crepes

This recipe contains gluten as it uses wheat semolina instead of rice. Make the flavored dosa without the topping and enjoy it with a chutney or sambar. Add a topping of your choice and turn it into an uttapam. Here is a special paneer topping for you to try. **Note**: Recipe contains gluten and dairy. Recipe is kid-friendly.

2 flavored dosas: 160 Cal | 8g protein | 3g total fat | 4g fiber
1 paneer uttapam: 260 Cal | 16g protein | 10g total fat | 4g fiber

Servings: 6 (12 dosas/6 uttapams)   **Soak: 4 hours, Ferment: 8-10 hours**   **Cooking Time: 45 mins**

Flavored dosa
½ cup black gram dal or urad dal (with or without skin)
1 cup wheat semolina
1" ginger + 1 chili, ground to paste
1 tsp fenugreek seeds
2 tbsp oil or 1 tbsp ghee
Salt to taste

Paneer topping for uttapam
1 onion, finely chopped
1½ cup crumbled paneer (¼ cup per serving)
1-2 green chilies, chopped
¾ cup cilantro, chopped
Salt and black pepper to taste

Soak and ferment the black gram dal and wheat semolina per the idli recipe (page 145).

Add salt and ginger-chili paste to the fermented batter and mix well. Skip the ginger-chili paste for making plain dosa or uttapam. For dosas, you can add water if the batter appears thick.

Grease and heat a non-stick pan. Spread a ladleful of batter before the pan gets hot. You can add the batter to the center of the pan and make concentric circles with your ladle to make thin crepes or use a crepe spreader. Alternatively, add ladle to one side of the pan and swirl the pan to spread it all over the pan. Cover with a lid and let it cook on medium heat.

Flip the dosa after 1-2 minutes when the dosa is easy to flip. If it does not peel off easily with your spatula, then allow it to cook for some more time. Then flip and cook it lightly on the other side uncovered for a crisp dosa. Repeat this process for rest of the batter, greasing the pan a bit each time to prevent sticking. Serve with sambar or chutney.

Variations: If you prefer very crisp **PAPER DOSA**, then make the dosas super-thin so that they crisp up and cook all the way. As such, they can be served without flipping.

UTTAPAM: Prepare the topping by mixing all the topping ingredients. Do not add any water to the batter or make sure the batter is thick. Spread 2 ladles of batter on the greased pan to make one uttapam. Add the toppings, cover with a lid and let it cook on medium heat. When it is ready to flip, sprinkle a few drops of oil on the topping and then flip it. Cook the other side on low heat without the lid. When done, serve with chutney or sambar.

TOMATO OMELET
eggless, vegetarian omelet

This is an eggless, gluten-free omelet that can be enjoyed as a crepe or pancake in place of an egg omelet. Try a tomato omelet toast or sandwich for some interesting ways to serve it, especially for children. The spice powders and onion add to the deliciousness of this omelet. However, you may omit the onion if you need to.
Note: Recipe is kid-friendly.

Per serving: 150 Cal | 7g protein | 5g total fat | 4g fiber

Servings: 4 (4 omelets)   **Cooking time: 30 mins**

Main ingredients
1 cup gram flour (besan) or kala chana besan (black chickpea flour)
½ onion, thinly sliced
1 tomato, thinly sliced
A few sprigs of cilantro, chopped

Spices
⅛ tsp turmeric powder
½ tsp red chili powder
½ tsp coriander powder

Staples
1 tbsp ghee or butter
Salt to taste

Make a paste of besan with water, by adding the water slowly to avoid lumps. Then add all the ingredients (except ghee) and adjust the water, to make a flowing, yet thick consistency batter. Taste to see if the salt is optimum.

Heat a pan and melt a few drops of ghee. Pour 1½-2 ladles of batter on the pan when it is warm, but not hot, and swirl the pan to make an omelet. Cover with a lid and let it cook on medium heat.

After 1 or 2 minutes, lift the omelet with a spatula to see if the bottom side has turned light brown. Then add a few drops of ghee on the top side, and flip the omelet. Let it cook without the lid, so that it becomes a little crisp.

Once the other side also turns light brown, transfer it to a plate. Repeat the steps for rest of the batter.

Enjoy this omelet plain, or serve with chutney or ketchup. Pair with a smoothie or an apple to add fiber and more nutrients and make it a balanced breakfast.

Variations: Make **TOMATO OMELET SANDWICH** by toasting slices of whole grain bread, applying some chutney and adding this tomato omelet after folding it. Add some shredded cheese for a kid's lunch box. Add chopped spinach, or grated squash or any other vegetables to make **SPINACH OMELET, SQUASH OMELET, ETC.**
Instead of spices, add dried herbs such as oregano, basil, etc. to make interesting new flavors for kid's lunches.

NUTRIENT-DENSE THALIPEETH / MULTIGRAIN PANCAKES
well-balanced, gluten-free savory pancakes

Thalipeeth are traditional Maharashtrian pancakes made with mixed grain and legume flours. Here is a nutrient-dense, well-balanced recipe to bump up the protein and fiber content. Serve with crushed peanut or garlic chutney, raw onion and some yogurt for a rustic meal experience. If you have access to a grinding mill, then you can roast and grind whole legumes and grains for a more authentic taste and higher nutrient content. Roasting is important, especially if you are using whole grains and legumes, in order to reduce the anti-nutrients. Nutrient profile could not be calculated for this recipe as some values were unavailable.

Servings: 6-8 pancakes **Cooking time: 30 mins**

Main ingredients
¼ cup amaranth (rajgira) flour
¼ cup sorghum (jowar) flour
¼ cup bajra (pearl millet) flour
¼ cup gram flour (besan)
¼ cup mungo bean flour (urad flour, black gram flour)
½ onion, finely chopped or grated
1 cup cabbage or spinach, finely chopped or grated

Spices
½ tsp red chili powder
½ tsp coriander powder
½ tsp cumin powder
2 tbsp sesame seeds or 1 tbsp flaxseed powder

Staples
1½ tbsp oil or ghee
Salt to taste

Mix all the ingredients (except oil) and make a thick batter that does not fall easily as you drop a ladleful.

Heat some oil in a pan, and when it is warm add 2 ladles of batter and press with ladle to make medium size pancakes. Fit in as many as you can on your pan; alternatively make them on an electric griddle or cook on two pans. Cover and let them cook on medium heat (2-3 minutes).

Drizzle a few drops of oil over the pancakes before flipping them over. If they are not easy to flip, wait for a minute and then try again. Cook the other side without the lid, until they are done. Transfer to a dish and repeat the steps for rest of the batter.

Enjoy with garlic chutney, yogurt, and sliced onion for a rustic meal experience.

Variations: Add any leafy greens or grated vegetables of your choice. For sweet pancakes, please refer to page 182 (Vanilla Pancakes with Mango).

Tip: Since jowar and bajra flours have lower fiber content than whole wheat flour, amaranth flour helps boost the nutrients in this gluten-free recipe.

OATS DOSA / OATS CREPE
healthier oats dosa recipe

Here is another nutrient-packed crepe that you can try and yes, it is gluten-free if you use gluten-free oats. Rolled oats and steel cut pats are preferred over instant oats. They add fiber to urad dal, making this crepe a great breakfast, especially for those with diabetes or high blood cholesterol. My mother-in-law shared this recipe with me, and now, here it is for you to try. Check out my instant version as well. **Note:** Recipe contains coconut or dairy.

Per serving: 170 Cal | 7g protein | 5g total fat | 5g fiber

Servings: 6 (6 dosas) **Soak: 2 hours** **Cooking Time: 45 mins**

Oats Dosa
1 cup rolled oats
⅓ cup urad dal
½ cup mung sprouts, optional
2 tbsp rice flakes (pohe)
2 tbsp dry coconut powder
1½" ginger piece
1 green chili
½ cup cilantro, chopped
1 tsp fenugreek seeds
1½ tbsp ghee or oil
Salt to taste

Instant Oats Dosa
1 cup rolled oats
½ cup urad flour
½ cup yogurt, optional
1½" ginger piece
1 green chili
½ cup cilantro, chopped
1 tbsp roasted flaxseeds
1½ tbsp ghee
Salt to taste

Wash the urad dal and pohe, and soak them along with oats and fenugreek seeds in 2½ cups water for 2 hours.

Then add rest of the ingredients (except oil or ghee) and grind to make a smooth batter. Adjust water slowly. Use the batter to make dosas right away or refrigerate it to make them the following day.

Heat the oil in a pan and grease it lightly with some oil. When it is warm add 2-3 ladles of batter and gently spread it with the ladle to make a dosa. Cover and let it cook on medium heat (1-2 minutes).

Drizzle a few drops of oil before flipping. If the dosa does not loosen easily, then wait for a minute. Slide the spatula underneath to loosen from all sides and then try to flip it. Cook the other side without the lid. Transfer to a dish when done. Repeat steps for rest of the batter.

Enjoy the dosas with chutneys (page 93, 190) or serve with chutney podi (page 191) doused in some melted ghee.

Variations: For the **INSTANT OATS DOSA**, grind oats along with flaxseeds, ginger, chili and cilantro, and make a coarse paste using a small amount of water. Then add urad flour, yogurt, and water slowly and make a thick, flowing batter. Add salt and beat the batter to incorporate some air. Then make dosas and serve right away with any chutney, ketchup, or hot sauce. These dosas are so flavorful, I prefer to enjoy them plain with my favorite smoothie.

For sweet crepes, please refer to page 180 (Chocolate Crepes).

INSTANT METHI CHILLA / FENUGREEK CREPE
another delicious crepe

This is another vegetarian crepe, flavored with the slightly bitter fenugreek leaves that go very well with carom seeds, especially in the winter as the carom seeds tend to generate heat in the body. Winter is the best time to enjoy the harvest of fresh fenugreek when it is easily available. I like to have fenugreek handy all year round. So I buy a few extra bunches in the season, pick the leaves, wash and pat-dry them, and then store them in the freezer. They last well for a few months. **Note**: Recipe contains gluten. Recipe is kid-friendly.

Per serving: 140 Cal | 6g protein | 4g total fat | 4g fiber

Servings: 4 (4 crepes) **Cooking time: 30 mins**

Main ingredients
½ cup gram flour (besan)
½ cup whole wheat flour
1 cup fenugreek leaves, wash and pat dry

Spices
½ tsp red chili flakes
1 tsp coriander seeds
⅛ tsp turmeric powder
⅛ tsp carom seeds (ajwain), optional

Staples
1 tbsp ghee
Salt to taste

Make a paste of gram flour and wheat flour with a small amount of water, and then increase the water slowly to make a thick batter. Whisk the batter if there are any lumps.

Coarsely pound the red chili flakes and coriander seeds in a mortar, and add them to the batter together with the rest of the ingredients (except ghee). Adjust water, if needed, to make a thick yet flowing consistency batter. Taste to see if the salt is optimum.

Heat a pan and melt a few drops of ghee. Pour 1½-2 ladles of batter on the pan and spread it evenly. Cover with a lid and let it cook on medium heat.

After 1 or 2 minutes, lift the crepe with a spatula to see if the bottom side is cooked. Then add a few drops of ghee on the top side, and flip the crepe. Let it cook without the lid, so that it becomes a little crisp.

Once the other side also turns light brown, transfer to a plate. Repeat the process for rest of the batter.

Enjoy with garlic chutney or ketchup, or serve with a sweet and sour pickle. Pair with a smoothie for breakfast, or pack this crepe for lunch with some yogurt and a fruit salad.

Variations: Use any other leafy greens and spices to create new flavor combinations.
Substitute the carom seeds with fennel seeds to enjoy this crepe in the warm months.
For sweet crepes, please refer to page 180 (Chocolate Crepes).

Tip: The proportion of flours is balanced to reduce carbohydrate load.

INSTANT RAGI DOSA / INSTANT FINGER MILLET CREPE
instant crepe with some calcium

This dosa can be made with soaked, ground and fermented urad dal batter, or you can make an instant version to serve as a healthy breakfast. Fermented urad dal dosa is nutritionally more favorable than the instant version as it increases vitamin content and makes the protein and carbohydrates easier to digest. Ragi (finger millet) is a good source of calcium, especially for those who do not consume dairy (milk, yogurt, paneer, cheese, etc.). Nutrient profile could not be calculated for this recipe as some values were unavailable.
Note: Recipe contains dairy. Recipe is kid-friendly.

Servings: 6 (6 dosas)　　　　　　　　　　　　　　　　　**Cooking time: 15 mins**

Main ingredients
½ cup ragi flour (finger millet flour)
½ cup urad flour (black gram flour)
¼ cup gram flour
½ cup yogurt
2 scallions (spring onion), chopped
1 cup shredded zucchini or any other vegetable

Spices
½ tsp red chili powder
½ tsp cumin powder

Staples
1 tbsp ghee or oil
Salt to taste

Combine all the ingredients (except ghee) in a bowl and make a flowing batter by adding water slowly. Whisk well to avoid lumps.

Heat a pan and grease it lightly with some ghee. When it is warm spread 2-3 ladles of batter to make a crepe or dosa. Cover and let the dosa cook on medium heat (1-2 minutes).

You will see that the edges peel away from the pan when it is time to turn the dosa over. Drizzle a few drops of ghee on the dosa before turning. If the dosa does not peel off easily, wait for a minute before trying again. Cook the other side without the lid until it is done. Transfer the dosa to a plate and repeat the steps for rest of the batter.

Enjoy the dosas with chutney and yogurt for breakfast, or with sambar or beans curry and a side salad or vegetable stir-fry (subzi) for lunch.

Variations: Substitute zucchini with any other shredded vegetables or leafy greens.
For sweet crepes, please refer to page 180 (Chocolate Crepes).

Tip: The proportion of flours is balanced to reduce carbohydrate load. This recipe can be used to replace roti or any flatbread to increase your protein intake.

SQUASH & OATS CREPES / PANCAKES
nutrient-packed crepes or pancakes for your lunch box

Try these pancakes or crepes for your lunchbox. They are gluten-free if you use gluten-free oats. Oats add fiber to the gram flour, and yogurt makes it more nutritious with calcium, good quality protein, vitamin A, and B-complex vitamins, especially B-12, which vegetarians may be consuming in lower amounts. Vegetables added to the batter make these crepes or pancakes delicious and nutritious. And, of course, curry leaves, cumin and garlic make for a great mix of flavors. **Note:** Recipe contains dairy.

Per serving: 200 Cal | 7g protein | 9g total fat | 4g fiber

Servings: 4 (4 large crepes or 24 pancakes) **Cooking time: 30 mins**

Main ingredients
1 cup rolled oats, ground to coarse powder
½ cup gram flour (besan or kala chana besan)
¾ cup yogurt
1 cup grated squash, bottle gourd, or any other vegetable
20 curry leaves, roughly chopped
2-3 green chilies, finely chopped
4 large cloves of garlic, grated, optional

Spices & Staples
1 tbsp flaxseed powder
1-2 tsp cumin seeds
1 tbsp oil or ghee
Salt to taste

Mix all the ingredients (except oil) in a bowl and make a thick batter. In order to avoid lumps, whisk the batter well and increase the water gradually to obtain the desired consistency. The batter will thicken as the oats absorb the water and swell. You may need to add more water and adjust salt, as you prepare the crepes or pancakes.

Heat some oil in a pan and swirl the pan to grease it evenly. When it is warm add 2-3 ladles of batter and gently spread with the base of the ladle to make a crepe. To make pancakes, spread 1 tablespoon of batter and flatten it to make a pancake. Fit as many pancakes as possible. Then cover the pan and let the crepes or pancakes cook on medium heat.

Flip the crepe or pancakes over when the first side is uniformly browned. Pancakes are easy to flip, however, it takes a long time to make a big batch using a single pan. Try using two pans or an electric griddle. Large crepes can be cooked quickly but may be a little tricky to flip. Choose a method that works for you.

Drizzle a few drops of oil before flipping. Cook the other side without the lid, until it is evenly browned. Press the pancakes or crepes gently. Transfer them to a dish and repeat the steps for rest of the batter.

Enjoy them plain, or serve with chutneys or ketchup for breakfast. Pair these crepes with a light vegetable soup, for example, carrot soup or gazpacho (from my website, quicklydelicious.com).

Variations: Use any seasonal vegetables such as red amaranth, colocassia leaves, etc.
For sweet pancakes, please refer to page 182 (Vanilla Pancakes with Mango).

totally TOFU

This section focuses on tofu, a product of soybean that makes for a hassle-free addition to your meals. It is a good source of protein, especially for vegetarians. Just 1 cup of diced tofu can provide nearly half of your daily protein requirement. It also contains good amounts of iron, calcium, magnesium, omega-3 fatty acids, and phytochemicals.

However, tofu does not contain much fiber, so add those high fiber vegetables to your meal or pair with whole grain cereals, millets, nuts, and seeds. Raw, pan-fried, and sautéed tofu is better than deep-fried tofu.

Tofu is a convenient and versatile ingredient to work with. It can take on the flavors of any marinade, curry powders or stock, and so can be easily adapted to any cuisine. If you do not like the taste of raw tofu, here is a trick – substitute tofu in your egg or paneer specialties, and you might actually like it because it absorbs the flavors of the curry or sauce. You can also pan-fry it and then serve in your curries and soups.

Other ways to incorporate tofu in your diet would be to substitute part of your meat, poultry, or seafood with tofu, or add it to meals that do not contain protein rich foods.

If tofu is not easily available, then consider using soy nuggets or soy granules. They can also help increase your protein intake. For health benefits and recipes for these soy products, please refer to pages 8-9 and 111-122 respectively.

So, shall we check out some tofu recipes? Be sure to subscribe to my website (quicklydelicious.com) for more tofu recipes like Schezwan Tofu Bites, Tofu Manchurian, Thai Tofu Salad, Tofu in Chili Garlic Sauce, etc that will posted soon.

TOFU IN THAI GREEN CURRY
tofu immersed in Thai flavors

If you enjoy Thai food, like I do, then you are sure to like this green curry. It is inspired by Thai flavors and adapted to the ingredients that are easily available. **Note:** Recipe contains coconut.

Per serving: 170 Cal | 8g protein | 13g total fat | 3g fiber

Servings: 4 **Cooking Time: 30 mins**

Main ingredients
1 cup firm tofu, diced
½ onion, diced
4 cups of vegetables of your choice
(1 cup broccoli florets + 1 cup green beans, sliced to 1" pieces + 1 large carrot, cut into round slices + 1 cup Cremini mushrooms, sliced)
¼ cup coconut milk
A handful of basil leaves, coarsely chopped
4 tsp fresh lime juice or 2 tsp lemon juice

Spices
¼ tsp cumin powder
¼ tsp coriander powder
¼ tsp red chili flakes, optional

Staples
1 tbsp oil
1 tsp honey or sugar
Salt and ground pepper to taste

Green curry paste
(use half, and freeze the remainder)
1 cup cilantro leaves and stems
1½" ginger piece
2 large cloves of garlic
1-2 green chilies, optional

Wash the cilantro and chilies, and peel the ginger and garlic. Grind them to a coarse curry paste adding only a small amount of water (less than ¼ cup). Cilantro stems are packed with flavor. So be sure to include them in the curry paste.

Heat the oil in a steel stock pot and add the sliced onion. Sauté the onion on high heat for a minute. Then add all the vegetables, dry powders, green curry paste, and salt. Mix well and sauté on medium heat for 2 minutes.

Add 2 cups of water and cover the pot. Cook the vegetables lightly on medium heat (~5 minutes). Turn off the heat when the carrots are cooked. Allow the curry to cool down before you add coconut milk, otherwise it may curdle.

Add coconut milk and additional water if necessary (½-1 cup of water) and adjust the salt. Bring it to a boil and let it simmer for a minute on medium heat. Mix in the tofu, chopped basil, lime juice and honey to create a beautiful balance of flavors. Garnish with chopped basil and serve with brown rice.

Variations: You can vary the vegetables and also add fish, shrimp, chicken pieces, or boiled egg to this curry. Boiled egg can be added towards the end, along with the tofu. However, seafood and chicken should be added along with the vegetables, and ensure they are cooked properly.
If kaffir lime leaves and galangal are easily available, then you can add them for an extra zing.

TOFU IN THAI YELLOW CURRY
Thai-inspired yellow curry

This delicious creamy, yellow curry is also inspired by Thai flavors but adapted to ingredients that are easily available. For a more authentic taste add the core Thai ingredients such as galangal and lemon grass. This is a great dish for vegetarians as it does not contain any fish sauce. For the non-vegetarian version, add chicken pieces, shrimp, fish, or boiled egg along with tofu. **Note:** Recipe contains coconut.

Per serving: 170 Cal | 7g protein | 13g total fat | 3g fiber

Servings: 4   **Cooking Time: 20 mins**

Main ingredients
1 cup of diced tofu
½ medium onion, finely chopped
1 cups broccoli florets and stalks
1 cup red bell pepper, diced
1 large carrot, peeled and diced
1 cup sprouts or sliced mushrooms
1-1½" ginger, mashed
A few sprigs of cilantro, chopped
¼ cup coconut milk
1-2 tsp lemon juice

Spices
¼ tsp turmeric powder
½ tsp red chili powder
½ tsp coriander powder
¼ cup roasted peanuts (whole or crushed), optional

Staples
1 tbsp oil
1 tsp sugar
Salt to taste

Heat the oil in a pot and add the onion and cilantro. Sauté for a minute on medium heat and then add vegetables, salt and spice powders. Mix well, cover and cook until the carrots soften a bit.

Then add the tofu cubes, ginger, coconut milk, and some water and let the curry simmer on medium heat for a few minutes so that the flavors get infused in the coconut curry. Stir occasionally to avoid splitting of the coconut milk.

Finish with lemon juice and sugar. Adjust salt and garnish with roasted peanuts before serving with cooked brown rice.

Variations: Vary the vegetables – you can use green beans, snap peas, carrots, red, yellow or orange bell peppers, bok choy, mushrooms, etc.
You can also add some pineapple or lychee pieces.
Use galangal and lemon grass whenever available.
You may add chicken, fish or shrimp as well – add them along with the vegetables, but make sure that they are cooked properly. You may also add boiled eggs at the end.

PALAK TOFU / TOFU PAKORAS IN SILKY SPINACH GRAVY
tofu fritters in finger-licking spinach gravy

Many people enjoy palak paneer in restaurants or make it often at home. This spinach gravy is easy, nutritious and super tasty even without the addition of cream, which is usually added for the creamy consistency. Cook this unique recipe on special occasions or for special guests by adding tofu pakoras to the silky spinach gravy. Pakoras can be a little time consuming and more calorie-dense, so add raw tofu or lightly pan-fried tofu pieces instead of the pakoras to make a quick, lower calorie version.

Per serving Palak Curry: 70 Cal | 3g protein | 5g total fat | 2g fiber
Tofu Pakora: 100 Cal | 6g protein | 6g total fat | 1g fiber

Servings: 6 **Soak time: 8-10 hours** **Cooking Time: 30-40 mins**

Palak gravy:
1 whole bunch spinach or 5 cups frozen spinach
½ onion, diced
2 medium tomatoes, diced
1" ginger piece, diced
1 large garlic clove, diced

Spices
⅛ tsp turmeric powder
¾ tsp red chili powder
¼ tsp garam masala
2 tsp kasuri methi

Staples
2 tbsp oil
Salt to taste

Tofu pakora (2 per servings):
12 slices of firm tofu, ½" thick, 2" wide
½ cup gram flour (besan)
⅛ tsp turmeric powder
¼ tsp red chili powder
2 pinches of carom seeds (ajwain), optional
1½ tbsp oil for pan frying
Salt to taste

For the palak gravy, heat the oil in a steel pan and add the diced onion. Allow it to turn golden brown on medium heat. In the meantime, wash and chop the spinach and tomatoes. Dice the ginger and garlic.

Once the onion turns golden brown, add the tomatoes, ginger, garlic, spices and salt, and sauté on high heat until the tomatoes soften. Add the spinach and mix well. Cover the pan and let the spinach cook on low heat for about 1-2 minutes. Turn off the heat and uncover the pan to let it cool.

In the meantime, cut the tofu slices and prepare the gram flour batter. In order to avoid a lumpy batter, add water slowly and whisk it well into a smooth paste. Then add the remaining spices and salt.

Heat the oil for the pakoras in a large pan. Dip each slice of tofu in the batter, coat it well and then fry on the pan on medium heat. Flip the pakoras when first side is done. When both sides are golden brown, transfer them to a plate.

Use a blender to turn the cooled spinach mixture into a homogeneous, smooth purée; add water to make a thick gravy. Bring it to a boil in the same steel pan that you used for cooking the spinach. Adjust the salt and serve with hot pakoras, whole grain phulkas or rotis and a side salad of vitamin C rich vegetables.

Variations: Use this spinach gravy recipe to make **PALAK PANEER WITH GREEN PEAS, PALAK CHOLE, MIXED VEGETABLES IN SPINACH GRAVY,** etc.
Mix in other leafy vegetables (fenugreek leaves, mustard leaves, etc.) for variety.
Add tofu pakoras to your salad for some good quality protein.

TOFU BRUSCHETTA
a creative appetizer for your next party

Hummus, guacamole, and salsas are commonly served at parties, right? Do you want to surprise your guests with something novel? Transform my red bell pepper salsa into a delicious tofu bruschetta for your next party and buckle up for the compliments from your guests.

Per serving (excludes crackers): 45 Cal | 3g protein | 3g total fat | 1g fiber

Servings: 4   **Cooking Time: 15 mins**

Main ingredients
1 large red bell pepper, deseeded, diced to ½" pieces
1 large garlic clove, chopped
½ cup medium firm tofu, crumbled
A few basil leaves, chopped
A few pinches of mixed dried herbs

Staples
1 tsp olive oil
2 tsp vinegar
Salt and pepper to taste

Wash and deseed the red bell pepper. I usually cut the crown and pull out the whole bulb of seeds and tap to remove any loose seeds. Then dice it to ½" pieces. Chop the garlic.

Heat the oil in a pan and add the chopped garlic. Let it sizzle on medium heat and, before it turns brown, add the diced bell pepper. Sauté on high heat until the pieces soften a bit. Don't let the bell pepper get burnt or overcooked. Turn off the heat and let it cool down.

Then sprinkle salt, freshly ground black pepper, dried herbs and vinegar, and mix well. Mix in the crumbled tofu and chopped basil, adjust salt and serve over whole grain crackers.

Variation: You can use it as a filling for sandwiches and wraps as well.

TOFU BHURJEE / TOFU SCRAMBLE
a delicious scramble for wraps, sandwiches, buns, etc.

This is a spiced scramble recipe that you can use for tofu, paneer, or egg. I like to add vegetables to my scrambles to make them more wholesome. You can add any vegetables (mushrooms, spinach or kale, frozen green peas, carrots, tomato, etc.) of your choice. Alternatively, keep the scramble simple and serve the vegetables on the side as a salad or soup.

Per serving: 160 Cal | 11g protein | 11g total fat | 2g fiber

Servings: 4   **Cooking Time: 15 mins**

Main ingredients
2 cups crumbled tofu
1 medium onion, finely chopped
1 cup broccoli florets
1 green bell pepper, diced
1 cup shredded cabbage
1 cup sliced mushrooms
½ green chili, sliced (optional)
A few sprigs of cilantro, chopped

Spices
¼ tsp cumin seeds, optional
⅛ tsp turmeric powder
½ tsp red chili powder
¾ tsp garam masala or Kitchen King masala
½ tsp coriander powder

Staples
1½ tbsp oil
Salt to taste

Heat the oil in a pan and add the cumin seeds. Once they sizzle add the chopped onion, green chili and chopped cilantro leaves, and sauté for a minute. The cilantro leaves when added with the onion impart a beautiful flavor to the dish.

Allow the onion to caramelize and then add the vegetables, spice powders, and salt. Mix well and let the vegetables cook on medium heat; cover if needed. Add the crumbled tofu, mix and serve as a filling for a whole grain wrap, sandwich or bun.

Enjoy with a vegetable soup – carrot soup from my website (quicklydelicious.com).

Variations: If you run out of vegetables, don't fret! You can still use this recipe to make a bhurjee with just onion and tomatoes, which are staples in any Indian pantry.

MINIMALIST SCRAMBLE: This scramble uses the same recipe but you can easily skip the tempering and the spices, except for the Kitchen King Masala. Use any vegetables on hand or simply sauté cabbage and mushrooms and season with salt and Kitchen King Masala. A delicious scramble is ready within minutes.

TOFU FRIED RICE: Transform this recipe into a fried rice by adding 1½ cups of cooked brown rice. Pair with my carrot soup (on my website)

KOREAN-STYLE HOT TOFU SOUP
a simple Korean soup

My husband and I love this soup and we order it every time we go to a Korean restaurant. Here, I have tried to recreate the soup from our favorite Korean restaurant. And, the best part is that it is ready in no time. This soup is quite comforting and nourishing, especially when you are busy and want to eat well in spite of your deadlines. Try it with some smoked red chili powder or add some kimchi for a more authentic kick. Either way, it will still taste great with a small side of rice (plain or as fried rice). **Note:** Recipe contains egg.

Per serving: 260 Cal | 17g protein | 17g total fat | 2g fiber

Servings: 2 **Cooking Time: 30 mins**

Main ingredients
1 cup diced tofu (soft or firm)
2 eggs, boiled
½ medium onion, diced
2 spring onions (scallion), sliced
1 medium green bell pepper (capsicum), diced
2 tomatoes, puréed
2-3 large garlic cloves, minced

Spices
½ tsp hot red chili powder (smoked if available) or red chili flakes

Staples
Salt to taste
1 tbsp oil
1 tsp sugar to balance the tanginess of tomatoes

Boil some water in a small steel pot; ensure that it is enough to submerge the eggs. Add the eggs gently with the help of a ladle into the boiling water and cook them for 10 minutes on high heat. Cover the pot partially.

Once the eggs are cooked, drain off the water and transfer the eggs to a bowl with cold water to prevent a green ring forming around the egg yolks. When cooled, crack open the shells and slice into halves.

While the eggs are cooking, purée the tomatoes and set aside. Heat the oil in a pot and add the garlic. When it turns golden, throw in the sliced onion, scallions and capsicum, and sauté on medium heat until the onion turns light brown.

Then add the tomato purée and red chili powder and mix well. Cook the purée for a minute on medium heat, and then add some water for desired consistency. Immerse the egg halves and tofu into the soup and let it boil for 2 minutes.

Serve hot with a garnish of chili flakes. Enjoy it with kimchi fried rice and steamed broccoli, or brown rice and stir-fried bok choy (see recipes on my website: quicklydelicious.com).

Variation: For an egg-free version, replace the eggs with 1 cup tofu.

QUINOA TOFU PULAO
a delicious wholesome meal

Quinoa and tofu make a great combination, not just in terms of palatability, but also as a good source of complete protein and other nutrients for vegetarians or for anyone who wants to cut back on meat or non-vegetarian options. Quinoa, considered a pseudo-cereal, is a grain crop grown originally in the South American region. It can be used in place of low fiber wheat products such as semolina, vermicelli, rice, and pasta. Try this simple recipe or make more interesting pulaos using your biryani recipes for quinoa and tofu combination.

Per serving: 420 Cal | 24g protein | 17g total fat | 7g fiber

Servings: 3 **Cooking Time: 30 mins**

Main ingredients
1 cup quinoa, washed and rinsed
1 cup diced tofu
½ medium onion, finely chopped
2 cups kale, chopped
1 cup Brussels sprouts, chopped
1 red and 1 yellow bell pepper, chopped
1 large clove of garlic, chopped
3 tbsp feta cheese, optional
1-2 tsp lemon juice, optional
A few sprigs of cilantro leaves, chopped

Spices
½ tsp red chili powder
½ tsp cumin powder

Staples
Salt and black pepper to taste
1 tbsp oil

Wash and rinse quinoa 2-3 times otherwise it can have a bitter after-taste. In a pot, add the quinoa and 2½ cups of water and bring it to a boil. Simmer for 15-20 minutes on low heat until the quinoa is cooked. Cover the pot if needed.

In the meantime, heat the oil in a pan and sauté the garlic and sliced onion until golden brown.

Then add rest of the vegetables and spice powders. Sauté for a minute and then cover to steam the vegetables on medium heat for about 2 minutes. Mix in the tofu and set aside.

Once the quinoa is cooked, add it to the vegetables and tofu. Season with salt and black pepper and finish with feta cheese, and cilantro. Taste before adding the lemon juice.

Variations: Try other vegetables such as green beans, carrots, green peas, mushrooms, zucchini, squash, spinach, broccoli, cabbage, etc.
Add garam masala to make the flavor more intense.
Follow any pulao or biryani recipe for quinoa and tofu combination, or simply use pulao or biryani masalas in this recipe.

for the SWEET MOMENTS

I confess that I have a sweet tooth (like many of us). I personally know very few people who are not particularly fond of sweet foods. Most of us somehow find a way to get our hands in the cookie jar, or grab a quick dessert, or even a sweet snack. If we stock sweet treats at home, we can easily pop them in our mouths for no special reason. Here are some relatively healthier recipes, but they do contain some sugar. Use a sweetener prescribed by your physician to substitute sugar in these recipes.

As you may know, the Indian calendar is marked by many festivals and special occasions to celebrate life. We love to express our good wishes by sharing sweet treats. Most sweets are loaded with sugar, fat, and calories and may be low in fiber and/or protein. When you prepare sweets at home, try to balance the dish with some fiber, protein, and other nutrients to make it more balanced or nutrient-dense. By making some legume-based sweets, you can add fiber and protein to your desserts, besides other vitamins and minerals, thereby making them healthier. However, they are still packed with calories because of the sugar and/or fat content, so exercising portion control is highly desirable. Making sweets at home with lower amounts of sugar and fat is also worthwhile. Check out my recipes to make relatively healthier sweet dishes.

Continue to celebrate life and good health, and do send your best wishes to your family and friends with a platter of fruits, dry fruits, and nuts along with your healthier homemade treats.

PURAN PEDA / A SWEET TREAT
puran to peda

Peda is a flattened, sweet ball of deliciousness that is considered a symbol of joy in the Indian culture. A box of pedas is shared with close friends and family to announce good news, whether it is the birth of a child in the family or success in an examination. Typically, the pedas are made by simmering whole milk for a long time until it becomes a dry and crumbly mixture (khoa). Sugar, various flavors, or nuts are then added to make different types of pedas. Here is a dairy-free peda made using puran, a sweetened mixture of yellow split peas. Puran is used to stuff puran polis, a flatbread (page 175). Try this dairy-free peda or continue to the next recipe to turn this into a puran poli.

Per peda: 60 Cal | 2g protein | 1g total fat | 1g fiber

Servings: 10 (10 pedas) **Soak: 1 hour** **Cooking Time: 30 mins**

Ingredients
½ cup chana dal (yellow split peas, split chickpeas)
~ ⅓ cup jaggery, crushed
A few mixed nuts- almond, cashew, walnut, pistachio (whole and crushed)
A few strands of saffron
¼ tsp cardamom powder (ground green cardamom seeds)
2-3 pinches of salt

Soak ½ cup chana dal for 1 hour in ¾ cup of water.

Then, pressure cook the dal along with the soaking liquid for 5 minutes on low heat after the first whistle, or after the pressure regulator starts to rock. Turn off the heat and let it cool down.

Transfer the cooked chana to a pan, add crushed jaggery and salt, and heat it until it becomes semi-dry. Turn off the heat before it becomes crumbly like a powder because it will thicken as it cools down.

Add the saffron and cardamom powder, and mix well. Once cooled, add crushed nuts and portion out to make 8-10 balls and flatten them. Serve with a garnish of nuts. You can use this puran to make sweets of any shape. (Picture is on page 173)

Tip: Salt enhances the sweetness of sugar and so we can add lower amounts of sugar.

PURAN POLI / SWEETENED FLATBREAD
a flatbread stuffed with sweetened split peas

Puran poli is a sweet flatbread popular in the western and southern regions of India. Of all the traditional Maharashtrian sweets, these sweetness-filled flatbreads are my favorite, not because they are nutritionally balanced, but because they turned out so well in my very first attempt! It felt like a eureka moment! This is how it began – I was craving some homemade puran polis. So I called my mom and my mother-in-law to get their recipes, combined their ideas and started making my first ever puran poli. There are many ways to makes these flat breads – some methods can be quite complex. Here is the simplest way to make them successfully.
Note: Recipe contains gluten.

Per puran poli: 220 Cal | 6g protein | 8g total fat | 5g fiber

Servings: 5 (5 puran polis) **Cooking Time: 1-1.5 hours***

Puran
½ cup chana dal (yellow split peas, split chickpeas)
⅓ cup jaggery, crushed
3 pinches of salt
¼ tsp cardamom powder
A few strands of saffron

Polis
1 cup whole wheat flour
3 pinches of salt for dough
1 tsp oil
1 tbsp ghee

Prepare the puran (filling) in advance to make things easier. Prepare the puran (page 174), but do not add any nuts to the puran. Set it aside.

Add salt to the flour and knead a soft dough with about ½ cup of water. Then apply some oil to coat the dough and knead again. Cover the dough and let it rest for at least 20 minutes.

Portion out the dough and the puran to make 5 balls (portions) each. Roll out the dough ball to 4" diameter. Place the puran ball at the center and flatten it. Fold the remaining dough to enclose it. Seal it well and then roll out again to make a flatbread of about 8" diameter. Roll out gently with uniform pressure. Don't worry if a portion of the puran surfaces; it will taste just fine and look rustic and appealing. Another method to roll out the puran polis is to divide the dough into 10 balls. Roll out each ball to the size of flatbread you want, spread one portion of puran on one flatbread and place another flatbread over it. Seal it by pressing on the edges. Pick a method that works for you (photos on page 176).

Heat a pan and transfer the flatbread only when it is hot. Then turn down the heat to medium and let it cook. Drizzle some ghee over the flatbread and on the sides. Flip it over when the bottom side is cooked (golden brown). Cook the other side as well and apply some more ghee if needed. Repeat the process for the rest of the dough.

Variation: For colorful versions, add some puréed spinach, grated carrot or beetroot to the dough. Spinach is mild in flavor and since the amount used is very small, it will not be perceptible.

*30 minutes if the puran is prepared in advance.

STRAWBERRY / BLUEBERRY / SPINACH SMOOTHIE
a great start for any morning

What better way is there to start your day than with a nutrient-dense smoothie? This smoothie is packed with antioxidants from the berries. The fat from soy milk will facilitate the absorption of the antioxidants and also provide satiety, so you will feel full for quite some time. Soy milk also contributes valuable protein, calcium and iron while banana and peaches provide the natural sweetness and fiber. This sounds super nutritious, and trust me it is super delicious as well. It is now time to grab a smoothie.

For one serving: 250 Cal | 10g protein | 4g total fat | 6g fiber

Serving: 1 **Cooking Time: 5 mins**

Ingredients
1 banana or 2 peaches, diced
1 cup strawberries, blueberries, blackberries or mixed berries, or 2 cups spinach
1 cup soy milk
A handful of mint leaves, optional

Wash and prepare the fruits. Place all the ingredients in your blender and process to make a homogenous smoothie. Pour it into a glass and enjoy slowly, or share it with your partner to complement your savory breakfast. Pair this smoothie with some nuts – almonds, walnuts, cashews – to keep you full for a few hours. I sometimes add mint leaves to my smoothie and it tastes great, especially with the strawberry smoothie. Pair with legume-based breakfast options for some extra protein and fiber.

Variations: You can substitute soy milk with dairy milk or almond milk. However, almond milk is low in protein and calories, so be sure to have plenty of nuts or pair with a legume-based crepe or puffs (recipes on page 134-161) to ensure good amounts of protein in the most important meal of the day.

KESARIYA MUNG DAL KHEER / SAFFRON-INFUSED MUNG PORRIDGE
a healthy porridge for your next special occasion

Kheer is a very popular Indian dessert served as ambrosia or prepared for festive occasions in many regional cultures. This comforting porridge is usually made with rice, vermicelli, nuts, carrots, calabash, etc. Have you tried any dal kheers? If not, then give this silky, smooth dessert a try for your next special occasion. This dish is especially nourishing for children, adolescents, pregnant, and lactating women. Keep in mind that the serving size here is smaller than usual. **Note**: Recipe contains dairy.

Per serving: 100 Cal | 5g protein | 2g total fat | 0g fiber

Servings: 4 **Cooking Time: 10-15 mins**

Ingredients
1 cup cooked mung dal, thick and plain (fresh or leftover, no spices or seasoning)
1 cup whole milk
2 tbsp sugar, more if you prefer sweeter, or a sweetener recommended by your doctor
A few pinches of cardamom powder
A few strands of saffron
A few almonds for garnish

Save a portion of your cooked dal from the previous day or cook some fresh dal. Make sure it is cooked plain, without any turmeric, asafetida, or other seasonings. Mash the dal well and combine it with milk, saffron, and cardamom in a pot and bring it to a boil. Add sugar per your taste preference.

Cook the kheer on medium heat while stirring constantly. Turn off the heat as the kheer begins to thicken. It will thicken further as it cools. If you prefer a runnier consistency, add more milk and adjust the sweetness. Garnish with chopped, whole or grated nuts and enjoy it warm.

MOCHA TOFU SOUFFLÉ
for those who love tofu

This is a high protein and nutrient-packed dessert made with tofu; however, it does retain the distinct taste of tofu. I feel the flavor of tofu grows on you, or at least it did for me after the first few bites. This soufflé is unique because it is steamed and ready in no time. Of course, you will need to refrigerate it before you serve. **Note:** Recipe contains dairy.

Per serving: 170 Cal | 12g protein | 8g total fat | 0g fiber

Servings: 2   **Freezing Time: 1 hour**   **Cooking Time: 30 mins**

Ingredients
1 cup diced tofu (medium firm)
½ cup milk
3-4 tsp sugar
1 tsp unsweetened cocoa powder
½ tsp instant coffee
½ tsp vanilla essence

Combine all ingredients and blend to make a smooth purée. Pour the purée into ramekins and pressure cook until the first whistle or until the pressure regulator starts to rock steadily. Turn off the heat and let the cooker cool down.

Once the pressure is released, carefully remove the ramekins and let them cool down a bit before refrigerating them for at least one hour. Serve cold with grated chocolate or enjoy as is.

CHOCOLATE CREPES
eggless crepes with strawberry sauce & banana

Crepes are so quick and easy to make that I like to make them often. Fresh fruits or homemade fresh fruit sauces go very well with these crepes. Make these for your Sunday breakfast or serve them for brunch. **Note:** Recipe contains dairy.

Per crepe: 160 Cal | 7g protein | 7g total fat | 3g fiber
For filling: 150 Cal | 2g protein | 1g total fat | 5g fiber

Servings: 2 (total 2 crepes)　　　　　　　　　　　　　　　　　　　　　**Cooking Time: 15 mins**

Crepe
½ cup gram flour (besan or kala chana besan)
½ cup milk
A pinch of salt
1 tsp honey
½ tbsp unsweetened cocoa powder
1 tbsp butter

Filling
2 bananas
2 cups strawberries, puréed
1 tsp honey or maple syrup

Add milk to the flour very slowly and whisk until you have a smooth batter. Add rest of the crepe ingredients, except butter, and mix well.

Heat some butter in a pan. Use a pan with a 7"-8" base width to make medium thick crepes. Use a larger pan for thinner crepes, but they can be difficult to flip.

When the butter melts, swirl it around to coat the pan. Add 2-3 ladles of batter and swirl around. Cover and let the crepe cook for 1-2 minutes on medium heat. The crepe will turn dry and loosen up as it cooks. Then gently flip it over with your spatula.

Cook on the other side until done and then serve. Repeat the process for rest of the batter. If you are making a large batch and are comfortable with multi-tasking, then heat up two pans or use an electric griddle. Serve the crepes with diced bananas and fresh strawberry purée or sauce.

STRAWBERRY PURÉE: Blitz the strawberries to a smooth purée and pour over the crepes. You can add 1 tsp of honey or maple syrup if the strawberries are too tart for your preference. My husband and some of my friends love it without any sweetener.

STRAWBERRY SAUCE recipe is on my website (quicklydelicious.com). In a snapshot, dice some strawberries and boil them in a small amount of water with some sugar. Sugar quantity will vary with the tartness of your strawberries.

Continued.

Variations: Choose any sweet fruit purée to serve as a sauce, for example, mango purée, peach purée, etc.

You can make plain pancakes (small size fluffy crepes) with this recipe by omitting the cocoa powder. Top them with your favorite fruits, nuts and some chocolate sauce, or chocolate almond butter.

Substitute banana with **CARAMELIZED PEARS.** Cut pears into slices and pan-fry in some butter on low heat. Cover and let the pears soften a bit. Sprinkle some sugar and water, if needed. Caramelize until brown and crisp and then transfer to your crepes. Enjoy with chocolate almond butter.

Substitute chocolate with other beautiful flavors – cardamom and saffron (in any season), nutmeg and ginger powder (in the winter), etc.

Make **SAVORY CREPES** by making crepes without the cocoa powder and serving them with a savory filling such as pan-fried vegetables, mushrooms, and some grilled chicken. Spread some pesto sauce, add crumbled feta cheese or garnish with shredded cheese.

VANILLA PANCAKES WITH MANGO
mangolicious pancakes

Baking soda, soda bicarb, or fruit salt (which is nothing but soda bicarb) is invariably used in pancakes as a leavening agent (raising agent). However, it reduces valuable B-complex vitamins in the food. By using egg, we can skip this ingredient and make pancakes that are packed with protein, vitamin A, and B-complex vitamins. This recipe uses only one egg for two servings. **Note**: Recipe contains dairy and egg.

Per serving (3 small pancakes): 220 Cal | 12g protein | 9g total fat | 4g fiber
Per topping: 180 Cal | 4g protein | 7g total fat | 3g fiber

Servings: 2 (total 6 small pancakes)   **Cooking Time: 15 mins**

Pancake
- ½ cup urad flour
- 1 egg
- ½ cup milk
- ½ tsp vanilla essence
- 1 tsp honey or maple syrup
- 2 pinches of salt
- 1 tbsp butter

For topping
- 1 mango, diced
- 2 tbsp or nuts of your choice
- 4 tsp honey or maple syrup (2 tsp per serving)

Beat the egg well until it is light and fluffy, or separate the egg white and yolk and beat them separately before combining.

Gradually add flour and mix well. Add milk and rest of the ingredients, except butter, and whisk until smooth.

Heat a small amount of butter in a pan or electric griddle. Beat the batter lightly each time you spread a ladleful of batter to make pancakes. They cook rather quickly, so keep an eye. Cook them on medium heat and flip immediately when one side is done. The other side will also cook quickly.

Transfer the pancakes to a plate and serve with diced fruits, nuts, and some honey or maple syrup. Go easy on the syrup or honey as it is just another form of sugar.

Variation: Transform this recipe into crepes by adding some more milk (about ½ cup milk).

BADAM MUNG DAL KULFI / ALMOND MUNG DAL ICE CREAM
a healthier, lower calorie kulfi

Kulfi is a denser and creamier version of ice cream, popular in parts of South Asia and the Middle East. Kulfis can be made at home with condensed milk or cream, however, they are very high in calories and saturated fat. Half a can of condensed milk contains 80g sugar, which is about half a cup of sugar. Mung dal or masur dal can pack in the goodness of legumes in this dessert. Are you ready to experiment with a wholesome kulfi? **Note:** Recipe contains dairy.

Per serving: 160 Cal | 6g protein | 6g total fat | 1g fiber

Servings: 2 **Freezing Time: 2 hours** **Cooking Time: 15 mins**

Ingredients
½ cup cooked mung dal or masur dal (thick and plain, fresh or leftover, no spices or seasonings)
½ cup whole milk
10-12 almonds or cashews
2 tbsp sugar
A few strands of saffron
2 pinches ground cardamom
A few almonds for garnish
Honey to serve with the lightly sweetened version

Grind the almonds or cashews to a paste using a small amount of water. Try to make it as smooth as possible. If you want to use almonds without the skin, then you can blanch them before making a paste. (**BLANCHING ALMONDS** – boil the almonds in water for a minute, strain them and then peel the skin.)

Save a portion of your cooked dal from previous day or cook some fresh dal. Make sure it is cooked plain, without any seasonings or flavors (turmeric, asafetida, salt, etc.)

Combine the cooked dal, nut paste, milk, saffron, and cardamom in a pot and bring it to a boil. Add sugar and dissolve it well. Let it simmer for a few minutes.

When it thickens, taste to see if the sweetness needs to be adjusted (be careful as the liquid will be hot). Note that foods taste less sweet when frozen, so you may need to add a little extra sugar before freezing. Alternatively, garnish with honey or maple syrup when you serve the kulfi. Pour the mixture into kulfi or popsicle molds and freeze for at least 2 hours.

Remove the kulfi from the freezer and place them in warm water for ~1 minute to help release them from the molds. Run a knife around or pat gently to remove the kulfi on to a serving plate. Garnish with honey or maple syrup, if necessary.

Variations: Make **PISTA KULFI** by using pistachio (24 kernels).
For rose kulfi use rose syrup and omit the sugar.

hot off
THE PAN

A lot of people are fond of multigrain rotis that are made by mixing cereal, millet, and legume flours or grinding the whole grains. Homemade combinations are better than store-bought ones as you have better control on the combinations and can vary them as and when you like. Make sure your multigrain flours contain substantial quantities of legume flours rather than just a few tablespoons in order to pack in more health benefits.

Sorghum (jowar) and pearl millet (bajra) have lower protein and fiber content than whole wheat flour, but higher than white rice. Whole wheat is an important source of fiber, B-complex vitamins, iron, and selenium. Finger millet (ragi) flour has good calcium content, but it is also more calorie-dense and lower in fiber than wheat. Complementing lower fiber millets such as jowar, bajra and ragi with whole legumes or high fiber vegetables can help balance the meal. Consuming millets to add variety is a good idea but make sure you pair them appropriately. They also make for a better alternative to white rice or white bread. Experiment with oats flour, amarantha (rajgira) flour, buckwheat flour, etc. to see if you like the taste.

When choosing a commercially produced bread, roti, pasta, or tortilla, read the product information to see if it has at least 3g fiber per 100 calories, if it is made of whole grains, and the ingredient list is short with minimal additives.

A gluten-free diet is prescribed for those with Celiac disease. There is no need to label gluten, wheat, or any other whole foods as fattening. No foods can really be fattening unless they are consumed frequently, in disproportionately large amounts without being paired with enough protein and fiber from legumes, fruits, and vegetables. Evaluate the meal as a whole. One must consider diet and other lifestyle factors, rather than eliminating any whole foods, unless prescribed to do so.

LOW GLYCEMIC, NUTRIENT-DENSE ROTIS OR TORTILLAS
flatbreads good for diabetes, hypertensives, PCOS

Make way for these super nutritious rotis. Soybean flour adds protein, potassium, folate, and all the goodness of soybeans to these rotis. They have lower carbohydrate content, making them great for diabetics. Additional potassium may help hypertensives gain better control over their blood pressure. Flaxseed powder adds omega-3 fatty acids and lignans that can help regulate hormonal imbalances. This is important for women with PCOS and menstrual problems. **Note**: Recipe contains gluten.

Per roti: 100 Cal | 4g protein | 4g total fat | 3g fiber

Servings: 8 rotis **Resting time: 15 mins** **Cooking Time: 30 mins**

Ingredients
1 cup whole wheat flour
½ cup soybean flour, full fat
2 tbsp flaxseed powder, as needed
1 tbsp ghee, butter or oil

Combine all the ingredients with only half the amount of ghee and knead to a soft dough. Add water as needed (little less than ¾ cup). Cover the dough and set it aside for at least 15 minutes.

Then make 8 equal size balls and roll out the rotis. If the dough seems fragile, then knead it further or sprinkle with some more wheat flour.

Heat a pan and roast the rotis on medium to high heat until golden brown on both sides. Apply ghee while roasting or afterwards. Note that these rotis will not puff up like phulkas. Serve with a vegetable stir-fry (subzi) and dal.

Variations: Substitute flaxseeds with sesame seeds to incorporate lignans.
You may use soaking liquid of dals or whole beans, or a small amount of milk to make the dough.

MISSI ROTI / PROTEIN-PACKED ROTIS OR TORTILLAS
flavored flatbread with more protein and potassium

Here is another great way to enjoy a roti that has slightly more protein and potassium. You can use regular besan or kala chana besan (besan from roasted black chickpeas). Flaxseeds add lignans and omega-3 fatty acids, making this roti a great food for those with PCOS. **Note**: Recipe contains gluten.

Per missi roti: 100 Cal | 4g protein | 3g total fat | 3g fiber

Servings: 8 (8 rotis) | **Resting time: 15 mins** | **Cooking Time: 30 mins**

Main ingredients
1 cup whole wheat flour
½ cup gram flour (besan) or kala chana besan (black chickpea flour)

Spices
2 tbsp flaxseed powder or
2 tbsp sesame seeds
2 tbsp kasuri methi
½ tsp red chili powder
¼ tsp turmeric powder
½ tsp carom seeds (ajwain) or nigella seeds (kalonji)
½ tsp coriander powder

Staples
Salt to taste
1 tbsp ghee, butter or oil

The process remains the same for all rotis – combine, rest, roll out, and roast. Combine all the ingredients with only half the amount of ghee and knead to a soft dough. Add water as needed (little less than ¾ cup). Cover the dough and leave it aside for at least 15 minutes.

Make 8 equal size balls and roll out the rotis. If the dough seems fragile, knead it further and sprinkle with some more wheat flour.

Heat a pan and roast the rotis on medium to high heat on both sides until golden brown. Apply ghee while roasting, or afterwards. Note that these rotis will not puff up like phulkas. Serve with a vegetable stir-fry (subzi) or curry for lunch, or with a small amount of Indian pickle and yogurt for breakfast.

Variations: Grate any seasonal vegetables and add them to the dough. You may use soaking liquid of dals or whole beans, or a small amount of milk to make the dough.

DAL PUDINA THEPLA / MINTY DAL FLATBREAD
basic yet delicious

Dal theplas are a great way to utlilize leftover dals. Complement these delicious flatbreads with your favorite curries for lunch, or just enjoy with pickle and yogurt for a quick breakfast. Knead, roll out, pan-fry, and consume. Add chopped spinach or any leafy greens to the dough, roast, and pack for lunch, with some yogurt and fruit. **Note**: Recipe contains gluten.

Per dal paratha: 100 Cal | 3g protein | 4g total fat | 3g fiber

Servings: 6 (6 parathas)	Resting time: 15 mins	Cooking Time: 30 mins

Main ingredients
½ cup cooked dal (thick)
1 cup whole wheat flour
¼ onion, grated
¼ cup cilantro + mint, finely chopped

Spices
½ tsp red chili or
1 green chili, finely chopped
⅛ tsp turmeric powder
1 tbsp sesame seeds or
1 tbsp flaxseed powder

Staples
1 tbsp ghee
Salt to taste

For making dal parathas, you can either use freshly cooked dal or leftover dal; either plain or lightly tempered. Make sure it is not runny, otherwise thicken the dal by boiling it to the desired consistency. Allow the dal to cool down before you start preparing the dough. If the dal contains turmeric, then you need not add more turmeric, as excess turmeric can impart a bitter taste or a very bright color to the parathas.

Combine all the ingredients with only half the amount of ghee and knead to a soft dough. Add water (~¼ cup) as needed. Cover the dough and leave it aside for at least 15 minutes.

Make 6 equal size balls and roll out the parathas. If the dough seems fragile, then add some flour and knead further so that it is easy to roll out.

Heat a pan and roast the parathas on medium to high heat until golden brown on both sides. Apply ghee while roasting. Serve with a vegetable stir-fry (subzi) or curry. You can even enjoy it with a vegetable raita or with plain yogurt (curd), small amount of Indian pickle, and a side salad. (Picture on page 185)

Variations: Add some puréed spinach, or chopped fenugreek or other leafy greens. You can also add grated carrots, radish, beet, cabbage, calabash (doodhi), or any vegetables of your choice. Add ½ tsp of garam masala for more flavor. Pack the theplas for lunch with some tempered yogurt and fruit.
Alternatively, you can use dry, spiced dal as a stuffing in your paratha to make stuffed parathas. Roll out the parathas by following the puran poli procedure (page 175-176).

call them
CHUTNEYS or DIPS

Cooked or roasted legumes can be ground to create delicious dips or chutneys. Flavor them with herbs and/or spices, with or without vegetables to make a smooth pasty spread like hummus, or a chutney to dip. Make a chutney podi to sprinkle over salads, wraps, or serve with idlis and dosas.

CURRY LEAVES & CHANA DAL CHUTNEY
curry leaves-flavored Indian hummus

This is a low calorie yet nutrient-dense protein dip. It goes very well with idlis, dosas, or uttapam. My mom makes this often and I especially love it with uttapam.

Per serving: 40 Cal | 2g protein | 2g total fat | 0g fiber

Servings: 4-6 servings **Total time: 10 mins**

Main ingredients
½ cup roasted chana dal (yellow split peas)
1 garlic clove
1 green chili or ¼ tsp red chili powder
6-8 curry leaves
¼ cup lightly packed cilantro leaves

Tempering
⅛ tsp mustard seeds
A pinch of asafetida
2 tsp oil
Salt to taste

Use a blender to grind roasted chana dal, garlic, green chili or red chili powder, curry leaves, and cilantro leaves with ½ cup of water to make a smooth paste. Add additional water (~¼ cup) and grind again, if you prefer slightly runny.

Heat the oil in a small steel pot or tadka pot. When it is hot enough, but not smoking, add mustard seeds and turn off the heat. After the seeds crackle, add a pinch of asafetida.

Allow the tempering to cool down and then pour it over the smooth chana dal chutney and mix well. Serve the chutney with idlis, dosas, uttapam, or appe.

CHANA DAL & PEANUT CHUTNEY
a nutty chutney

Per serving: 60 Cal | 2g protein | 4g total fat | 0g fiber

Servings: 4-6 servings **Total time: 10 mins**

Ingredients
¼ cup roasted chana dal (roasted yellow split peas)
¼ cup peanuts (skin removed)
1 large clove of garlic
½ inch ginger piece
1 green chili

Tempering
4-6 curry leaves
A pinch of asafetida
⅛ tsp mustard seeds
2 tsp oil
Salt to taste

Use a blender to grind all the ingredients, excluding those listed under tempering, along with ½ cup of water to make a smooth chutney. Add additional water (~¼ cup) and grind again, if you prefer slightly runny.

Heat the oil in a small steel pot or tadka pot. When it is hot enough, but not smoking, add mustard seeds and turn off the heat. After the seeds crackle, add asafetida and curry leaves, and pour it over the chutney. Serve this chutney with idlis, dosas, appe, or uttapam!

Variation: You can temper this chutney with cumin seeds, asafetida, curry leaves and red chilies.

INSTANT CHUTNEY PODI / INSTANT DRY CHUTNEY
a roasted dal powder

This is my take on the traditional South Indian chutney podi, customized to a smaller batch. Traditionally dried red chilies, tamarind, and different spices are used to create regional variations and mixes for idlis, dosas, etc.
Note: Recipe contains coconut and peanut.

Per serving: 160 Cal | 8g protein | 5g total fat | 9g fiber

Servings: 6   **Cooking Time: 15 mins**

Ingredients
½ cup chana dal (yellow split peas)
¼ cup urad dal (black gram dal)
¼ cup dried coconut
¼ cup roasted peanut powder
1 tbsp roasted flaxseed powder
¼ cup curry leaves, washed and pat-dried
1 tsp red chili powder
1 tsp amchur powder (dry mango powder)
2 tsp sugar or jaggery
2 tsp oil
Salt to taste

Dry roast the chana dal in a pan on low heat until light brown. Transfer it to a plate. Roast the urad dal and coconut separately in the same pan until light brown and transfer it to the plate.

Heat the oil and pan-fry the curry leaves until toasty. Transfer them to the plate.

If you don't have roasted peanut and flaxseed powder, then lightly roast some peanuts and flaxseeds on the same pan. Transfer to a separate plate and peel the skin of the peanuts when cooled.

Once all the roasted ingredients are cooled, grind them along with rest of the ingredients to a coarse powder. If you think the chutney podi is not spicy enough, then add some more red chili powder and grind again to mix well. Store in an air-tight jar and keep in the refrigerator for longer shelf-life.

Serve as a flavoring for idli or dosa by mixing this chutney with melted ghee. Sprinkle over yogurt to serve as a dip. Add some podi to the Instant Toasty Idli recipe (Page 143) for a very tasty variation.

Variations: Temper mustard or cumin seeds in oil and add it to the roasted ingredients.
Substitute amchur powder with tamarind, and red chili powder with dry red chilies. The red chilies need to be roasted in oil.

HUMMUS
a dip for every party

Hummus is a Mediterranean dip made with cooked chickpeas and sesame seeds; served either plain or flavored with herbs and roasted veggies. It pairs very well with whole wheat pita bread. It will surely bring the crowd to the table for the few seconds it will remain there.

Per serving (2 tbsp): 50 Cal | 2g protein | 2g total fat | 2g fiber

Servings: ~ 1 cup (15 tbsp) **Total time: 10 mins**

Ingredients
1 cup cooked chickpeas
2 tbsp tahini or sesame paste (untoasted)
1 garlic clove
2 tsp lemon juice
½ tsp red chili powder or paprika
1 tbsp olive oil
Salt to taste

To make **TAHINI**, grind sesame seeds with a small amount of water and make a thick paste. Store in a jar and pour some oil to form a top layer for preservation. It will keep in the refrigerator for a few weeks. Use it in hummus, as a salad dressing, or add it to thicken a gravy or chutney.

Grind the chickpeas with tahini and garlic into a smooth paste. Add other flavors now if you want to make flavored hummus – mint leaves, cilantro, jalapeño, roasted bell pepper, etc. and blend again. Transfer to a bowl. Add lemon juice and salt, and taste to make sure the flavor is balanced. Pour olive oil and sprinkle red chili powder. Serve right away with veggies, pita bread, pita chips or store in the refrigerator for a healthy snack dip. It will keep in the refrigerator for 2-3 days.

HUMMUS VARIATIONS
dips to complement your party theme

Add ½ cup cilantro or ¼ cup mint leaves for **CILANTRO HUMMUS** or **MINT HUMMUS**; or make it spicy cilantro with a zing of green chilies.

For a lightly sweetened flavor, make **ROASTED BELL PEPPER HUMMUS**. Deseed a medium size red pepper, rub it with 1 tsp olive oil and roast on a pan. When lightly browned on all sides, allow it to cool before blitzing with rest of the ingredients. Use well-drained cooked chickpeas, or dry them out a bit in the microwave as red bell pepper holds moisture and can make your hummus runny. Use only half of the bell pepper and add more only if needed.

Use hummus as a spread in your wraps (such as chicken, shrimp or veggie wrap) or sandwiches in place of mayonnaise. Serve as a dip along with whole grain toast, pita bread or pita chips, or vegetables for a lower calorie option.

REFERENCES

Krausse's food and nutrition therapy, 12th edition. L. Kathleen Mahan and Sylvia Escott-Stump. Published by Saunders Elsevier in 2008.

Essentials of human nutrition, 3rd edition. Edited by Jim Mann and A. Stewart Truswell. Published by Oxford University Press in 2007.

Nutritive value of Indian foods. C Gopalan, B. V. Rama Sastri and S. C. Balasubdramanian. Revised and updated by B. S. Narasinga Rao, Y. G. Deosthale and K. C. Pant. Published by National Institute of Nutrition in 1999.

Soy foods, isoflavones, and the health of postmenopausal women. Mark J. Messina. American Journal of Clinical Nutrition 2014;100(suppl):423S–30S.

Dietary lignans: physiology and potential for cardiovascular disease risk reduction. Julia Peterson, Johanna Dwyer, Herman Adlercreutz, Augustin Scalbert, Paul Jacques, Marjorie L McCullough. Nutrition Reviews 2010; 68(10): 571–603. doi:10.1111/j.1753-4887.2010.00319.x.

Legumes and soybeans: overview of their nutritional profiles and health effects. Mark J. Messina. American Journal of Clinical Nutrition 1999;70(suppl):439S–50S.

The effect of flaxseed supplementation on hormonal levels associated with Polycystic Ovarian Syndrome: a case study. Debra A. Nowak, Denise C. Snyder, Ann J. Brown, Wendy Demark-Wahnefried. Current Topics in Nutraceutical Research 2007; 5(4):177-181.

Legumes. Jane Higdon. Updated by Victoria J. Drake. Reviewed by James W. Anderson. Linus Pauling Institute Website. http://lpi.oregonstate.edu/mic/food-beverages/legumes. Accessed Dec 10, 2016.

ChooseMyPlate.gov Website. U.S. Department of Agriculture. www.choosemyplate.gov. Accessed Dec 10, 2016.

International Year of Pulses Website. Global Pulse Confederation. http://iyp2016.org. Accessed Dec 10, 2016.

2016 International Year of Pulses Website. Food and Agriculture Organization of the United Nations. http://www.fao.org/pulses-2016/faq/en. Accessed Dec 10, 2016.

USDA National Nutrient Database for Standard Reference, Release 28. Version Current: September 2015, slightly revised May 2016. US Department of Agriculture, Agricultural Research Service, Nutrient Data Laboratory. http://www.ars.usda.gov/nea/bhnrc/ndl, https://ndb.nal.usda.gov/ndb/foods. Accessed Dec 10, 2016.

GLOSSARY

aam	mango	black pepper	kali mirch, mira
adrak	ginger	black-eyed peas	cowpeas, chawli
ajwain, ova	carom seeds	bottle gourd, doodhi, lauki	calabash
akrod	walnut		
all-purpose flour	maida, refined wheat flour	brinjal, baingan	eggplant
almonds	badam	butter	makhan
aloo	potato	buttermilk (Indian buttermilk)	Indian chaas, flavored or plain thin lassi
alsi	flaxseeds		
amaranth	rajgira	calabash	bottle gourd, doodhi, lauki
amchur	dry mango powder	capsicum	green bell pepper (sweet pepper)
amti	Maharashtrian curry		
ananas	pineapple	caraway seeds	shah jeera
anar dana	dried pomegranate seeds	cardamom(green)	elaichi (hari)
anjir	fig	carom seeds	ajwain, ova
appe	similar to aebliskiver/ aebliskives -danish pancake puffs, spheres of cooked batter.	carrot	gajar
		cashew	kaju
		cereals	does not refer to the commerical breakfast cereals, but the cereal grains that include wheat, rice, oats, rye, etc.
appe pan	paniyaram pan, aebliskiver pan		
apple	seb	ceviche	Latin American appetizer, typically seafood, that is marinated/cooked in a citrus juice
arhar dal	pigeon pea, toor dal		
asafetida	hing		
atta	flour		
badam	almonds	chaas/ chaach	Indian buttermilk
baingan	brinjal, eggplant	chakra phool	star anise
bajra	pearl millet	chana	chickpea
bath	cooked rice	chana dal	split chickpeas
bay leaf	tej patta	chaunk	tempering, vaghar,
bell pepper (red, yellow, orange, green)	capsicum (red, yellow, orange, green), sweet peppers	chawli	cowpeas, black-eyed peas
		chickpeas	Bengal gram, kabuli chana, garbanzo beans
Bengal gram, kabuli chana, garbanzo beans	chickpeas	chickpeas	garbanzo beans, kabuli chana, Bengal gram
besan	gram flour		
bhatura	fried bread (large, usually made of maida or all-purpose flour)	chilla	crepe made with soaked and ground dal batter
black chickpeas	kala chana	chilkawali dal	dal with skin
black gram dal, split mungo beans	urad dal	chivada	roasted Indian snack
		chopping	finely diced
black gram, mungo bean	urad	chutneys	dips, sauces
		chutney podi	powdered chutneys

GLOSSARY

cilantro	coriander leaves, hara dhania, kothimbir	dry mango powder	amchur
cinnamon	dalchini	eggplant	brinjal, baingan
cloves	laung, lavang	elaichi (hari)	cardamom (green)
coconut	nariyal	enchilada	Mexican tortilla rolled with filling and doused with a chili pepper sauce
coconut milk	nariyal ka dudh, narlache dudh	fajitas	Mexican stir-fry
cookies	sweet biscuits	falafel	Middle Eastern fried chickpea balls
coriander leaves, hara dhania, kothimbir	cilantro	fansi, french beans, farasbi	green beans
coriander powder	dhania powder		
cowpeas, black-eyed peas	chawli	farsaan	fried and spiced Indian snacks
cucumber	kakdi	fennel seeds	saunf, badishep
cumin powder	jeera powder	fenugreek leaves	methi
cumin seeds / cumin	jeera	fenugreek seeds	methi dane
curry leaves	kadi patta	fig	anjir
dal	split beans, with or without skin (chilka)	finger millet	ragi, nachni
		flaxseeds	alsi
dal with skin	chilkwali dal	flour	atta
dalchini	cinnamon	fresh or frozen green peas	matar
dhaba	road-side eatery		
dhania powder	coriander powder	fritters	pakoras
dhokla	steamed savory cakes	gajar	carrot
dice, dicing	cut into medium size chunks	garam masala	ground mixed spices, commonly available
doodhi	lauki, bottle gourd, calabash		
dosa	Indian crepes served plain, stuffed or flavored.	garbanzo beans	chickpeas, Bengal gram, kabuli chana
dates	khajur	garlic	lehsun, lasun
dried green peas	hara vatana	ghee	clarified unsalted butter
		gheun	wheat
dried peas	sukha vatana	ginger	adrak
		gram flour	besan
dried pomegranate seeds	anar dana	green beans	fansi, french beans, farasbi
		green bell pepper (sweet pepper)	capsicum
dried white peas	safed vatana		
drumsticks	shevagyachya shenga, pods of moringa oleifera, saijan ki phalli	green gram dal, mung bean dal	mung dal
		green gram, mung bean	mung
dry coconut powder	kopra, khobra, desiccated coconut	groundnut	peanut, singdana, shengdana

GLOSSARY

ground mixed spices, commonly available	garam masala	kasuri methi	dried fenugreek leaves
		kesar	saffron
Gujarat	state in the western region of india	khajur	dates
		kheema	minced
Greek yogurt	strained yogurt	kheer	porridge
haldi	turmeric powder	khichadi	soft rice and beans dish
hara nimbu	lime	kidney beans	rajma
hara vatana	dried green peas	kimchi	Korean fermented spicy cabbage
hara vatana ki dal	split, dried green peas		
hare mung	mung, green gram, mung bean	kofta	fried balls typically served with a curry or gravy, or meatballs made of red meat or poultry
hing	asafetida		
honey	shehad, madh		
hummus	Mediterranean chickpeas spread	kopra, khobra, desiccated coconut	dry coconut powder
guacamole	Mexican side made with avocados	kulfi	dense Indian ice-cream
		lady's fingers, bhindi, bhendi	okra
idli	steamed disc or lens shaped cakes		
		black cardamom	masala elaichi
idli rice	parboiled rice	lassi	thick yogurt based beverage, sweet or salty
imli	tamarind		
Indian cottage cheese	paneer	lauki	doodhi, calabash, bottle gourd
Indian stir-fry	subzi		
Indian bun	pav	laung, lavang	cloves
jaei	oats	lehsun, lasun	garlic
jaggery	unrefined sugar	lemon	nimbu
jaiphal	nutmeg	lentils	masur
jeera	cumin seeds	lime	hara nimbu
jalapeño	Mexican green chili pepper	madh	honey, shehad
jeera powder	cumin powder	Maharashtra	state in the western region of india
jowar	sorghum		
kabuli chana	chickpeas, Bengal gram, garbanzo beans	Maharashtrian curry	amti
		Maharashtrian dry stir-fry	usal
kaddu, bhopla	pumpkin		
kadhi	tempered, spiced yogurt sauce	maida, refined wheat flour	all-purpose flour
		mango	aam
kadi patta	curry leaves	masala elaichi	black cardamom
kaju	cashew		
kakdi	cucumber	masur	lentils
kala chana	black chickpeas	masur dal	pink lentils
kali mirch, mira	black pepper	matar	fresh or frozen green peas
kalonji, onion seeds	nigella seeds	matki	moth beans, moth

GLOSSARY

methi	fenugreek leaves	paprika	red chili powder that is less spicy and typically used in Mediterranean cuisine
methi dane	fenugreek seeds		
millets	include sorghum (jowar), bajra (pearl millet), ragi (finger millet), amaranth (rajgira) etc.	paratha	thick flat bread, plain or stuffed
		parboiled rice	idli rice, ukda chawal
minced	kheema	pav	Indian bun
mint	pudina	peanut	groundnut, singdana, shengdana
mira	black pepper, kali mirch		
miso	Fermented soy paste used for making soups	pearl millet	bajra
		peda	flat round Indian sweet
mohari	mustard seeds, raai, sarson	phulkas	light, puffed flat breads
moth beans, moth	matki	pigeon pea, arhar dal	toor dal
mung	green gram, mung bean, hare mung	pineapple	ananas
		pink lentils	masur dal
mung dal	green gram dal, mung bean dal	pista	pistachio
		pistachio	pista
mungo bean	urad, black gram	pohe	rice flakes
mustard leaves	sarson	potato	aloo
mustard seeds	sarson, mohari, raai	puda	crepes
nachni	finger milllet, ragi	pudina	mint
namak	salt	pulao	spiced rice preparation
nariyal	coconut	pumpkin	kaddu, bhopla
nariyal ka dudh, narlache dudh	coconut milk	Punjab	state in the northern region of india
natto	Japanese breakfast food made from fermented soy beans	puri	fried bread (small, usually made of whole grain flours), flat and crisp fried crackers
nigella seeds	kalonji, onion seeds	pyaj	onion
nimbu	lemon	raai	mustard seeds, mohari sarson
nutmeg	jaiphal		
oats	jaei	ragi	finger milllet, nachni
oil	tel	raita	a yogurt dip with vegetables, fruits, herbs with or without ground spices.
okra	lady's fingers, bhindi, bhendi		
onion	pyaj		
pakora	fritters	rajgira	amaranth
palak	spinach	rajma	kidney beans
pancake	small pudas	rehydrated tamarind pulp	imli, dried tamarind is soaked in warm water to soften and pulp is extracted by squeezing the tamarind
paneer	Indian cottage cheese – made by curdling hot milk with an acid- vinegar, lemon juice or yogurt		
paniyaram pan	appe pan		

GLOSSARY

rice	chawal	star anise	chakra phool
rice flour	chawal ka atta	subzi	Indian stir-fry with spices
road-side eatery	dhaba	sukha vatana	dried peas
roti	Indian flat bread	sugar	shakkar
sabut masur	whole lentils	tadka, vaghar	tempering
safed vatana	dried white peas	tahini	sesame seed paste used in Mediterranean cuisine
saffron	kesar		
saijan ki phalli	shevagyachya shenga, drumsticks, pocds of moringa oleifera	tamarind	imli
		tapas	Spanish appetizers served in small plates with drinks
salsa	Mexican sauce	tej patta	bay leaf
salt	namak	tempeh	fermented soy food
sarson	mustard leaves	tempering	tadka, vaghar, chaunk
sarson, mohari, raai	mustard seeds	thalipeeth	Maharashtrian multigrain pancakes
saunf, badishep	fennel seeds		
sesame seeds	Til	thepla	flavored thin, flat bread
sevayan	vermicelli	til	sesame seeds
shah jeera	caraway seeds	tofu	Asian soybean curd
shakkar	sugar	toor dal	pigeon pea, arhar dal
shehad	honey, madh	tortilla	Mexican flat bread typically made of corn
shevagyachya shenga, moringa oleifera, saijan ki phalli	drumsticks		
		turmeric powder	haldi
		tzatziki	Greek yogurt and cucumber dip
shrikhand	strained / sweet Greek yogurt		
		unrefined sugar	jaggery
singdana	groundnut, peanut, shengdana	urad	black gram, mungo bean
		urad atta	urad flour
shengdana	groundnut, peanut, shengdana	urad dal	black gram dal, split mungo beans
sorghum	jowar	urad flour	urad atta
soy beans	soyabean	usal	Maharashtrian dry subzi
soy flour	soyabean ka atta	uttapam	thick dosas, served plain or topped with vegetables
soyabean	soy beans		
soy sauce	dark colored condiment made from fermented soybean paste mixed with other ingredients	vadi	dried legume cakes
		vaghar	tadka, tempering
		vermicelli	sevayan
		walnut	akrod
spinach	palak	wheat	gheun
split beans, with or without skin (chilka)	dal	whole lentils	sabut masur
		yogurt	curd, dahi
split chickpeas	chana dal	yellow split peas	chana dal, split chickpea
split, dried green peas	hara vatana ki dal		

INDEX

A

acidic foods 13
acidity 43
active lifestyle 4
  marching 4
  walk 4
aebleskiver pan 27
aged varieties 15, 16
almonds 5, 73, 177, 178, 184
amaranth 34, 157
animal proteins 13
anti-nutrient 7, 13
anti-nutrient 13
antioxidants 43, 177
appe 14, 15, 17, 18, 22, 27, 32, 45, 93, 133, 134, 136, 137, 138, 141, 142, 143, 146
appe pan 27, 32, 134, 136, 137, 138, 141, 142, 143, 146
appe pan 27
appetizer 45, 89, 98, 109, 121, 122, 168
apple 4, 34, 73, 155
arugula 119
asafetida 41

B

B-12 (vitamin) 21, 33, 161
bake 13
baking powder 13, 22, 28
baking soda 13, 22, 28
balanced ix, xi, xii, 9, 30, 47, 48, 61, 83, 90, 97, 123, 124, 132, 133, 138, 145, 155, 157, 159, 160, 173, 175, 192
balancing meals 30
banana 177, 180, 181
basil 43, 97, 164, 168
B-complex vitamins 4, 7, 8, 9, 12, 20, 21, 22, 63, 81, 123, 161, 182, 185
beetroot 55, 102, 104, 108, 119, 151, 175
bell pepper 53, 60, 61, 69, 83, 87, 90, 96, 97, 102, 109, 115, 117, 124, 131, 132, 168, 169, 171, 172, 192
black beans 2, 45, 82, 83, 89, 109, 132
black chickpeas 5, 53, 79, 82, 96, 108, 109, 131, 187
black-eyed peas 5, 16, 76, 82, 127
black gram 5, 7, 18, 19, 50, 56, 112, 128, 134, 141, 143, 145, 149, 154, 160, 191
black gram dal 19, 56, 128, 141, 145, 149, 154, 191
blood cholesterol 3
blood hemoglobin 7, 63
blood lipids 16
blood pressure 12, 16, 30, 43, 63, 88, 133, 137, 138, 186
blueberries 2, 177
bone health 8
bottle gourd 61, 77, 161
breakfast 27, 32, 45, 133, 134, 136, 155, 158, 159, 160, 177, 180, 187, 188

broccoli 32, 83, 97, 117, 124, 131, 146, 164, 165, 169, 172
brown rice 4, 9, 34, 61, 112, 123, 124, 126, 129, 145, 149, 164, 165, 169
buckwheat 185
burger 45, 109, 122
butter 27, 50, 67, 79, 88, 97, 155, 180, 181, 182
buttermilk 20, 22, 31, 40, 90

C

cabbage 20, 32, 50, 52, 53, 63, 71, 96, 102, 104, 112, 114, 127, 131, 157, 169, 172, 188
canned beans 12
capsicum 53, 61, 96, 104, 115, 131, 132, 171
caraway 41
carbohydrates 3
  carbs 3
  oligosaccharides 3
cardiovascular risk 7
carom seeds 4, 37, 102, 106, 159, 166, 187
carrot 4, 22, 55, 56, 61, 69, 83, 85, 88, 94, 102, 104, 106, 129, 143, 146, 151, 164, 165, 169, 175
cashews 177, 184
celiac disease 185
chana dal 3, 14, 15, 33, 42, 44, 45, 58, 71, 77, 78, 81, 93, 122, 134, 136, 143, 174, 175, 190, 191
cheese 9, 19, 30, 36, 67, 83, 87, 88, 92, 97, 109, 121, 122, 124, 126, 138, 149, 151, 153, 155, 160, 172, 181
cherries 92
chicken 23, 30, 56, 74, 83, 112, 114, 117, 118, 119, 121, 122, 149, 151, 153, 164, 165, 181, 192
chili peppers 43
chili powder 40
chutney 15, 20, 22, 33, 64, 89, 90, 92, 93, 94, 102, 106, 107, 122, 128, 134, 136, 137, 138, 143, 145, 146, 151, 153, 154, 155, 157, 158, 159, 189, 190, 191, 192
cilantro 43
cocoa powder 179, 180, 181
coconut 2, 35, 44, 61, 69, 74, 79, 93, 100, 128, 142, 151, 158, 164, 165, 191
coffee 13, 28, 179
colds 43
colon cancer 3
constipation 3
cooking practices 7
coriander 40
coughs 43
croutons 88, 90
cucumber 20, 60, 90, 109, 119
cumin 40
curry leaves 41
curry paste 164

D

dairy 6, 13, 15, 30, 47, 53, 77, 81, 92, 93, 94, 104,

INDEX

141, 142, 143, 154, 160, 161, 174, 177, 178, 179, 180, 182, 184
dairy-free 47
dals 2, 14
dal with skin 33, 55, 56, 58, 71, 112, 126, 134, 137, 145, 151
dhals 14
dhoklas 14, 15, 17, 18, 32, 133, 137
diabetes 4, x, xi, xii, 3, 30, 133, 158, 186
dosas 14, 15, 17, 18, 22, 32, 33, 42, 45, 61, 133, 136, 137, 138, 143, 146, 149, 151, 153, 154, 158, 160, 189, 190, 191
draining and rinsing 12
dried legume cakes 19
dried peas 2, 4, 5, 17, 34, 38, 64, 66, 73, 79
drumsticks (vegetable) 61, 77
drumsticks (chicken) 112

E

egg 5, 30, 97, 155, 163, 164, 169, 171, 182
eggplant 58, 61, 85, 112, 123, 127, 128

F

fat 5
fava beans 82, 83
fennel 4, 37, 41, 43, 73, 77, 94, 117, 122, 138
fenugreek 41, 42, 44, 56, 58, 61, 67, 73, 78, 104, 112, 122, 134, 137, 138, 141, 145, 149, 154, 158, 159, 188
fenugreek leaves 42, 78, 112, 159
fenugreek seeds 41
fermentation 13, 20, 21, 145
fermented batters 21, 133, 146
fermented foods 20
fermented vegetables 21
fiber 3, 4
  soluble fiber 3
finger millet 34, 160
flatulence 3, 4, 9, 12, 14, 20, 33, 36, 41
  ginger 4
flaxseeds 134, 137, 138, 141, 145, 149, 151, 157, 161, 186, 187, 188, 191
flour 7, 8, 9, 18, 34, 36, 47, 92, 96, 102, 104, 106, 133, 143, 155, 157, 159, 160, 161, 166, 175, 180, 182, 185, 186, 187, 188
folate 7, 52, 69, 186
food pairings 5, xi, 7, 12
fruit salt 28, 141, 143, 146, 182

G

galangal 43
gallstones xii, 6
garam masala 40
garlic 43
gas 4
germination 13, 20, 92
ghee 27, 50, 52, 55, 56, 58, 67, 71, 73, 74, 76, 78, 79, 81, 100, 102, 104, 106, 112, 115, 118, 126, 127, 128, 129, 131, 145, 146, 149, 153, 154, 155, 157, 158, 159, 160, 161, 175, 186, 187, 188, 191
ginger 4, 43
gluten 15, 47, 97, 102, 106, 109, 143, 154, 155, 158, 159, 161, 185, 186, 187, 188
gluten-free 47
glycemic index 3, 9, 34, 50, 63, 82, 83
glycemic load 18, 133
gram flour 18, 34, 92, 102, 104, 143, 155, 157, 159, 160, 161, 180, 187
greek yogurt 20
green beans 2, 52, 71, 123, 126, 128, 131, 164, 165, 172
green bell pepper 53, 60, 61, 96, 115, 117, 131, 169, 171
green peas 2, 15, 33, 64, 66, 79, 81, 115, 126, 129, 131, 153, 169, 172
greens 22, 35, 56, 67, 73, 78, 90, 94, 104, 109, 119, 157, 159, 188
green split peas 112

H

heart disease x, xii
herbs 15, 20, 22, 43, 44, 45, 47, 85, 87, 88, 89, 97, 119, 121, 122, 124, 136, 143, 155, 168, 189, 192
high fiber 33
honey 20, 22, 44, 73, 77, 87, 97, 104, 114, 121, 164, 180, 182, 184
hormonal imbalances 8, 186
hypertension 4, x, xi, xii

I

idlis 14, 15, 22, 27, 33, 42, 61, 93, 133, 143, 145, 146, 149, 189, 190, 191
idli stand 27
immunity 3, 7, 20, 66
indigestion 43
iron 7, 8, 9, 13, 27, 32, 50, 52, 53, 58, 60, 63, 69, 76, 123, 137, 138, 163, 177, 185

J

jaggery 15, 44, 69, 76, 77, 78, 93, 174, 175, 191

K

kaffir lime 43
kale x, 2, 32, 35, 60, 66, 67, 77, 82, 83, 108, 117, 122, 124, 169, 172
Kashmiri red chilies 112
kasuri methi 42, 50, 60, 63, 112, 115, 118
kebabs 32, 41, 45, 109, 122, 137, 138
Kitchen King masala 40, 126, 169
khichadi 6, 126, 127
kidney beans 2, 5, 17, 50, 63, 83, 109

INDEX

kimchi 20

L

lactation 5
large beans 17
lassi 20
LDL cholesterol 5
legumes 2
lemon 43
lentils 2, 3, 4, 5, 30, 33, 34, 38, 52, 58, 85, 88, 92, 106, 112, 124, 129, 134, 184, 197, 198, 199
lentils 7, 17, 38, 52, 124
lettuce 90, 94
lima beans 87
lime 43
lower fiber 33
low glycemic index food 3

M

magnesium 7, 8, 9, 69, 123
mango 73, 92, 181, 182, 191
maple syrup 180, 182
meat 3, 5, 6, 8, 13, 15, 23, 30, 53, 109, 111, 115, 118, 119, 122, 149, 151, 153, 163, 172
milk 5, 8, 9, 30, 36, 69, 142, 160, 164, 165, 174, 177, 178, 179, 180, 182, 184, 186, 187
millets 33, 163, 185
minerals 7
mint 4, 20, 22, 43, 85, 90, 92, 93, 102, 106, 112, 114, 118, 122, 142, 143, 177, 188, 192
miso 20
moderate fiber 34
monounsaturated fatty acids 5
moth beans 16, 69, 73, 92, 100
multigrain 157, 185
mung beans 7
mung dal 2, 3, 19, 33, 38, 55, 56, 58, 71, 74, 112, 126, 127, 134, 137, 141, 178, 184
muscle weakness 6
mushrooms 87, 97, 117, 124, 131, 155, 164, 165, 169, 172, 181
mustard 41

N

navy beans 82, 83
niacin 7
nigella seeds 41
nut-free 47

O

oats 2, 4, 30, 34, 36, 117, 158, 161, 185
obesity xi
omega-3 fatty acid 5, 9, 163
one-pot 24, 52, 126
onion 43
orange 87, 98, 137, 146, 165
oregano 43, 87, 88, 121, 155

P

pair 13, 37, 81, 85, 90, 97, 98, 100, 123, 127, 138, 141, 151, 163, 185
pairing ideas xi, 4, 6, 9, 12, 21, 30, 33, 34, 36, 47
pakoras 14, 15, 17, 18, 74, 102, 104, 134, 136, 166
pancake puffs 27
panch phoron 73
paneer 9, 30, 36, 60, 73, 77, 81, 151, 154, 160, 163, 166, 169
paniyaram pan 27
parboiled rice 34, 61, 126, 129, 145, 149
parsley 43, 87, 97, 119, 122
pasta 33, 36, 97, 109, 118, 122, 172
PCOS 4, xi, xii, 3, 8, 16, 30, 36, 186, 187
peaches 177
peanuts 2, 5, 93, 165, 190, 191
pearl millet 33, 34, 157, 185
pears 181
physical activity 5, 30, 31
phytochemicals 8
pigeon peas 7. See also split pigeon pea
pink lentils 2, 58, 85, 112, 134
pinto beans 82, 87
pistachio 182, 184
planning ahead xi
pomegranate 92, 96
potassium 4, 7, 9, 12, 18, 63, 111, 137, 138, 186, 187
potato 22, 35, 64, 85, 92, 121, 151, 153
prebiotics 3
pregnancy 5
preservatives 12
pressure cooking 15, 22
    pressure cooker 22, 23, 24
    pressure regulator 23
    whistle 23
probiotics 20, 21, 33
proportion 5, 22, 33, 40, 55, 123, 133, 145, 149
protein 5
pulses 2
pumpkin 55, 61, 77, 112, 128

Q

quick fixes x

R

radish 32, 50, 56, 63, 102, 104, 188
raita 20, 22, 50, 60, 106, 188
rancid 7
recuperation 5
rice 4, 6, 9, 12, 15, 19, 22, 23, 24, 30, 31, 33, 34, 52, 53, 55, 60, 61, 64, 69, 82, 92, 112, 123, 124, 126, 127, 128, 129, 131, 132, 134, 137, 138, 141, 143, 145, 149, 154, 158, 164, 165, 169, 171, 172, 178, 185
rice flakes 15, 92, 158
right perspective x
roasted bengal gram 7

INDEX

rolled oats 4, 158, 161
rosemary 43
rotis 18, 31, 33, 34, 60, 71, 77, 81, 89, 100, 102, 104, 166, 185, 186, 187

S

salad 13, 15, 17, 20, 22, 31, 32, 44, 50, 55, 56, 63, 64, 69, 73, 76, 79, 85, 88, 89, 90, 94, 96, 97, 102, 108, 109, 112, 114, 115, 119, 122, 124, 126, 127, 129, 160, 166, 169, 188, 192
sauce 8, 9, 21, 24, 40, 41, 89, 90, 102, 109, 136, 165, 180, 181
sauerkraut 20
scallions 131, 160, 171
scramble 118, 169
selenium 185
semolina 18, 33, 100, 134, 143, 145, 149, 154, 172
sesame seeds 41, 157, 186, 187, 188, 192
shrikhand 20
small beans 16
soaking 14, 16
soaking or cooking liquid 12
soda bicarb 13, 143, 146, 182
sodium 9, 13, 88, 111
sodium bicarbonate 13, 143, 146, 182
sore throats 43
sorghum 33, 34, 157
soybean flour 9, 186
soybean meal 9
soybean nuggets 9
soybeans 5, 8
soy chunks 8, 9, 19, 34, 36, 118
soy flour 9
soy granules 8, 9, 19, 34, 111, 115, 118
soy milk 9, 177
soy sauce 9
spices 40
spinach 4, 56, 60, 67, 74, 90, 117, 119, 122, 143, 146, 151, 155, 166, 169, 172, 175, 177, 188
split beans 2
split dried green peas 2, 15, 66, 112
split dried peas 15, 66
split legumes 14
split mung beans 2, 3, 71, 134, 137, 141
split pigeon peas 2, 3, 58, 61, 71, 77, 78, 134
split pulses 14
split yellow peas 3, 134, 136, 174, 190, 191
sprouts 19, 32, 92, 98, 124, 131, 158, 165
squash 52, 155, 161, 172
stamina 6
standardized 47
steam 27
steamer 27
steamer basket 24
stir-fries 19, 32, 41, 42, 89, 131, 153
stove top boiling 14
strawberries 32, 73, 177, 180
strength 6

sugar 3, 12, 15, 22, 35, 36, 44, 50, 56, 60, 63, 69, 76, 77, 82, 83, 93, 104, 123, 133, 142, 164, 165, 171, 173, 178, 179, 180, 181, 182, 184, 191

T

tahini 192
tarragon 43
tea 13, 15, 28, 41, 45, 60
tea-time 45
tempering 44
textured vegetable protein 9
thiamin 7
thyme 43
tofu 8, 9, 13, 22, 34, 36, 74, 118, 163, 164, 165, 166, 168, 169, 171, 172, 179
turmeric 40
tzatziki 20

V

vadis 19
vegetarians xii, 5, 8, 13, 21, 31, 118, 161, 163, 165, 172
versatile 47
vinegar 97, 168
vitamin c 13, 20, 21, 28, 32, 37, 50, 52, 63, 69, 114, 132, 137, 166
vitamins 4, 7, 8, 9, 12, 13, 14, 18, 20, 21, 22, 63, 81, 123, 143, 161, 173, 182, 185
  folate 7, 52, 69, 186
  niacin 7
  thiamin 7

W

water 14, 16, 36
weight gain 6
weight loss 16, 133
whole beans 2, 17, 111, 131
whole grain bread 4, 5, 64, 67, 88, 115, 117, 155
whole legumes 3, 4, 6, 7, 14, 16, 17, 18, 19, 28, 30, 36, 89, 134, 138, 185
whole lentils 2
whole wheat 5, 9, 34, 50, 55, 60, 64, 106, 122, 126, 157, 159, 175, 185, 186, 187, 188, 192
wraps 47, 89, 102, 104, 106, 118, 119, 168, 169, 189, 192

Y

yoga asanas 4
  pavan muktasana 4
yogurt 20, 22, 53, 92, 93, 94, 104, 117, 142, 143, 157, 158, 160, 161, 187, 188, 191

Z

zinc 7, 13
zucchini 52, 87, 97, 102, 119, 172

Made in the USA
San Bernardino, CA
26 April 2017